THE
FINE ART
OF
CAMOUFLAGE

A Memoir

by

Lauren Kay Johnson

MILSPEAK BOOKS
An Imprint of MilSpeak Foundation, Inc.

Manufactured in the United States of America

Library of Congress Cataloging-in-Publication Data
Johnson, Lauren Kay
Library of Congress Control Number: 2022943491
ISBN 979-8-9857941-6-8 (paperback)
ISBN 979-8-9857941-7-5 (epub)

Editing by: Margaret MacInnis
Cover design and formatting by: Michelle Bradford Art

Portions of Chapter 2 and the Epilogue first appeared in "I grew up with my mom's war stories. What will I tell my kids about my deployment?" the Washington Post (Aug. 23, 2021).

Portions of Chapters 2 and 19 first appeared in "Inheritance of War," Drunken Boat and in "Leaving Home, Coming Home, and Finding Home in Between" Folio (Dec 2016).

Portions of Chapter 10 first appeared online in "American Export: Elections," the Atlantic (Nov. 8, 2016).

Portions of Chapters 8 and 15 first appeared in "I helped write the official lies to sell the Afghanistan war," the Washington Post (Dec. 13, 2019).

Portions of Chapter 23 first appeared in "Home from War, but Not at Peace," Glamour (Nov 2013).

Portions of Chapter 24 first appeared in "On the Western Front," Mason's Road (Aug. 2012).

MilSpeak Foundation, Inc.
5097 York Martin Road
Liberty, NC 27298
www.MilSpeakFoundation.org

For my daughters, because you deserve more than sound bites.

"*I had become an expert at camouflage. My precocity allowed me, chameleonlike, to be to each what they required me to be.*"

—BRYCE COURTENAY, *The Power of One*

Additional Praise for *The Fine Art of Camouflage*

"*The Fine Art of Camouflage* heralds the arrival of a sharp new literary voice. From her family inheritance of duty to country, to her inner conflicts between being a good public affairs officer and a decent human being, to her chronicles of day-to-day life as a counterinsurgent in Afghanistan, Johnson writes with a fascinating blend of how-it-was immediacy and astute reflection. What a great memoir."

—MATT GALLAGHER, author of *Empire City* and *Youngblood*

"An astonishing glimpse into the daily life of America's military women. A moving chronicle of a mother-daughter relationship. A powerful coming-of-age tale. Johnson has pulled off a hat trick with her haunting debut. I couldn't put it down."

—JOANNA RAKOFF, internationally bestselling author of *My Salinger Year*

"Johnson has written the rare first-person account of a woman going to war, but *The Fine Art of Camouflage* is so much more than that. It's a deeply moving memoir of having her own mother go off to war when Johnson was a child. It's a ruthlessly honest portrait of life in a war zone and of information warfare in particular. And it's an unflinching recounting of Johnson's growing doubts about the war in Afghanistan and her service there, of losing faith and attempting to find it again. I'm so glad I read this."

—AMY WALDMAN, author of *A Door in the Earth* and *The Submission*

"Beautifully crafted and deeply moving, *The Fine Art of Camouflage* is a memoir of Johnson's dual deployments—one to help bring stability to a war-torn land, the other to discover the true meaning of service to country. Courageous and difficult undertakings both; thus, the wisdom and insight they yield are as captivating as they are hard-won."

—JERALD WALKER, author of *How to Make a Slave and Other Essays*, National Book Award finalist

"In *The Fine Art of Camouflage*, Johnson writes movingly about her time serving in Afghanistan, as a woman who worked actively in a combat zone—a perspective we don't hear enough about in media or literature. Her respect for the people she worked with in Afghanistan is admirable, and her cultural observations are riveting. There is so much more to this book too: thoughts on family, legacy, connection, efforts, and, ultimately, the way we care for the people we love. It is a gorgeous book."

—ANDRIA WILLIAMS, author of *The Longest Night*

AFGHANISTAN

Administrative Divisions

UZBEKISTAN

TAJIKISTAN

★ DUSHANBE

CHINA

TURKMENISTAN

JOWZJĀN
Shibirghān

Mazār-e
Sharif

KUNDUZ
Kunduz

Taloqān

Faizābād

BALKH

TAKHĀR

BADAKHSHĀN

Aibak

FĀRYĀB

Sar-e
Pul

SAMANGĀN

BAGHLĀN

Maimanah

SAR-E PUL

Pul-e
Khumrī

PANJSHIR

Pārūn

BĀDGHĪS

Bāzārak

NŪRISTĀN

Qal'ah-ye Now

Chaghcharān

Bāmyān
BĀMYĀN

Chārikar
PARWĀN

Mahmūd-e
Rāqī
KĀPĪSĀ

Asadābād
KUNAR

Herāt

HERĀT

GHŌR

WARDAK

KABUL
★ KĀBUL

Mehtar Lām
LAGHMĀN

Jalālābād
NANGARHĀR

IRAN

Nīlī
DĀYKUNDĪ

Maidān
Shahr

LŌGAR

Pul-e'Alam

ISLAMABAD
★

INDIA

1972 Line of Control

Ghaznī
GHAZNĪ

Gardez
PAKTIYĀ

KHŌST

Khōst

Tarīn
Kot

URUZGĀN

Farāh

FARĀH

Sharan

PAKISTAN

ZĀBUL

PAKTIKĀ

Lashkar
Gāh

Qalāt

Kandahār

Zaranj

NĪMRŌZ

HELMAND

KANDAHĀR

	International boundary
	Province (welāyat) boundary
★	National capital
●	Province (welāyat) capital

Afghanistan has 34 provinces (welāyat).

Scale 1:6,900,000

*Dilaram District is reported to be administered from Farah Province,
but the Government of Afghanistan does not recognize its existence.

Boundary representation is
not necessarily authoritative.

LAMBERT CONFORMAL CONIC PROJECTION, STANDARD PARALLELS 30°25' N 37°10' N

803283AI (G00878) 12-08

Author's Note

To protect the privacy of those involved, names and identifying details have been changed. Conversations and quotes have been recreated to the best of my ability. In writing this book, I reviewed hundreds of emails, official correspondence, documents, and other primary sources in an effort to accurately capture the events portrayed. I fully acknowledge and take responsibility for the fallibility of my memory. In the absence of exact details, I trust the integrity of the emotional landscape.

This manuscript uses the spellings Paktia and Khost for the Afghanistan provinces, although alternative spellings exist. In 2009-2010, Provincial Reconstruction Team Paktia recognized fourteen districts in Paktia Province, including three unofficial districts.

Part One

HOME *noun*

Definition: Common

1. A dwelling place; a person's house or abode; the fixed residence of a family or household; the seat of domestic life and interests.

2. The place where one lives or was brought up, with reference to the feelings of belonging, comfort, etc., associated with it.

3. A refuge, a sanctuary; a place or region to which one naturally belongs or where one feels at ease.[1]

Definition: in Military/War

1. An altogether fluid thing; a transient residence.

2. The place where the Travel Management Office ships your household goods.

3. A storage unit in Pensacola, Florida.

4. A location where one used to reside, or where one's family resides, or where one's three cats reside in the care of one's family, etc.

5. [Accidentally referred to as] a larger-than-tiny room on a remote Afghanistan Forward Operating Base.

1

Combat Barbie

(May 2009)

I LAY FLAT ON MY STOMACH BEHIND A GRASSY MOUND. The grass was wet with dew. Water seeped through my military uniform at the knees, thighs, and elbows. My body armor pressed hard against my chest. I sucked in a deep breath of thick Indiana air, winded from my sprint across the field, and felt the Kevlar shell constrict. I winced. My boobs hurt. The armor was designed for men and for obvious reasons didn't fit perfectly. My pulse thumped beneath my helmet. I slid my rifle into prone firing position in front of me. It slapped against the ground in protest.

I'd been issued two weapons a month earlier at the start of this military pre-deployment training, to instant dislike. The clunky M4 carbine rifle strung across my chest rattled with every step. My hands didn't seem big enough to hold it properly. I barely passed the weapons qualification, firing erratically at the green figures that popped up in my lane at the shooting range, the rifle's kick beating a bruise into my shoulder. The M9 pistol was less invasive, slipping smoothly into the holster around my right thigh, and I was somewhat familiar with its quirks. As an Air Force officer, I had an annual M9 training requirement. Before I left my Air Force base in Florida for this training in Indiana, I'd qualified as an expert marksman. But that title was deceptive.

A public affairs officer, I mostly served behind a desk. My weapons were "command messages" and "strategic communication." I fought battles in press releases, phone calls with angry local citizens, and arguments in the commander's briefing room. I was used to clearing email inboxes, not clearing weapons. Even once in Afghanistan, I would be a non-combat

1

soldier. I shouldn't need to rely on a firearm to keep me alive, but I had to be prepared, just in case.

So, throughout my three months in Indiana, I carried my two weapons everywhere, even to the bathroom. On several occasions, I nearly left my M9 in a port-a-potty after detaching my thigh holster to pee. To foster a more amicable relationship, I named my weapons. My M4 became Annie, after *Annie Get Your Gun*, and my M9 was Janie, in homage to Aerosmith.

During the training exercise, behind the grassy mound, Annie grunted into place in front of me, and Janie dug into my thigh, and I cursed them both. I cursed myself for not being more comfortable six weeks into training. I cursed myself for being a spoiled Air Force desk job chick who should never have volunteered to go to war. Then I told my inner critic to shut up. I angled Annie at the plywood wall of the mock village up ahead, which we were supposed to clear of enemy insurgents, and looked through the sights. No movement. Yet.

A young Army corporal skidded in beside me, breathing hard. He positioned his rifle to provide cover fire. I glanced forward to the next mound, where the other two soldiers assigned to my tactical team waited. One of them leaped up, my cue to follow, and began running to the outer wall of the makeshift village. I tried to mimic his nimble bound from behind my own knoll, but every joint protested. I lumbered forward with the grace of an arthritic buffalo, fumbling Annie to forty-five degrees "at the ready," and sprinted—or attempted to sprint—to the next knoll. I wasn't out of shape. A twenty-five-year-old competitive swimmer-turned-triathlete, I'd even completed a marathon just a few months prior. But that was on paved Houston roads. I'd worn a tank top, shorts, and high-end running shoes. Here, sludge caked to the bottom of my combat boots. I humped half my body weight in armor and supplies. My arms pumped awkwardly around the first aid kit and extra ammo magazines fastened to the sides of my bulletproof vest. The flimsy hair bun at the base of my helmet wiggled loose. My glasses fogged in the humidity.

I reminded myself that conditions would be worse in Afghanistan. In a few weeks, I was headed to Forward Operating Base (FOB) Gardez in southeastern Paktia Province, at an altitude of roughly 8,000 feet. The air would be dry but brutally hot or cold. Mud would be replaced by powder-fine Afghan dust, notorious for clogging weapons. The bullets would be real, not the blanks we were using for this exercise.

I knew my deployed experience should more closely resemble the classroom portions of training. We sat through hours-long PowerPoint presentations on Afghan culture, politics, and tribal dynamics, waded through military doctrine, and held think tanks on campaign planning. As a Provincial Reconstruction Team (PRT), our unit wasn't meant for combat. A joint service Army-Air Force team, combined with representatives from the U.S. Department of State, the U.S. Agency for International Development, and the Department of Agriculture, we were assigned to one of Afghanistan's twenty-six provinces to mentor government officials there, talk to locals to build support for the government and erode support for the insurgency, and oversee construction projects and training programs to increase access to basic services. My job as the PRT information operations officer was to document those efforts and liaison with the Afghan and international audiences, providing information beyond insurgent propaganda.

Ours was a nation-building unit, as the counterinsurgency slogan went, a "war for hearts and minds." It was the stuff of Greg Mortenson's *Three Cups of Tea*, the bestselling 2007 memoir about an American mountaineer building schools in Afghanistan and Pakistan, which was practically required reading for military personnel assigned to these missions. In 2011, long after the war in Afghanistan and my own idealism had grown stale, the book came into controversy over alleged inaccuracies and embellishments. In 2009, though, I'd read Mortenson's account and fallen head over steel-toed boots for the softer side of war, the help-them-help-themselves, shake hands/kiss babies, sing-Kumbaya-and-change-the-world kind of battle. While Special Forces soldiers were clearing villages of enemy insurgents, the PRT would be one town over, drinking tea in the tribal leader's living room. Still, we had to be ready to fight. Even the seven women on our team, who per military regulations weren't authorized to serve in frontline combat positions, could find ourselves in ambushes or seeking shelter from mortars or small arms fire.

Crouching behind the second grassy mound in Indiana, I didn't feel ready. I understood generally what this training exercise involved: Approach the village. Clear the village. Provide cover fire. I knew what those phrases meant, in theory; but I didn't trust my mind, my body, my weapons to execute the commands. I didn't have time to dwell on uncertainty. Annie, Janie, and I were alone for only a moment behind the mound before the corporal careened in beside me.

My next move would take me to the back side of one of the buildings. The plywood village looked bigger, more intimidating from here. More real. The corporal aligned his weapon for cover fire and whispered, "Ready, Lieutenant." I took off rattling toward the building and skidded into a crouch at the base of the wall. I paused to suck in a gulp of humid air and then inched forward, rifle poised at my shoulder, until I was next to the petite Sgt. Maria Rivera and another soldier assigned to my tactical team. When the corporal fell in behind me, we were ready to advance.

We crept toward the village entrance. Other four-person teams were already inside. I could hear barked commands and the shuffle of gravel underfoot. Doors banged open. Men yelled in English and Pashtu.

"Stop!"

"Wuhdaraygah!"

We rounded the corner, moving quickly now, rifles angled down in case our fingers jumped at the sight of our own soldiers. Activity strangled the narrow gravel walkway. Camouflaged bodies darted swiftly and confidently between buildings and around actors dressed in baggy blouses and bright scarves, simulating Afghan civilians. I didn't know where we were going. I was glad I wasn't in the lead. We stopped at one of the buildings and slid along the wall until we approached the door. The soldier in front ran his hand over the frame, checking for wires or booby traps. We listened for movement inside. All I heard were commands and crunching gravel, my heartbeat and heavy breathing.

"Ready?" the first soldier asked.

"Ready," we all repeated.

He backed up, took a step, and rammed his foot into the door. It flung open, and the rest of us ran in ahead of him, each moving to a different corner of the room. Empty. I was surprised at my disappointment.

"Clear!" someone yelled. "Let's move out!"

I spun around and fell back in line outside the door. I was now in position two, behind Sergeant Rivera. I would be first to enter the next building. Sergeant Rivera led us along the outer wall, ducking under a window cut out of the plywood. She stopped at the door and traced her hand over the frame, then nodded at me.

"Ready?"

"Ready."

She kicked open the door. I didn't think twice about charging in—because this was training and I knew I was safe, or because training and adrenaline took over, I don't know. I lunged inside, rifle aimed at the back right corner. I heard the door slam into the wall and then a loud pop, like a gun shot. A blast of air hit my right side. I fell to my knees, stunned.

"You're dead," a voice said. "Just lie down."

Before I left my Florida Air Force base, I met with an officer who'd been through a similar three months of training before deploying with the Army. His advice was to "embrace the suck."

The Army training base, Camp Atterbury, Indiana, lacked the creature comforts I'd grown accustomed to as a city girl growing up outside Seattle and attending college in Los Angeles, and as an Air Force officer stationed amidst the tourist hub of Florida's Gulf Coast. The Army base had one gym, a tiny convenience store, and a clubhouse with three TVs, two pool tables, and six Ethernet cables to share among roughly 1,000 trainees. The club sold alcohol, but we weren't authorized to partake. We slept in World War II-era open bay barracks. The men of each of the twelve PRTs bunked with their teammates. As the vast minority, the women all bunked together. Our different training schedules meant a constant chorus of Velcroing body armor, creaking beds, and buzzing alarm clocks. We joked that our standard of living would be higher in Afghanistan.

Entertainment at Camp Atterbury came in the form of nightly bus trips to the nearest Walmart, half an hour away in Columbus. Out of principle, I told myself I would not wait in line to ride a bus to Walmart. Then I ripped a head-sized hole in the Army-issued pillowcase covering the lumpy Army-issued pillow on the creaky metal Army bunk bed and learned that the Columbus, Indiana Walmart had an impressive selection of bedding.

A month into training, I found myself outside my team's male barracks. Pizza boxes, Subway wrappers, and chicken wing cartons littered the courtyard picnic tables. Music blared from someone's laptop, shifting between R&B, country, and salsa, depending on who hopped up to play DJ. People danced and laughed. I stood with a group in the corner, leaning against the laundry bin, smoking a cigar and feeling normal.

For me, smoking cigars was not normal. I'd smoked maybe four in my life, the cheap kind, laced with blueberry and gone in fifteen minutes. Even those fruity fumes irritated my lungs, and I felt clumsy balancing the chubby stick between my fingers. Surrounded by my teammates, though, it just seemed right. There was a bonding element in seeing our smoke blend together, in cutting or lighting each other's cigars. We were strangers who, after weeks of eating, sleeping, and training together, weren't strangers anymore. Smiling around my spicy Nicaraguan stogie, I felt myself relax.

By the end of training, alternating periods of competence and cluelessness became a predictable cycle. The shocking and unfamiliar dulled into a new, heightened sense of routine. I, who once crashed my car into a parked car in a Starbucks parking lot, earned my Humvee driver's license. In case Annie and Janie failed me in my time of need, I learned ten different ways to break arms or choke people in hand-to-hand-combat. The Combat Lifesaver Course certified me to apply tourniquets, start IVs, or relieve the pressure of a sucking chest wound. Bolstered by the shield of "just in case," I didn't balk at the prospect of needing these skills. Instead, I felt a surge of pride to share each accomplishment with my mom, a retired Army officer who deployed during the first Gulf War.

In all the moments of training, the memory that stands out most prominently is my death in the plywood village. After the booby trap exploded, spewing pink paint across my right side, I felt like I lay there for a long time. Long enough for my heartbeat to slow. Long enough for me to realize that I wasn't dead, but that I could be, if the village wasn't made of plywood. Long enough to notice the pink paint that surrounded and covered me in a PG version of blood.

The paint was everywhere: in my hair, in a sticky film over my glasses, even in my ears, a bouquet of camouflage against my pale skin. Paint filled Annie and Janie's every crevice and gave my boots a rosy tint. One of the trainers told me OxiClean would take the dye out of my uniform and body armor. In the bathroom of the women's barracks, I stayed up well past midnight rubbing sudsy water into the fabric until my arm ached. It was useless. I would need a new uniform. I was angry with the trainers for using permanent dye, for wasting my limited time. I was angry with Sergeant Rivera for missing the booby trap and at my dumb luck for being first through the door. Yet those feelings were short-lived.

Like confusion and frustration, the pink paint would stay with me throughout the deployment. I don't know who came up with the nickname Barbie. Pink Mist came a close second, but I liked the contradiction of Barbie in combat. She was feminine, and not, subverting expectations. Nuance aside, to be given a nickname to be used as a "call sign" in deployed communications was flattering in itself, a sign of acceptance. Still, that's not why the incident stands out.

When I crawled into bed that night, careful not to creak the springs of the rickety bunk, I stared at my uniform draped over the bed frame. Even in the moonlight the fabric glared pink. I thought back to bursting through the doorway, to the *pop!* and the shot of air. One of the training evaluators took a video from a perch at the open roof of the building. He showed it to me afterwards. I watched the door shoot open, and an instant later I charged in, rifle raised to my shoulder, until a blast of pink powder sent me stumbling sideways. I sat for a second, dazed, and then the evaluator told me I was dead. I curled up on my side. The gravel beneath me bled pink.

At first there was no response. Then a commotion started outside.

"What happened?"

"I don't know."

"Don't stop, keep coming!" the evaluator yelled from behind the camera.

"There's a bomb in here!"

"Lieutenant Johnson's down!"

"It already went off."

"Medic! Medic!"

Less than twenty-five seconds had passed on the camera's clock.

Before my teammates entered the room to carry me out, the video ended, trailing off with the chuckling laughter of the evaluator, the camera shaking in his hands.

In bed, exhausted but unable to sleep, I replayed the scene in my mind. The instructor's southern drawl. Sergeant Rivera's concerned face hovering over me. The awkward strain when she lifted my legs and another soldier grabbed my torso. The shifting of gravel as they blundered Dead Weight Lauren toward the door. The pink splotch on the plywood wall that finally made us laugh. I wrote in an email to family and friends a few days later that the training exercise was "an extremely harrowing experience for all of us knowing that if the device had been real, I would be seriously injured . . . or worse." Not wanting to worry anyone I made sure to add: "But be comforted—it would be a very weird, and very bad day if we were in charge of clearing a village."

I didn't mention, though, the other feeling that edged into my consciousness the night of the exercise, with my head resting on my Walmart pillowcase, staring at the yellowing mattress above me. In the evaluator's video, I appeared more badass than Barbie. When I charged into the room, I looked professional and confident, like I belonged. And for once since arriving in Indiana, I didn't feel out of place. I didn't feel like a displaced Air Force desk officer, or a city girl, or even like a woman. I felt like a soldier.

2

Inheritance of War

I SWORE I WOULD NEVER BECOME A SOLDIER LIKE MY MOTHER. She called it a blip, a few months out of an otherwise enjoyable career with the Army. No one saw the blip coming. Both of my grandfathers served in the military, but their wars stayed cold. My mom's reserve unit, Seattle's Fiftieth General Hospital, with 750 personnel, was too big, too expensive deploy, the very reason she'd chosen the unit. After three years as an active-duty Army nurse, she wanted to start a family. The Fiftieth promised stability; for them to deploy, it would take World War III.

On Thanksgiving weekend of 1990, my mom got a phone call. She had been receiving practice calls ever since Saddam Hussein invaded Kuwait, drills to make sure the phone tree was accurate, to keep everyone prepared. This time, the call wasn't a drill. The unit was put on alert for deployment orders. My sister, brother, and I were asleep, so we didn't see the white-faced shock when Mom answered the phone. We didn't watch her crumple into Dad's arms when she told him or see the shock mirrored in his own face as questions of her safety, the family's well-being, single parenthood flooded his mind.

Mom and her hospital unit wouldn't receive orders right away. They would spend Thanksgiving with their families, worrying and hoping—hoping World War III would dissipate with the holiday weekend; hoping their orders would leave them as local backfill for active-duty soldiers who deployed or send them to Germany, the unit's assigned overseas operating location based on the Cold War model; hoping their orders would be short.

None of these hopes materialized. Mom's orders were for Riyadh, Saudi Arabia, for an undetermined length of up to two years.

I hardly recall the Army's presence in our family before Desert Storm. The Army slipped in and out one weekend a month and two weeks a year when Mom put on green clothes and went "camping." Sometimes we ate hotdogs and pretended to camp too. With that Thanksgiving phone call, though, the Army consumed us. I had just turned seven, my sister, Shavonne, was eight, and my brother, Matt, barely two. Suddenly, we were no longer a regular young family. Mom had always been the center mass around which we all orbited, and now our gravity field had shifted. In preparation for the deployment, she took frequent trips to the local Army base, sometimes for days at a time. Big green Army bags piled up in the living room where we used to build puzzles and pillow forts. Instead of driving to school with Mom, Shavonne and I went to daycare with Matt early in the morning when Dad left for work. Neighbors stopped by our house to drop off funny-tasting casseroles. They said nice things like, "We're praying for you," and "Let us know if you need anything." I just needed my mom. I was restless in school and gymnastics practice, anxious to get home and hug Mom and hold onto her forever.

Before she left for Saudi Arabia, I told my mom I hated the Army. "Oh sweetie," she said, "I know it feels like the Army is being mean, but it's the Army's job to go help people. A bad man invaded another country, and we need to go help the people there and get him out." With that, she redirected my hatred to Saddam Hussein. The Army wasn't taking Mom away; a bad man was making her leave. Shavonne and I even learned a song about that man and how much we all hated him. We sang the song over and over, and Mom laughed the hardest:

> *Joy to the world, Saddam is dead!*
> *We barbequed his head!*
> *Don't worry 'bout the body*
> *We flushed it down the potty,*
> *And round and round it goes . . .*

I don't remember this, but my parents tell me that before she deployed, I asked Mom if she could die. I imagine myself climbing into her lap. In my mind she's wearing the soft blue bathrobe she had when I was growing up. I'm clutching it, nuzzling into her brown permed curls. Mom wraps her fuzzy blue arms around me, and I can feel her heartbeat, strong and serious. She gazes out through her thick-framed glasses, her eyes light like mine above the long, sharp nose and freckles inherited by Shavonne. Mom purses her lips. She's thinking about my question, about my life—all our lives—without her. She's thinking about the briefings the hospital unit received, the expectations of chemical weapons and massive casualties, the potential for an attack on Israel and an ensuing holy war of nuclear proportions. She's thinking this might be a suicide mission. Mom pulls me closer and strokes the top of my head, trying to memorize the feel of me. She's weighing her need to protect her child with a desire for honesty.

She answered my question: "I'm going to do the best I can to come back to you as soon as I can."

"Don't tell her that!" my dad said. "Tell her no!"

But my mom couldn't lie.

Just before she left, Mom wove Shavonne's and my hair into double French braids, like she did when we had soccer or T-ball games, the only thing that would keep my thin hair and Shavonne's unruly curls in place under helmets and through trips up and down the field. These braids were special, though. They held the memory of Mom's touch: her gentle fingers brushing across my scalp, the nail of her little finger drawing a part down each side, her soft breath on the back of my neck. I wanted to keep the braids forever. I promised Mom I would. It would be our connection while she was gone, and every time I looked in the mirror I would think of her.

Mom deployed right after Christmas. Christmas has always been my favorite holiday, and the occasion carried extra weight in 1990 because we had Mom with us. The Christmas morning snowfall seemed magical to us kids but made a treacherous drive for our relatives, who commuted several hours for everyone to be together. I don't know if our house has ever been so full; it's funny how war brings people together. We had an epic snowball fight with my cousins, opened presents, ate roast beef and mashed potatoes and gravy, and took pictures around the Christmas tree, just like every year.

A few days later, we watched Mom board an Army transport bus. She waved to us through a grimy window until her pale face was lost to camouflage and dust and distance. On the bus she was surrounded by other moms and dads, sons and daughters, brothers and sisters, and a single twenty-something medic. The medic had no family to wave to through the grimy window, but he saw us: a man with red-rimmed eyes standing next to two girls with double French braids. Both girls clung to the man and cried. In the man's arms was a small boy. The young soldier couldn't hear it, but the boy repeated, "Where's Mommy going?" over and over, long after the bus rolled out of sight.

"Looking at your family when we left was my war moment," the medic later told my mom. "Seeing how heartbroken they were."

My memories of Mom's deployment blur into a fuzzy background, punctuated by snapshot images of clarity. I remember cheese quesadillas, "cheese pies" I called them, cooked in the microwave. A neighborhood mom who watched us after school served them to us while we waited at her house for Dad to pick us up. One day while there, I got the stomach flu. The neighbor tucked me into a nest of blankets on the couch with Gatorade and a bucket, but I kept getting up. I walked to the hallway and threw up. I threw up in the living room. I kept walking, looking for my mom.

As the days passed, oil slickened my hair and my precious braids started to unwind. I remember an angry fit of protest, and an ultimate compromise. Every few days the gracious neighbor cleaned and re-braided my hair. It looked exactly the same. But it wasn't.

I cried every night in bed after Mom's tape-recorded voice finished reading a bedtime story. I saw the school counselor for a few weeks. I don't recall her name or what she looked like or even what we talked about, but I remember staring out her window at the snow-crusted ground. My classmates were at recess, throwing snowballs, having fun. For the first time I did not feel normal.

We were the only local kids who had a parent deployed. Neighbors took turns babysitting and delivering meals. A yellow ribbon hugged the big maple tree in front of our elementary school. When she returned, my mom would cut the ribbon off to a whooping chorus of cheers from our classmates. But while she was gone it hung there, through rain and wind and snow. I saw the ribbon every day, and I hated it.

We lived for weekly calls from Mom, letters, occasional pictures, anything to let us know she was safe. Each trip to the mailbox was its own tiny Christmas, marked by expectation and, too often, when no letters came, disappointment. At one point, Mom sent Shavonne and me matching T-shirts with pictures of camels wearing combat boots and gas masks. I still have that shirt, a child's size small, buried in the back of a drawer. Dad pointed out Saudi Arabia on our office globe. Mom was there, inside the little star that represented the capital of Riyadh. It didn't look very far away.

We watched news reports every evening on TV. Headlines that spring covered topics that interest me now as an adult: an escalation of violence in Sudan following the imposition of nationwide Islamic law, an historic meeting between Nelson Mandela and Zulu Chief Mangosuthu Buthelezi, Haiti's appointment of its first elected president, the controversy over Dr. Jack Kevorkian's assisted suicides, the Exxon Valdez oil spill. In 1991, I could focus only on the war. My world expanded exponentially when Mom deployed; I wasn't yet ready to stretch beyond the Middle East. Besides, the Middle East was everywhere, dominating TV, radio, and newspaper reports. In a letter home Mom noted that we were probably getting more news of the war than she was; TV was censored in Saudi Arabia, and she didn't have free time to watch anyway.

In the States, we witnessed a new era in broadcasting, the first time war received real-time coverage from reporters on the ground. They showed awesome footage of planes taking off from aircraft carriers and terrifying shots of exploding missiles. All around were people in camouflage, but not the green and black my mom wore on Reserve duty. These uniforms were brown like dirt. There was a lot of dirt on the news when they talked about the war. I thought it must be hard for Mom to stay clean. I had never watched the news before. Sitting on the couch, my legs curled beneath me, I got my first exposure to the industry of which one day I would be a part. As a public affairs officer I would be there, against the dusty brown backdrop of war, ushering reporters, directing camera angles, providing talking points to the people in camouflage, filtering conflict for the families back home.

Operations Desert Shield and Desert Storm represented a new era in warfare too. Mom was part of the largest reserve component ever activated in support of an armed conflict, and the first involuntary call requiring reservists to report to active duty since the dissolution of the draft. In total, the government activated more than 227,000 reservists. The Army provided the bulk of personnel, nearly 140,000, with around fourteen percent in medical specialties like Mom's hospital unit.[2] Mom was also part of the largest contingent of U.S. military women ever to deploy. By war's end, 40,000 women had served overseas, almost as many as had been on active duty during the height of America's last large-scale conflict, the Vietnam War.[3] Desert Storm saw two American women held as Prisoners of War, and thirteen killed in action.

Sometimes on the news they talked about people dying. At recess one day I was by myself, as I often was during that time, wandering along the edge of the concrete basketball court, when my class bully sauntered up to me. "Hey, I heard about a lady that got killed in the war," he chided, "Do you think it was your mom?"

I hadn't heard about the lady. Had she been on the news the night before? No one had called to tell us something bad had happened. Wouldn't they call? But what if they *had* called; what if Dad answered and didn't want to tell us before school? What if they knocked on our door but no one was home? Maybe the bully had seen a news report that I'd missed? The thought of never seeing my mom again overwhelmed me, and I sat down on the concrete and cried for a long time.

While Mom was gone, we made up games to make time and distance not seem so massive, to trick ourselves into feeling like we might have some sort of control. For "When will Mom come home?" the whole family—my dad, sister, brother, grandparents and I—scribbled our return date guesses across the calendar. My sister's prediction, March 12, 1991, was the earliest, three and a half months after Mom's departure. The rest of us hoped but doubted she was close.

As March arrived, we only got a couple days' notice that Shavonne's guess was exactly right. As suddenly as war had swooped into our lives, it ended. We let ourselves be consumed by frenzied preparations for Mom's homecoming, spending hours tracing letters and gluing glitter onto bright sheets of poster board. There were trips to Party City to buy trunk-loads of yellow ribbons and American flags. We must have alerted the relatives, the elementary school, my Girl Scout troop, the whole neighborhood, and Mom's college roommate, because hordes of them showed up at McChord Air Force Base outside Seattle on the morning of March 12.

Together we stood behind a chain link fence, a crowd of hundreds, watching the empty runway. Shavonne and I held signs and chattered with our classmates. Matt, too young to understand where Mommy had been or why, just knew that this was the day she was coming home. He coiled his tiny hands around the fence and rocked back and forth, back and forth, eyes glued to the tarmac. His expectant little face, framed by a puffy black and red jacket, became a popular clip on local news segments.

I don't know how long we waited before we heard the drone of an approaching aircraft. The crowd hushed. We twisted our heads frantically and shielded our eyes from the sun. A dark speck emerged on the horizon, and we erupted into a cacophony of cheers. The dark speck got bigger and turned into a place that drifted slowly across the landscape. As it inched closer, the crowd grew wild. We screamed and shook the fence. My dad scooped up my brother. Someone, a grandparent maybe, grabbed my hand. Reporters yelled into their microphones. We were supposed to stay behind the fence, but when the plane landed and the first camouflaged figure emerged, we stampeded the runway. All I could see was legs: jeans and khakis and sweats, then a trickle of camouflage moving upstream, and then a pair of legs that stopped and dropped a bag and bent and hugged and cried, and then I was in her arms and nuzzling my face into her hair and the world was whole again.

For a while after her deployment, I screamed every time Mom put on her uniform. Then, gradually, the Army faded into the background again, one weekend a month, two weeks a year. The blip, Desert Storm, followed us all like a shadow, not unpleasant, but always there.

We were extra thankful on Thanksgiving when the phone didn't ring. We got teary-eyed whenever Lee Greenwood's "God Bless the U.S.A." came on the radio, an anthem for Mom's unit. For years, our schools asked Mom to give Veterans' Day speeches, and Shavonne and I modeled Saudi Arabian clothes she'd brought back as souvenirs: black draping capes and veils that covered everything except a square around our eyes, similar to the burqas I'd see eighteen years later in Afghanistan. I loved being a part of Mom's experience, if only from under the veil. I liked to twirl and see the fabric billow around me. Mostly I liked watching my mom.

She talked about how difficult life was for women in Saudi Arabia. "They have to cover all their skin, even when it's really hot outside," she said. "If they don't, the police can arrest them! And they aren't allowed to drive!" Even as an American, Mom said, she couldn't go certain places because she was a woman. She told our classmates about the armed guards on the hospital buses and around the compound to help keep the doctors and nurses safe. Mom shared that she was afraid at first to take care of Iraqi prisoners, but she learned that they only fought because their families were threatened by Saddam Hussein. I thought how brave she was and how lucky I was to have a mom who was more than just a mom, but also a soldier, a healer, and a hero who helped save people from that mean man. After Mom finished speaking everyone clapped for her, and I beamed under my veil.

I didn't know how painful those events were for my mom. I didn't realize she struggled diving back into her roles as wife and mother and everything else we heaped on her. She didn't discuss her terror at nightly air raids, or her aching loneliness, or her doubts about her ability to handle combat. I didn't know she carried trauma with her every day, even after she returned home. I didn't understand her earnestness when we made a family pact that no one else would join the military, because one deployment was enough.

3

Home, Sweet FOB

ON THE AFTERNOON OF SEPTEMBER 11, 2001, I pulled my boxy 1980s sedan out of the parking lot of my high school, where I was two weeks into my senior year. The day had left me numb. I felt sad and angry, but detached, as though I had been sucked into a horror movie but resigned to watch, not play an active character. I opened my sunroof to let in the fresh, warm afternoon. That the sun would shine on a day where so many people had died, even 3,000 miles away, seemed wrong. The trees lining the suburban street were tinged with the first hints of fall. I flipped on the radio. The news reported nothing new, but I couldn't stop listening. My car eased through one school zone to the next. Approaching the elementary on the corner I heard honks from the main intersection, not angry, traffic jam honks, but a peppy beeping like at football tailgate parties. There were shouts, too, whooping cheers from all sides of the intersection. As I got closer, I saw them. Taking over the sidewalks in front of the elementary school and the gas station across the street, swarms of men, women, and children waved American flags and held "God Bless America" signs. A portly man on the left held a sign that read: "HONK IF YOU LOVE AMERICA," and before I knew what I was doing, I was honking and pumping my fist and pounding my steering wheel.

"Yes!" I heard myself shout, "God bless America!"

I turned at the intersection, still honking, and crested the hill toward home just as the first bars of a familiar song came on the radio. I couldn't remember the last time I'd heard Lee Greenwood's "God Bless the U.S.A." When Mom had given a presentation about Saudi Arabia to one of my school classes, perhaps, or when she last marched in the town Veterans' Day Parade. I knew every word, and as the first few crackled through the sedan speakers, I burst into tears. The swell of emotion was so powerful I nearly swerved off the road, overcome by a mix of sadness, nostalgia, pride, confusion, hope, and anger I couldn't name or understand, a force I hadn't felt since March 12, 1991, when Mom stepped off her military plane.

Something inside me awakened.

I thought of that day and of my broken family pact nearly a decade later as the UH-60 Blackhawk helicopter lifted off from Bagram Air Base, Afghanistan, to take me to a tiny province on the Pakistan border. I was going to war. My mind whirred like the rotor blades above me.

Watching the twin towers collapse from a TV in my high school auditorium. The Air Force ROTC contract signed a few months later...

Like the rest of the country, 9/11 left our community in shock, but on the West Coast most were untouched by the immediate aftermath. Classes started late. My boyfriend left school early to donate blood. At home, we watched news coverage, talked about how terrible it was and speculated, vaguely, how the government might respond. On some level I must have realized that the effects would trickle down into my life, that things were going to change for every American. Yet sitting on the living room couch surrounded by my family, I didn't feel the impact personally.

That fall, my senior class took a military aptitude test. I followed mine with an ROTC scholarship application—"Just to see," my parents and I agreed. Then came the full-ride offer to my dream school in Southern California. I was mesmerized by beaches and sun and Hollywood, and the fancy private-school lifestyle my parents' middle-class salaries couldn't support. I liked the ROTC instructors and cadets I met during my scholarship interview. I felt like I would fit in. At eighteen, I wanted nothing more. I wouldn't understand until years later the stirring inside me then, the force that had come alive on 9/11: a latent patriotism, the subconscious pull to serve, like my grandfathers had before me, and to emulate my hero, my mom.

My mom worried for me, but she was also proud. How could she enforce an agreement I'd made at age seven? How could she turn me away from a choice she herself had made? At the same time I defied her I carried on her legacy. Mom had loved the Army, besides the blip. She clapped along with my dad as I stood beside an American flag and three other incoming scholarship cadets, all raising our right hands and swearing to defend the Constitution against all enemies, foreign and domestic. War was brewing, but we couldn't feel the reverberations from the white-walled university reception area in Los Angeles. Afterall, it would be four long years before I graduated. Then I would be an Air Force officer; I'd never be on the front lines.

Lifting off from Bagram Air Base, the Black Hawk helicopter shuddered under the weight of the crew and ten passengers, armor, and luggage. The walls seemed too thin to shield us from the quickly chilling air, let alone from bullets or RPGs. Outside my window I got my first look at *real* Afghanistan, away from the relative safety of Bagram. The landscape loomed stark and desolate and brown. So much brown, like the glimpses of Saudi Arabia from my childhood newscasts. We wove through rocky hills dotted with patches of green that I assumed must be local settlements. The gunner shifted his weapon from patch to patch, alert for potential threats. I imagined villagers scrambling to their rooftops with rocket launchers. We climbed over a mountain range still frosted with snow even though it was July. I pictured an insurgent camp dug into a mountain cave with Osama Bin Laden himself issuing orders to attack the passing aircraft. Insurgents weren't known for their anti-aircraft capabilities, but at training they stressed everyone, everything, everywhere was a threat, and my mind spun to the extreme.

This wasn't my first military helicopter ride. I loved the rustic feel of helicopters: the crisscross of wires through the cargo compartment, the oil-slicked floor, the gunner silhouetted at the open door against a backdrop of trees or desert, ocean or river, the relentless *thwop thwop thwop* pulsing through my body. Helicopters were charming for their grittiness. Unlike sleek fighters or massive cargo planes, helos felt intimately rugged and tactical. I could imagine them at war.

As we whipped through war zone airspace, though, that grittiness became disconcerting. I sweated under my helmet, despite the frigid, altitude-thinned air. My mind whirred again . . .

Two years into my service, an assignment on a month-long training mission in the Republic of Mali, Africa. Playing soccer with schoolchildren. Hosting community health clinics. Feeling more purpose than I had in my entire life. Shortly

19

after I returned, an offer for deployment, "along the lines of what you were doing in Africa." I said yes.

Telling my parents I was deploying felt like an in-person conversation, but I was glad for the buffer of geography. I didn't want to watch Mom's face contort in fear and worry. I didn't want to acknowledge myself as the source of her pain. To deploy meant breaking our family pact all over again, this time without the excuse of being a naïve eighteen-year-old and without the shield of four years of college.

I gripped my cell phone like a stress ball and paced across my Florida living room, gathering courage. Then I took a deep breath and dialed.

"Hi sweetie!" My breath caught at my mom's chipper greeting. I tried to match her tone.

"Hi!"

"Let me see if I can find Dad."

"OK."

I swallowed hard around a fist in my throat. I could picture Mom smiling and prancing to grab the second phone from the family room to bring to my dad. She was excited for a weekend catch up session, and I was preparing to slay her.

"How are things in Florida?" she asked.

Tears burned behind my eyes. "It's a little chilly," I said, "but the sun's out." I looked to the sliding glass door across my kitchen where all three of my cats lounged on the sunbaked tiles. "Your grandcats say hi."

"Oh give them pets for me!" Mom's voice moved away from the mouthpiece as she spoke to my dad. "It's Lauren."

"Well, hello there!" he said. "How's the Floridian?"

"I'm OK." I hated the tremor in my voice. "I have some news."

"OK," my mom said.

"What's up?" my dad said.

"Well, I got deployment orders."

I heard the hiss of breath on the other end of the line. I squeezed my eyes against the tears, but an image of Mom's anguished face played behind my eyelids.

"Oh, Lauren," she sighed. "We were afraid that might happen."

"Where are you going?" Dad asked.

"Afghanistan."

"Oh . . ." My parents followed the news closely enough to know that Afghanistan was not a desirable vacation destination in 2009. They later confessed they hoped I would be sent to Iraq, where violence appeared to be declining and the Bush administration was making plans for withdrawal.

"I don't know exactly where yet," I continued. "But I'll be part of a Provincial Reconstruction Team. You should look it up. It's actually pretty cool! Working with the local population to build schools and stuff. Like *Three Cups of Tea*, Mom!" I knew Mom had read Greg Mortenson's memoir and that she threw herself into feel-good stories even more than I did. "We'll be on a secure base. Not on the front lines or anything."

"How long will you be gone?" I was grateful for my dad's logical checklist mind giving me concrete details to address.

"The deployment is nine months, and there's three months of training beforehand."

"Nine months!" Mom squealed, and I winced. "I thought Air Force deployments were short!"

"They're usually shorter," I said. "Public affairs is normally six months. But," I quickly added, "that's, like, sitting behind a desk writing press releases. I think this will be much more rewarding. More like what I was doing in Africa." I nodded to my living room wall, reminding myself I believed this. Everything I did at Hurlburt Field, the special operations base where I was stationed, happened on the periphery: supporting other people doing meaningful work, sharing *their* extraordinary stories. My yearning to belong, to contribute, to please could no longer be satisfied behind the window of my air-conditioned office.

"Oh, Lauren," my mom said again. "Couldn't you get pregnant? Or move to Canada?"

"Oh geez," Dad scoffed.

I laughed. So did Mom, though I sensed she was only partly joking. "I think there might be some long-term consequences associated with that," I said. Then my smile folded. I took another ragged breath. I'd been dreading this confession most: that I wanted to leave. Of course, the military would send me regardless. But the desire felt like a betrayal. Entangled with the part of me that wanted to serve and do extraordinary things was a part of me that wanted nothing more than to be a good daughter. Being a good daughter meant keeping myself safe. I chose my words carefully. "Besides," I said, "this is what I signed up for. It's my duty. It's something I need to do."

Mom's voice came back raw but firm: "I understand that." I could tell she wished she didn't.

Hovering above Afghanistan in the helicopter cargo bay I sucked in a deep breath, attempting to recapture my courage, and adjusted my gloved hands around the buttstock of my rifle. I still resented my weapons, but Annie and Janie had nonetheless become a sort of security blanket. They were more familiar than my other surroundings. The three of us were wedged into the helicopter's webbed seating next to a handful of my teammates. Following an additional week of training at Bagram, the military's main hub in Afghanistan, those of us requiring more extensive job turnover got the priority flights to Forward Operating Base (FOB) Gardez. Our departure had already been delayed when Army Sgt. Robert "Bowe" Bergdahl went missing from his base in the province adjacent to Paktia and air assets were redirected for the search efforts. Now with a mere three days overlap with the current PRT, we were anxious to cram in as much learning as we could. Most of our training had been general: deployed operations, Afghanistan history and culture, counterinsurgency tactics. I hoped the ensuing seventy-two hours would be enough for me to grasp the specifics of my information operations job.

My teammates on the helicopter seemed mostly calm. Some took pictures of the landscape or each other. Our head civil engineer appeared to be napping; his lanky form slumped against the metal wall. Our intelligence officer looked almost giddy. His body armor decked out with all the latest gadgets, he was a living exhibition of the Worst-Case Scenario Survival Handbook. It was strange to consider my teammates in this setting, in this helicopter taking us to war. These people I'd met only three months before felt almost like family, albeit a cruder, rowdier, tobacco-chewing, shit-talking version. They would stand in for my family for the next nine months, serving as advisors, supporters, confidants, and protectors. I would depend on them. And they would depend on me. Watching the pitching horizon, I resolved to at least pretend not to be terrified. Perhaps actual non-terrified feelings would follow.

The two-hour flight remained uneventful (if such a thing as uneventful travel were possible in a war zone). The mountains flattened into the dusty brown swath of Gardez Valley, a view that could be mistaken for the farmlands of the Midwestern United States, except the sparse fields lay cracked and brittle from lack of irrigation, and mud-brick forts, *qalats*, replaced big red barns. A single paved road cut across the landscape, merging in the distance with the small cluster of Gardez City, the provincial capital and the only population center in Paktia that could pass for a town by American standards, complete with generator power and a few multi-story buildings. The helicopter banked sharply, and I caught sight of what would be my home for the next nine months: FOB Gardez.

In many ways, the massive Bagram Air Base, my first introduction to Afghanistan, reminded me of Hurlburt Field back in Florida. In fact, Bagram was even more robust, boasting not one but three movie theaters, multiple dining halls, several fast food kiosks, and a sprawling Base Exchange that sold the latest movies, music, and magazines, imported American snacks, uniform supplies, and "authentic" Afghan souvenirs. Soldiers deployed at Bagram held sporting tournaments and dance lessons. American entertainers passed through on USO-sponsored "morale tours." (Morale wouldn't reach us in Gardez.) Main highways clogged with traffic jams. Bagram didn't just resemble a U.S. military base, but a major U.S. city.

I knew FOB Gardez would be different—"quaint" was the word my predecessor used in emails. Gardez made Hurlburt Field and even the Camp Atterbury training base seem like bustling urban centers. The FOB measured less than a mile in circumference. There was no fixed-wing runway, which was why we traveled by helicopter, no paved roads, no base store, Pizza Hut, or Dairy Queen. I'd savored one last glorious latte before leaving Bagram, where a cup of gourmet coffee seemed a mandatory uniform item. I'd seen pictures of the one-room FOB Gardez dining hall, the tent gym, and the fort-like qalat that would serve as our living and working space. Somehow that knowledge failed to prepare me for the reality of the small rural base where we were about to land.

I could see the FOB's entire perimeter through the open side door as we hung above the Helicopter Landing Zone (HLZ). I had never seen the perimeter of Bagram; the base stretched for miles in every direction. From

23

inside, you were at once a part of the faux metropolis and consumed by it. FOB Gardez looked more like it was striving to be part of the Afghan landscape, separated only by walls of giant reinforced sandbags—HESCO barriers—and spirals of concertina wire.

The Black Hawk lurched to the ground, leaving my stomach behind. The rest of me followed my teammates out. Ducking below the rotor blades, my body armor and backpack threatened to tip me over. Annie rattled her disapproval against my chest. I straightened and surveyed my surroundings. From the ground, this didn't feel like rural Afghanistan. The gravel felt the same against my boots as the gravel around our temporary sleeping quarters at Bagram and our barracks at Camp Atterbury, which felt the same as the gravel on the median of the main road at Hurlburt Field, and the same as the gravel walkway running through my parents' Seattle yard. Everything around me looked familiar: Military equipment, military weapons, dust, plywood buildings, military personnel.

The personnel walked quickly toward us. Our bags were tossed in a pile outside the helicopter, and someone yelled to load them onto a cart. I reached for mine, but several strong male hands beat me to it. A hot blush crept into my cheeks. When I'd carried my own duffel throughout the journey, my male teammates were impressed with my initiative. I didn't know whether to be flattered or insulted.

Since I was one of only two women on the helicopter, my soon-to-be predecessor, Major Catherine Rhodes, found me easily. She looked ecstatic to see me. I didn't think to take her exuberance as a warning.

"Lieutenant Johnson!" she squealed. "It's so great to meet you!" She was taller than I imagined, with a willowy stature that looked as though the rotor wash might blow her away. She extended a slender arm into a surprisingly firm handshake and then twirled and escorted me off the HLZ and around the bend of HESCO barriers that fed into the main base. I strained to process her exclamations through the haze of exhaustion and disorientation.

"Welcome to FOB Gardez! It's not much, but it's home!" Her voice lilted with a slight southern twang. "It'll take a while to get used to the altitude." She was right. I'd only walked a few yards and my lungs were heaving. At 8,000 feet Gardez sat almost twice as high in elevation as Bagram, which itself had been a challenge after the lowlands of Indiana and Florida. We rounded another corner of HESCO barriers, and there it was: the qalat. I'd heard about the fort and seen pictures, but nothing quite captured how cool it would be.

A qalat, Arabic for "fortified place," is a mud-brick compound common throughout Afghanistan and Southwest Asia. At most basic, the structure consists of four thick walls with built-in apartments for multi-generational families. FOB Gardez contained two qalats: the one in front of me where the PRT lived and worked, and a second that housed Army soldiers. Both were fairly simple in design—four outer walls with a tower at each corner—but the Army qalat was famous, as far as qalats go. In March 2002, just a couple months before my high school graduation, the Gardez qalat served as a planning and observation post for one of the first major combat operations of the Global War on Terrorism. Operation Anaconda aimed to seal off escape routes through Paktia's mountains into Pakistan and root out Taliban and al-Qaeda fighters entrenched there. Bad weather delayed helicopter flights, and enemy fighters exceeded expectations in numbers and resolve. The fighting ebbed and flowed for seventeen days, leaving eight American solders dead and more than fifty wounded. But coalition forces claimed control of the mountains. Military leadership declared the mission a success.

The Gardez location proved strategic, and the U.S. government leased the qalat and surrounding area for use in the continued Afghanistan campaign. The land included a second qalat, and in January 2003 Afghanistan's first PRT took residence in its walls. I was a freshman in college at the time. For an ROTC assignment, I gave a briefing on the public affairs career field, my first glimpse at the job that would ultimately take me to Afghanistan. Standing at the front of a dimly lit classroom, itchy in my new starched Air Force blues uniform, I rattled off bullet points about working with media, leading tours, and writing for the base newspaper. "It's essentially PR and journalism for the Air Force," I professed, as if I knew anything about PR, Journalism, or the Air Force. I decided public affairs was the job I wanted, the best way to utilize my English major writing skills. Plus, I thought, it sounded fun!

Six years later I stood in front of the Gardez PRT qalat in dusty camouflage, ready to start a new position in information operations, a job that would call into question everything I thought I'd come to understand. By 2009, Operation Anaconda's footprint had dwindled; the Taliban, al-Qaeda, and the local warlord tribe of the Haqqani network had seized back the supply routes running across the border. The Army qalat appeared unfazed, its thick walls cutting a stately silhouette against the bright blue sky. The PRT qalat before of me wore its age with less regality. Three of the four corner lookout towers were crumbling. (After rainstorms, local workers would patch the melting walls with a sloppy paste of mud and hay.) Still, the fortress looked majestic, like something out of a history book or an *Indiana Jones* movie. The sentiment must have registered on my face.

"Pretty neat, huh?" Major Rhodes beamed. "Your room and your office are in here."

I followed her past a parking lot of Humvees basking in the qalat's shadow, past a row of steel freight containers, or connexes, used in war zones for storing practically everything—supplies, bathrooms, people—and through an archway at the center of the qalat's front wall. Inside, the fort split in half. To the left, the outer walls enclosed two small plywood buildings: the PRT office building, where I would work, and the Tactical Operations Center, where PRT senior staff and the co-located Army unit conducted mission planning. Major Rhodes led me to the right. There the walls formed a square around a sparse courtyard, and I saw doors carved into the mud every few feet. We walked down the gravel path along the center wall. The first apartment obviously belonged to the communications team; the door was marked by a tangle of cables and a sign advertising the Nerd Herd. We passed another room, turned right at the corner, passed another room, and then stopped. My room.

I swing open the flimsy wooden door and gasped. "Are you serious? This is all for me?" I'd anticipated a bed-sized rectangle to call my own, or a bunk bed to share with my new best friend, or a partitioned sixth of a "b-hut," the plywood barracks where our security forces and Air Force enlisted teammates bunked. I looked across the small office through a second door to the bedroom. I had a desk, a bed, a wardrobe, a wall of built-in shelves, and a window shaded by a colorful array of scarves, all to myself. My standard of living really would be higher in Afghanistan!

"One of the perks of being a woman," Major Rhodes said. "We all get to stay in the qalat."

The perks ended there. My room was 128 steps to the women's bathroom (I would count one morning). Major Rhodes led me back down the gravel path, around the center wall, past the PRT office building, and up a few wooden steps to the only women's bathroom in the qalat, containing the single toilet, shower, and sink serving the seven women of our PRT and our female interpreter. Eight months later, in the midst of the troop surge, the bathroom would serve eighteen women.

Major Rhodes gestured grandly at the facilities as if to say, *one day soon this will all be yours!* I grimaced at the sliver of mirror, the creaky, rotting floorboards, and the stained plaster. The outer door hung crooked on its hinges, the shower curtain reeked of mildew, and several nails poked haphazardly from a crude set of shelves. I was pleasantly surprised, however, at the contents of the shelves. Baskets heaped with sample bottles of shampoos and lotions and a stockpile of tampons and maxi pads.

"Any time packages come in with women's stuff they go in here," Major Rhodes said. "It's nice, especially since we don't have a base store. If you need anything else you'll have to get it shipped or order from drugstore.com. They deliver out here."

Between the Air Force gear I'd been issued at Hurlburt Field and the Army supplies added at Camp Atterbury, military luggage restrictions left limited space for toiletries. I'd only brought a few weeks' worth and hadn't thought ahead to replenishing my stash. While helping me pack, my mom had commiserated. "I remember trying to stuff like six months' worth of feminine products into my ruck sacks," she said. "And I had no idea if even that would be enough. Guys have it easy! They don't need to worry about things like that!"

Across my Florida living room my dad waggled one of my combat boots. "Yeah," he said, "but our shoes are bigger."

As Major Rhodes and I left the bathroom, I made a mental note to talk up the supply shelves when I spoke with my parents to put their minds at ease about my accommodations. Outside, we moved toward the back corner of the qalat. There, the walls opened up, and I found myself in a maze of plywood buildings and connexes. We passed the back of the dining hall and the small white chapel that held Sunday service when the provincial chaplain rotated through. Before even stepping inside my first Sunday in Gardez, the little building comforted me, like the *Daily Walk Bible* in my luggage, like the cross tattooed on my left forearm.

I didn't grow up in a religious family. Between my parents, sister, brother and me, our spirituality came in the form of togetherness, athletics, and patriotism. I remember going to a church service to hear a neighbor woman sing and being terrified by a sermon about the fires of hell. In Sunday school with a friend, we colored pictures of Jesus and Mary. Later, we learned that one of the food service workers had hepatitis, and all the kids had to get a shot. It's a wonder that I ever entered a church again. I didn't until middle school, when I stumbled into a youth group with Shavonne on the invitation of one of her friends. A horde of teenagers crowded into a church basement, we rocked out to live music, put on skits, and laughed at the youth pastor's cheesy jokes. I loved the singing. I loved the sense of community. Everyone was just so nice, not like the popular kids at school who teased me about acne and the stench of chlorine that stuck to my skin after morning swim workouts no matter how hard I scrubbed. I saw religion as kind people united in something greater than ourselves. At that point in my life, that was all I was capable of understanding. It was all I needed.

A year later I stood in front of the church congregation in shorts and a baggy t-shirt, up to my knees in the lukewarm water of the baptism tub, pronouncing my love for God and acceptance of Jesus Christ as my savior. In my testimony, I confessed that I sometimes talked bad about people and told white lies, but I was on the right path now with God. I crossed my arms over my chest and closed my eyes as the pastor lowered me into the water in the name of the Father, the Son, and the Holy Spirit. Opening my eyes again, watching my parents clapping in the audience through drops that clung to my eyelashes, I felt strong. It's easy to be strong when you haven't been tested.

Beyond the Gardez Chapel, Major Rhodes led me by connex offices, connex barracks, tents, connex bathrooms, concrete tunnels serving as shelters for incoming fire, more tents, more connexes. I didn't understand how a base so small could be so confusing. Everything looked the same.

"You'll get your bearings quickly," Major Rhodes said. "The qalat is a good landmark." Then as we stepped into a connex, "This bathroom is much nicer, obviously. But it's a long walk, and I wouldn't recommend it at night."

She didn't need to elaborate. Military sexual assault was a well-broadcast deployment threat, particularly for women. I'd received a briefing before I left Florida and at least one more in Indiana. The women's residency in the qalat had more to do with safety than hospitality. I breathed in the connex bathroom's fresh Lysol scent and looked longingly at the row of six showers.

"You guys will come up with a schedule for the qalat bathroom," Major Rhodes said. "It worked fine for us."

My head spun as our tour continued. I tried to note recognizable structures and directions and wondered how long I could go without a shower. We approached the weight room, named for a U.S. soldier who had been killed while serving in Paktia. The connection struck me, and I froze at the doorway. Major Rhodes didn't notice. "I never come in here," she said, pushing the door open with a screech. "It's always packed with men. And it smells. Also, there's a camel spider that hangs out here."

The building clamored with sweaty, grunting men. Most eyes turned to us as we entered. The floorboards groaned beneath my feet. A dumbbell hit the ground across the room, and I wondered how it didn't break through. I left quickly, more interested in the cardio gym, where I could run or cycle out my stress. More primitive and a bit farther—past the laundry room, another mess of b-huts and connexes, and a towering pyramid of bottled water—the gym was merely a tent crowded with four treadmills, two recumbent and two upright stationary bikes, and two elliptical machines, but it was quiet and empty.

Finally, we made our way back to the qalat. "Just one more thing," Major Rhodes said. "This is super cool." The early morning helicopter ride, culture shock, and an empty stomach dampened my enthusiasm, but I followed her through a crooked waist-high gate and up a flight of wobbly wooden stairs. "This is the only qalat tower you can go in anymore," she said. "They don't use it for defense or anything. It's just a nice place to come when you need a break."

The old lookout tower failed to impress, just plywood over the mud-brick floor and a wooden railing reinforced with sandbags. But as I peered out from beneath the wood and sandbag roof, I was mesmerized. The walls of the qalat spread out beneath me. I could see the top of my room's door in the next section. There was the HLZ and the other half of the FOB I had yet to explore. To my left lay the land we'd covered on our tour. The maze of structures looked organized and straightforward from up here. Then beyond, the base fell away, and there was Afghanistan. A patch of smog and flickering generator-powered lights designated Gardez City, with the single road snaking outward. Miles of brown, hazy emptiness stretched through Gardez Valley, then burst into miles of mountains at the horizon. The sky seemed immense, all-consuming. For a moment, I felt almost peaceful.

Major Rhodes broke the spell. "We should get to lunch before it gets too crazy."

We shuffled back down the stairs, through the gate, out the back corner opening, and around to the front of the dining hall, where a line trickled out the door. A wooden sign advertised the Olive Gardez in looping cursive, the logo the only likeness to its American namesake. Inside we filtered across a muddy floor, through a hand washing station at a metal trough, and to a buffet line where soldiers heaped generous portions of steaming food onto our trays. I realized I was famished. I'd heard horror stories about deployed cooking, but I'd never been a picky eater. After three months of Camp Atterbury cafeteria slop and/or dehydrated meals, I figured I could stomach practically anything. I was thrilled to see a salad bar, though the contents had obviously been frozen. I plucked out some lettuce and a few crystallized tomato slices and smothered everything with Italian dressing.

On the spectrum of comfort, FOB Gardez fell somewhere in the middle. We lacked the amenities of Bagram and other national and regional hubs, but I knew of tiny combat outposts throughout Paktia Province where sleeping barracks were open-bay and bathroom facilities were holes dug into the sand. Some military forces camped for weeks in the mountains with no base at all.

At least we have hot meals, I reminded myself.

Later I waited in the dank, steamy bathroom for my turn in the shower. As I finally scrubbed the grime from my face in sulfur-scented water and my elbows banged against the narrow stall, I told myself: *At least we have running water.* When I rinsed my toothbrush from a bottle, below the warped mirror with the sign that read "WATER IS NOT POTABLE, DO NOT DRINK," I repeated: *At least we have plumbing.*

I trudged the 128 steps back to my room and collapsed into my new bed. The hard, springy mattress was covered with a thin foam topper that pleated under my back. The wood frame moaned with any movement. Still, as I'd gushed to my family in an email letting them know I'd arrived: "I'm so excited to sleep in a real bed and have less than sixty three roommates!!" I told them about the cool fort housing, the lookout tower, and the well-stocked bathroom shelves. Other details, like the knot corkscrewed around my stomach and the choke hold of fear on my mind, I left unsaid.

Gardez was designated a blackout FOB—no outdoor lighting to call attention to our location—but the moon hung nearly full. Through my makeshift scarf curtains the beams cast colorful, eerie shadows, which seemed to dance to a melody of helicopters, Humvee engines, and footsteps over gravel.

"This is Afghanistan," I whispered to the plywood ceiling. "This is my room. For 270 days. I can do this." I fell asleep not entirely confident, yet not doubting, that that was true.

4

Not In Kansas Anymore

MY FIRST MORNING IN GARDEZ, I woke to the jingle of my alarm clock. I lay on my side, staring at a blue-painted plywood wall. My nostrils tingled with the thick, musty scent of old wood and older dust. I heard no other voices or alarm clocks, the typical morning accompaniment at Camp Atterbury and during transit at Manas Air Base in Kyrgyzstan and at Bagram. Then I remembered. I was in Gradez. This was my new home. My stomach did a nervous flip.

I groped for my glasses on the shelf behind me, and then looked around at my room. The blue wall, the scarf curtains, the patchwork of red-patterned floor rugs; it had been a while since I'd seen so much color. My duffel bags and my camouflage uniform hanging on the wardrobe door slumped in more familiar shades of gray and olive green. I had to pee. I'd had to during the night as well, stumbling to the bathroom by the dim light of my red-tinted, blackout FOB-approved flashlight, tripping over a rogue sandbag, and crossing my arms over my bra-less chest as I passed the twenty-four-hour manned operations center. Between the dry air, the walking, and the salty food, I'd felt thirsty all through the previous day. Now my throat scratched again. I hoped my body and my bladder, along with the rest of me, would quickly adjust to Afghanistan.

I slipped on a bra beneath my Eeyore pajamas and padded the 128 steps in my Crocs. The steamy bathroom hummed with women in various stages of undress. Sgt. Maria Rivera chuckled as she pulled a brown undershirt over her thick black curls. "Good morning, ma'am," she said. "Welcome to the fray."

"Yeah, you too," I said, stepping aside to allow two women from the team we were replacing to exit. It seemed awkward to greet the room of mostly naked strangers but more awkward not to, so I hollered a cheery, "Morning, ladies!" as I sneaked into the toilet stall. I washed my hands and face in the sink, careful not to swallow any water, and then retreated to my room to finish getting ready.

I dressed in my drab camouflage and slicked my hair into a low bun to fit under my hat. Looking into the cracked slab of mirror next to my wardrobe, I patted on blush and concealer. I felt silly wearing makeup in a war zone and had almost not brought any. At the advice of my college roommate, who'd deployed to Iraq, I'd tossed in the basics. "You'll get to a point where you just want to feel like a girl," she'd said. A few months later I would be grateful for the makeup when I scrambled for anything to help me feel like some semblance of myself.

After breakfast at Olive Gardez, I joined Major Rhodes—who I noticed was wearing lip gloss and eyeliner—in my new office to begin our turnover. The major greeted me with the same cheery squeal as the previous day and pulled up an extra chair for me next to her desk. *My* desk. I sat down, my knees knocking against a set of drawers, and examined the space. Two shelves held binders of information operations documents and provincial data, books on Afghanistan history and culture, and a bowl of stale-looking M&M's. I would inherit two laptops, one connected to the non-secured network and the other on the secure network for files containing sensitive and classified information. A jumble of wires and red and blue (secure and non-secure) network cords ran up the wall and merged into a thick snarl with the computer and phone cords from the building's other workspaces. The entire band snaked across the ceiling and out the front door, leaping from the plywood office to the center wall of the qalat, where it grew into a larger bundle with wiring from the operations center next door. Over the qalat wall the mass finally ended at the communications office. At Hurlburt Field, we weren't allowed to turn on a secure computer within a several-foot radius of non-secured devices. Many secure devices were kept in lock boxes. Here, the laptops, phones, TVs, and Afghanistan Roshan cell phones all lived together in perfect, albeit messy harmony. The discrepancy made me smile.

Major Rhodes directed my focus to the secure laptop. "I thought the easiest thing would be to put everything you need to know all together in one place," she said. "So I made a PowerPoint." She opened the file. The slides numbered in the hundreds.

I stopped smiling.

In the ensuing whirlwind, I took comfort that I was among other bewildered newcomers, not like two-and-a-half years prior when I first reported to Hurlburt Field. Of course, back then, I had my rock. In 2006, my mom drove with me for ten days and nine states from Seattle to the Florida panhandle. The coast-to-coast road trip was by far the longest we'd taken together, and my first as a full-fledged college-graduated adult. Beside me in the car, Mom radiated the same calm I always knew in her presence. She'd steadied my nerves on many pre-dawn weekend mornings en route to championship swim meets and on the drive to Los Angeles for my first semester of college. All these years later, she remained my center mass.

As the familiar slid farther away with each mile marker, though, I felt the building pressure of expectations. Mom, too, had gone through ROTC in college. Like me, she had the pull to serve, plus the allure of a full college scholarship. I wouldn't consider my younger self "ferociously independent," like Mom describes hers, but I liked to pretend I was. After college Mom, too, trekked across the country, from Seattle to Washington, DC for Army nursing school. She signed on the dotted line to mark the beginning of a career that took her through twenty-two years, plus a blip. She carried on the military tradition of her father and his two brothers and her father-in-law. Now she'd passed the torch to me.

If this were fiction, I would write that Mom and I spent the car trip laying bare our fears. Me, adolescent fears of a cross-country move and starting my first job, but also of entering the family business. While the scenery flipped from mountains through forests to canyons and three days of Texas flatlands, I would admit that I was afraid I wouldn't be good at taking or giving orders, that I would fail, somehow, as a military officer, and in doing so I would betray my family history.

In the fiction, Mom would tell me that I didn't have to prove anything. We wouldn't make a dramatic getaway across the Mexican border (or maybe we would; it's fiction after all), but Mom would sit me down in a hotel room in Salt Lake City or Albuquerque or El Paso and look me square in the eyes with an intensity I've never seen from her. She would remind me that at my ROTC commissioning ceremony the commanding officers announced that, due to military downsizing, everyone in my class had been offered an out: no strings attached, no need to pay back scholarship money, no active duty commitment. She would confess that she wished I'd walked away. Then she would open up about the scars her deployment left, the trauma she carried back home and still wrestled with fifteen years later. "You signed a contract," she would say. "You can't undo that choice. But be careful, Lauren. The military always has an agenda." There would be a lot of tears and hugging, and then we would eat heaping bowls of ice cream with hot fudge, a shared favorite.

Would this have changed anything? If Mom had passed the torch to me slowly and deliberately, would I have felt its flames licking at my fingers? Like the choose-your-own-adventure books I loved as a child, could I have found an alternative storyline, one not so marked by confusion and pain? In difficult situations, parents must walk the tightrope between silence and the pummel of truth. At seven, I needed the illusion of normalcy. At eighteen, would I have been better served by blunt honesty? And how could Mom be expected to make that shift with barriers so deeply entrenched?

In reality, the cross-country drive was marked by laughter, not self-reflection. As she had when I was seven years old, mom weighed her options for protecting her daughter. This time, she gifted me enthusiasm to edge out my nervousness. We focused on exciting changes, like my impending mission of finding my first apartment and the less urgent task of finding a cat. The military came up when I tested my snazzy new ID card at base hotels along the way. "Oh my goodness!" Mom exclaimed upon entering our suite at Keesler Air Force Base in Biloxi, Mississippi. Then walking into the next room: "Holy cow! This is huge! Boy, I think the Air Force was definitely the way to go." (This wasn't the first or the last time she'd commend my choice of service branches.)

I laughed. "A little better than an Army tent?"

"I'd say so!" she said. "I bet the food's better, too! You can have ice cream at every meal!"

"Not if I want to fit in my uniform!"

The whole drive, I don't think we mentioned Mom's deployment. We didn't speculate on the potential for one of my own. The omissions didn't take up space in the packed Toyota Corolla. This wasn't me going to war; I was simply taking the next step toward independence, like the ultimate extended swim meet, or another round of college, just 3,000 miles away and with a uniform. Besides, I'd been told that public affairs officers rarely deployed, and certainly not as lieutenants. Of course, the military had made promises to Mom, too. Sometimes there's a fine line between optimism and denial.

I wasn't opposed to deploying; it was just such a vague notion, like most of what the patches on my uniform represented: Public Affairs, Air Force Special Operations Command. Stamped across the left chest pocket like a "property of" label: U.S. Air Force.

Mom and I actually drove past the Hurlburt Field base entrance initially, districted by the pristine sandy beach tracing the other side of the highway. My supervisor, a pretty blonde first lieutenant, laughed when I told her. "It's a small base," she said. "It kind of blends in with the surroundings."

The lieutenant showed Mom and me to our cozy suite at the base hotel. Less impressive than our Keesler lodging, it wasn't much bigger than my qalat room but equipped with a kitchenette, TV, and a queen-sized bed. Mom stayed one night. We ate fresh seafood at a beachfront restaurant, and then walked barefoot through powder-fine sand while the sunset split the Gulf into ripples of orange and red. "Wow," Mom said, nodding appreciatively. "Not a bad place to live." From the Southern California beach to the Gulf Coast, the military had indeed dealt me a fortunate hand.

When I reported to the Hurlburt Field public affairs office a few days later to begin my new career, I tried to draw strength from the ghost of Mom's goodbye hug, from the knowledge that she'd once been in these carefully shined shoes. I could sense my eyes widening every time the lieutenant introduced me to someone or pointed out another item on the to-do list. I gaped at the constantly-ringing phones, busy keyboards, and smiling all-knowingness of my coworkers, and at the high-ranking, frazzled importance of the base commander's staff next door. On base tours and media engagements, I found myself both a tourist and an attraction (*Everyone, meet our new L-T!*). Hurlburt Field chugged through an assembly line of training, deploying, training, deploying, training, deploying, executing the kind of high-impact, low-profile military missions I'd only imagined through Hollywood movies. I realized immediately that I was surrounded by super badasses. I, a mere mortal, had a lot of proving myself to do.

Two years later I was managing a public affairs and visual information office of twenty-nine people. I'd shamelessly emailed every junior woman officer on base and rallied a crew that met for potlucks, karaoke nights, and two-stepping at the local country bar. I'd rented a three-bedroom house and adopted a mother cat and her two kittens. I'd made myself a home. On base, I'd put my Johnson family perfectionist genes to use and established myself as a go-getter, volunteering for extra duties and weekend shifts. I slept with my Blackberry under my pillow, inviting all-hours alerts of base personnel involved in DUIs, domestic violence incidents, barfights, anything that could generate media interest. Twice, notifications of training mission plane crashes jolted me awake. No one died. Casualties weren't a concern; not yet. When I got overwhelmed, I repeated my mantra: *My job isn't life or death.*

I'd coordinated interviews with CNN and the *New York Times* and spent a month in the Republic of Mali, single-handedly providing public affairs support for 200 people and the first operational use of a new aircraft—an adventure my parents, grandparents, and I all raved about in our annual Christmas letters. After being promoted to first lieutenant, I'd welcomed a young second lieutenant with a similar introduction to the one I received, amazed at the knowledge and confidence and acronyms flowing from my mouth. The second lieutenant, on the other hand, looked as though he might collapse under the weight of information overload. Now in Gardez, I was again the one overwhelmed to the brink of toppling over.

Despite Major Rhodes' best efforts, nothing proved easy about my introduction to my job, FOB Gardez, or Paktia in general. The PowerPoint bible merely represented the chaos around me: a mishmash of people, places, tasks, and terminology more convoluted than the tangle of computer and telephone wires. In my two-and-a-half years of Air Force service, I'd become fluent in Air Forcean and even Special Opsian. I could rattle off full sentences in acronyms. The Army was a different beast, though, and different from the Army in a deployed environment, and different from the multi-service, multi-national, joint military-civilian International Security Assistance Force (ISAF) that encompassed the PRT.

The confusion began with my job title. As a U.S.-based public affairs (PA) officer, I danced between the pillars of media operations, community relations, and internal information. I served as documentarian, reporter, spokesperson, tour guide, and liaison, the point of contact and first line of communication for all things related to Hurlburt Field and its people. When necessary, I was damage control. In Afghanistan, I would still manage those pillars, but in a warped, fluid way, and by a different name: information operations (IO). I'd worked with IO before, a department whose stateside job was essentially to encourage security paranoia. They hacked into airmen's social media accounts, picked through our base website with a fine-tooth comb, and went dumpster diving for sensitive information. They revealed our security vulnerabilities, which in the military could endanger lives.

During my public affairs career training in 2007, I studied a different side of IO, one at the other end of the spectrum from PA. That IO centered on influence, using components like psychological operations and military deception, while PA, the instructors constantly stressed, dealt strictly with facts. PA relied on public trust, and overt attempts at influence eroded credibility. The Air Force didn't have career-trained IO officers, so when they were required to staff Afghanistan Provincial Reconstruction Teams, they chose the closest fit: public affairs.

When I reported to Camp Atterbury for PRT training before the deployment, I didn't know what my IO position would entail. After three months there, I still wasn't sure. I knew PRT IO was different, both from the paranoia-enforcers I'd worked with at Hurlburt Field and from the outdated Army IO doctrine used in training, based on Vietnam-era combat operations where the only "target," the audience, was the enemy. I knew IO was important. Our training briefings and even mainstream media touted Afghanistan as an information battle. If we were to win the war, we would need to win hearts and minds. We would win hearts and minds with information. (A simplified but not inaccurate example: *Afghanistan government good. Coalition forces good. Taliban bad.*) We would accomplish this without the help of mass media. As with much of the country, the literacy rate in Paktia lagged below twenty percent. Only pockets of Gardez City had electrical power to support television and radio connectivity, and only for about ten hours a day. Hand-crank radios disseminated by coalition forces and tuned to radio stations owned by coalition forces were the main source of information outside word of mouth, with the mouth belonging to tribal leaders and the local mosque. In the fight for hearts and minds, our opponents were the insurgents. They had distinct home field advantage, bolstered by widespread mistrust in the government and skepticism of coalition forces—both attitudes I would quickly begin to understand. Insurgents were also unhindered by bureaucracy or obligation to the truth.

At Hurlburt Field, the PA mission was concrete, with defined, logical steppingstones. We knew our audiences inside and out. We had situation-specific standard operating procedures, checklists, contingency plans, fill-in-the-blank press releases, and leadership guidance. We held crisis reaction exercises, crafted after action reports, and documented lessons learned. In Afghanistan, PRT IO officers seemed to be inventing the wheel. Guidance came in the form of vague directives: put together an IO plan for this mission or that construction project. Or, as a fellow IO officer quoted his commander in an email, "Sprinkle some IO dust on that." The particle type and method of sprinkling were for us to devise.

By summer 2009, the war had reached a critical tipping point. Violence had boiled over into Pakistan that winter when the Taliban took control of the Swat Valley, marching ever closer to Islamabad. Taliban leaders on both sides of the border united against coalition forces. Just before I reported to Camp Atterbury for training, newly-inaugurated President Barack Obama announced his strategy for Afghanistan, shifting the focus to counterinsurgency operations and training Afghan Security Forces. The administration would send 17,000 additional troops to Afghanistan and begin drawdown of forces in Iraq. Afghanistan's second democratic presidential election also approached, mere weeks after my team's arrival, an event billed by Defense Secretary Robert Gates as, "The most important objective for us in 2009 in Afghanistan."

In the States, public support was low, and apathy was high. In the seven years since I'd sworn my ROTC enlistment oath, war had swelled and faded in public consciousness. To most, Iraq and Afghanistan were interchangeable. Even plopped in the middle of the war, I couldn't yet fathom the enormity of the task at hand, its complexities, the tightness with which it would grasp me and refuse to let go, even when my feet landed back on American soil.

All I knew was that I was twenty-five years old, a lieutenant in a position designed for a major, two ranks above me and the equivalent of about six years' experience. Major Rhodes had replaced a captain who'd been removed because he "couldn't handle the job." I was the direct advisor to the PRT commander in all PA and IO matters. Most of my military service had involved working with a full PA staff in a military-friendly town on the beach in Florida. Even my deployment to Mali was low-threat, just a training mission, out of the public eye, a camera and pen my only weapons. I'd served in my traditional PA capacity supporting a unit I'd spent two years observing.

Watching Major Rhodes at her desk—my desk—my stomach curdled around the morning's pancakes. The major, in contrast, looked overjoyed. She flicked through the PowerPoint bible while I feverishly took notes about where to find important documents and who needed to know about what. "I won't go into detail, but this is the *Reader's Digest* version," she kept saying. She clicked past each slide with zeal, smiling and laughing and exclaiming, as if this was a presentation of family vacation photos, not the faces of local Afghan leaders, maps of tribal and ethnic boundaries, meeting schedules, report deadlines, and pending projects upon which the future of a fragile nation just might hang. (She did show me a few vacation photos, too: her on a beach with her husband, long dark hair blowing wild and carefree around her tan face.)

My biggest takeaway that first day was that, as evidenced by Major Rhodes' bible, much of my deployment would be represented by PowerPoint slides. Once a week, I would lead an hour-long, PowerPoint-guided IO Working Group to brainstorm communication strategies. I would attend a daily PRT Commander's Update Brief (CUB), where I detailed my activities on the designated IO slide. Every Thursday, I would participate in a virtual Brigade Update Brief (BUB) with the Army brigade staff at our Southeast Afghanistan regional headquarters. There was also a daily Provincial Update Brief among the Army teams stationed throughout Paktia, which I didn't attend, but I was privy to the post-meeting griping from my

Army colleagues, and I could appreciate the absurdity of the CUB/BUB/PUB triumvirate. For nine months, I would file reports and give presentations via PowerPoint. I would capture every Afghan community meeting, training program, groundbreaking and ribbon cutting ceremony in a tidy storyboard PowerPoint slide, *Reader's Digest*-style, with a few pictures and an event summary and analysis, to share with brigade headquarters. I would prepare a PowerPoint briefing for the U.S. ambassador to Afghanistan and for the Kansas City Chiefs Cheerleaders' morale visit (the latter which was ultimately canceled due to a security threat). I would joke that the best way for terrorists to disrupt coalition activities would be to plant a virus into Microsoft PowerPoint.

I know Major Rhodes' PowerPoint bible contained valuable information. Some made it into my notebook. Some I dug up later, called out by circumstance from the hard drive of my mind. But on that first day my eyes took in meeting agendas and manning charts and stale M&M's and bearded men and maps and vacation photos and slide number eighty-seven until it all blurred together like a movie on fast forward. The soundtrack came from ringing phones, the bleep of incoming emails, background chatter, and Major Rhodes' throaty laugh.

My brain, chock full of combat training, IO training, sleep-deprivation, and disorientation, could focus on one thing only: the thought that I was in completely over my head.

5

Solid(ish) Ground

I WAS USED TO BEING IN DEEP WATER—LITERALLY. A competitive swimmer, I spent a good chunk of my adolescence in pools. I was born for the water; according to my parents, if baby Lauren started crying, they simply took me into the bathroom and turned on the bathtub faucet and I stopped. The year after Mom deployed, I swam across the entire twenty-five-yard pool for the first time. During free time after lessons, the pool splashed with a mess of inflatable rafts and beach balls, thrashing arms and legs. I pushed off the wall and started cycling my arms and kicking my feet like the instructor had showed us. I swam a few yards and then popped up for a clumsy breath. A few more strokes, another bobbing gulp of air, a minor collision with a neon inner tube, and then there it was: the wall! I hadn't planned on making it all the way across, but when my fingertips touched the plaster I felt a surge of accomplishment. I was strong and powerful. If I could swim a whole pool length, I was sure I could do just about anything.

For years our house outside Seattle whirred in a cycle of activities, the changing of seasons marked by rotations of sporting equipment. At the end of summer I packed away my swimsuit, cap, and goggles, and grabbed my soccer cleats and shin guards. A few weeks later I laced up new high-tops for basketball, and then broke in my softball mitt come spring. Meanwhile, Shavonne and Matt ran, hit, shot, and tackled their way through their own seasonal cycles. I don't know how my parents kept the schedules straight, or how they maintained a stocked fridge to satisfy three always-ravenous athletes. Somewhere in between we found time for school, family ski trips, Disneyland vacations, and visits with the grandparents for nearly every holiday.

By middle school, our talents and favorites emerged. Shavonne would become a track and cross-country star. Matt would be the high school quarterback and a three-sport varsity athlete. Like my mom, I would be a swimmer. My mom's parents often came to watch me compete. They told me they enjoyed reliving Mom's swimming days. Mom and I even shared the same favorite event, the 100-yard breaststroke. Sometimes, Mom would tell me later, when my grandparents cheered for me they said her name instead of mine. "Go Debbie!" they screamed. "Go Debbie, go! I mean Lauren! Go Lauren!"

I had talent for swimming, and I liked the attention that came with success. I also loved sharing the sport with my mom. We compared times and training regimens, commiserated over aching shoulders and the infamous swimmer's tan lines that complicated prom dress shopping. I loved my teammates, too. We grew up together in the pool, our camaraderie unlike anything I've enjoyed beyond the military. Something deep and psychological also drew me to the sport. In the monotonous back and forth across the pool—sometimes as much as 150 laps, between four-and-a-half and five miles, both morning and evening—I found a soothing rhythm. I counted my strokes. Pool lengths were constant and measured. When my head dipped below the water, everything melted into a low gurgle in my ears and the splicing, bubbled lines of my hands in front of me. I liked the way the world looked through the water, especially during early morning workouts when the rising sun sliced into a million dancing prisms. Edges rippled and softened into a tempered, warped reality. The pool was sore muscles and red eyes and four-thirty a.m. wakeups, but it was also a sanctuary.

Approaching high school, I had everything planned out: I'd go to Stanford on a swimming scholarship and qualify for the Olympics. Then when I got old, around thirty, I'd retire from the sport and teach third grade, like my favorite teacher, Mrs. Fortin. Freshman year, the dream seemed feasible. Three other girls I swam with also started ninth grade at Meadowdale High School, and almost instantly we became something of high school swim team royalty. Over the next four years we broke nearly every school record and set a few district marks as well. We led the school to conference titles and strong finishes at the Washington State Swimming and Diving Championships and closed in on All-American times.

Steadily, though, along with the realization that I was good, but not good enough, other interests filtered in. Drama club, student leadership, a rigorous academic load, two years of track and passing the baton to Shavonne for her anchor leg in the 4x400 meter relay, my first boyfriend. "I'm probably the only parent who encourages her child to do less," my mom liked to say. After high school season my senior year, I appeared to finally listen. Swimming faded to a hobby. I accepted that I would need another way to pay for college. And I was ready for a new obsession.

In Gardez, shadowing Major Rhodes over those first three days, anticipation began to squeeze back in amidst the fear. I wrote in an email to my parents: "I'm looking forward to sitting down with our new team and hashing out all our processes the way WE want to do them. There's certainly a lot going on here, but exciting stuff! I can't wait to tell you more about it when we get settled in."

The rest of the PRT arrived, including Chris, a major I'd grown close to during training at Camp Atterbury. Chris was responsible for coordinating the PRT's day-to-day activities from the operations center next door to my office. He was my superior officer, which made our personal relationship inappropriate under military fraternization rules. On Chris's first evening in Afghanistan, we escaped to the privacy of the qalat lookout tower to watch the sunset.

"Wow," he said. "It's really beautiful from up here." I watched the pastel light play across his face. The son of Italian immigrants, Chris inherited the classic Mediterranean olive complexion and thick black hair, accented with striking green eyes. Still, he was attractive in an off-kilter way. His face was long and angular, too delicate a canvas for the piercing eyes, full lips, and prominent Roman nose. His muscular chest sat heavy and square on a slim frame, giving him the illusion of a perpetual shrug. Acne scars left remnants of an awkward youth. Some awkwardness carried over into adulthood; like me, Chris was prone to tripping over his own feet. Yet where I fought hard against my bumbling, he embraced his. He balanced endearing goofiness with a steady, anchored calm that reminded me of my mom. Perhaps that's why I latched onto him so strongly.

I let out a sigh I'd been holding for several days. "I feel so much better now that you're here," I said.

"So do I," Chris said. "It's crazy how much I missed you." He scooted his hand across the tower railing until it rested on mine.

"Me too!" I said. "Seriously, I have no idea what I'm doing, and this place is so confusing and overwhelming, and I'm freaking out a little bit." The stress and frustrations suddenly converged on me, and big, sloppy tears spilled down my cheeks. I swiped at them with my uniform sleeve. "I'm sorry. It's just so weird here. But knowing you're next door is such a comfort."

Chris pulled me into a hug. I pressed my face into his broad chest and breathed in his Old Spice scent. "It's gonna be OK," he said. "Nobody knows what they're doing right now. You'll get the hang of it. We all will. We've got a good team, and we'll make it through this. Together."

I was sure Chris was right. He'd grown up in multiple countries and been stationed around the world; he knew the nuances of culture shock. As mind-boggling as things seemed, I suspected the deployment would be similar to that first twenty-five-yard swim all those years ago: some rough water, not always graceful, but before I knew it I'd touch the wall. And afterwards, as they always did, I expected the sore muscles would go away.

Thankfully, I wouldn't be completely on my own with my job transition. I would partner with an Army sergeant from the Agribusiness Development Team (ADT) assigned to Paktia as well as two lieutenants from another Army unit that conducted ground operations, including combat missions, throughout the province. Both units had been in Gardez for several months. (They would return home six months into my deployment, to be replaced by new units bringing new priorities and leadership strategies. Three months after that, our PRT would change command. Deployments are a high-stakes game of leapfrog.)

On my introduction the IO office, the ADT sergeant, Drew Castillo, a middle-aged Hawaiian man with salt-and-pepper hair, rose from his desk to greet me. "It's very nice to meet you, ma'am," he said. Unlike to Major Rhodes' strong handshake, Drew's surprised me for its softness. His hand hugged mine tenderly, as though we were longtime friends, not new professional war zone colleagues. Drew, I would quickly learn, op erated with a warmth and laid-back air that seemed incompatible with a deployed environment: refreshing, but almost too casual for comfort.

I loosened my too-tight grasp. "Nice to meet you, too," I said. "I'm looking forward to working with you. It sounds like the ADT is doing some great work." My agricultural knowledge consisted of the Publix Super Market produce department, but I knew Paktia remained a largely agrarian province, and therefore the ADT played a critical role in local development.

The two Army lieutenants hovered behind Drew, sizing me up. Before either spoke I could tell they were stark opposites. Nick's desk backed up to mine, nearly empty except for a photo of his wife and a dip-spit cup. He was all Army, about my height but dense with muscle, brown hair shimmed in the classic high-and-tight. His uniform sleeves were rolled up to the elbows, and as I approached, he crossed his thick forearms slowly, deliberately. A wad of tobacco twitched in his cheek. Nick's colleague, Jacob, who worked in the operations center monitoring ongoing operations, leaned against the edge of Nick's desk, at once eager and shy. He was pale and freckled, with frizzy hair that refused to be tamed by his Army hat. All the places where Nick's uniform pinched tight, Jacob's rumpled. He looked like a boy playing dress up. I was relieved to think that he looked younger than me, and at least equally wide-eyed.

Nick made the first move, brusquely shaking my hand and then immediately re-folding his arms. "I'm gonna call you Larry," he said.

"Um . . . Okaaayyy," I stammered.

Major Rhodes laughed. "Oh, he's just being funny," she said, with a dismissive wave. "So, when I first told them your name he thought I said *Laurence* instead of *Lauren*. He thought you were a guy, which"—she gestured to me—"obviously you're not."

"So I'm gonna call you Larry," Nick said again.

"Hi *Lauren*," Jacob said, stressing each syllable ever-so-slightly and ever-so-slightly rolling his eyes. "It's good to meet you." He grinned, and I felt myself relax, ever-so-slightly.

The PRT relied on Afghan employees as well. As the IO officer, I oversaw two Afghan personnel, Aamir and Rahim, interpreters whose specialized job was to advise us on cultural issues: *Can I photograph that? Will this radio message resonate with the local population? Will it offend anyone? What colors should we use for this poster?* Almost everything we did or said went through the filter of Aamir and Rahim. The two were almost as different as Nick and Jacob. Rahim, tall and scrawny, shifted his eyes nervously between Major Rhodes and me, but he bowed and shook my hand vigorously when we met. Aamir stood more poised, with a round, kind face. He clasped my hand in both of his, a sign of trust and intimacy I would have trouble getting used to in Afghanistan, and looked me square in the eyes. "Pleased to meet you, ma'am," he said. "Thank you for coming to Afghanistan. We are at your service."

"Aamir and Rahim are both very hard workers," Major Rhodes said. "They've been extremely helpful to our team." Both men bowed at the compliment. The major explained that they lived on base but had a few days leave every month to visit their families sixty miles away in Kabul. Rahim had a wife and young children. Aamir would shortly be engaged. We paid them handsomely by Afghan standards, but our employment carried risk. Interpreters were routinely murdered for working with coalition forces—brutal, statement-making murders, like the tribal elder ally who would be slaughtered a few months into our deployment, his body parts scattered along a roadside. Rahim had been stopped once at an insurgent checkpoint on his way to Kabul. He managed to lie his way to safety, but when he recalled the incident, his face still pinched with terror.

Back at my desk I watched the last nine months in warp-speed through the PowerPoint bible: provincial government officials cutting ribbons, shaking hands, standing in front of crowded rooms of headscarves and *pakol* caps. The men's beards seemed to grow and shrink before my eyes as one face blended into the next. I couldn't keep track of who was in charge of what utility or security force, though it didn't seem to matter. For the most part, Major Rhodes lumped them all together as she spoke of the kindness and competence of the officials, praise we had been hearing from her team all through training. She went on about all the progress the PRT had made and what a privilege it was to work alongside the Afghans, including the provincial governor. "He really gets IO," she said. "He brings a media team everywhere he goes so they can play clips on TV and radio. He's a great ally." Though I'd heard this commendation before, I still recorded it in my notebook. I wrote "Gets IO" next to the governor's name and underlined it twice.

My closest local governmental colleague would be the director of information and culture, who managed the government radio and TV stations and oversaw the rest of Paktia's meager media infrastructure. The two of us could leverage each other's capacity, sharing information and collaborating on radio programming. Before our introductory meeting, Major Rhodes complimented the director, too. He had knowledge and aptitude beyond many Paktia officials, she said, which made him well-placed to bring the province into the next broadcasting century. As such, the PRT had promised the director a new multi-million-dollar media center in Gardez; it would be my job to see the promise through. Then she mentioned, almost off-handedly, that the director preferred working with men. I didn't want to pass judgment, but sitting across from him at the PRT conference room table, I couldn't shake the feeling that the director was glaring at me. He had a soft, handsome face, but his eyes shot lasers. As a cultural gesture, Major Rhodes and I both wore scarves over our hair, as PRT women would do at every meeting. While Major Rhodes said her goodbyes—"It's been *such* a pleasure working with you. You are doing *great* things for Paktia. I *so* look forward to hearing all about the media center when it's complete!"—I wanted to pull the scarf over my face to shield myself from the director's penetrating stare. Aamir, who interpreted the meeting, even mentioned the cold reception afterwards. I knew gender discrimination remained prevalent in Afghanistan, especially in conservative rural areas like Paktia, but experiencing hostility firsthand, and from someone I would be working with closely, was a punch in my gut that even body armor couldn't shield. I tried not to be discouraged, though it was becoming clear that many things about this deployment would be out of my control.

By the change of command ceremony on July 15, four days after my arrival in Gardez, I had full reign of the two laptops and my desk phone. I could make educated guesses at the names of my American and Afghan colleagues. I could find my way to the gym and the Olive Gardez and wind through the operations center hallways to say hi to Chris or Jacob. In my first official act as PRT Paktia information operations officer, I took photos of my commander shaking hands with the provincial deputy governor at the ceremony. We were stuffed into a small hangar next to the Helicopter Landing Zone, where high ceilings swallowed the speeches and the smell of grilled hamburgers mixed with body odor and gasoline. I let the buzzing layers of conversation envelop me, a swirl of English and Pashtu and Dari, and laughter that transcended language barriers. This was what I was here for, I thought. Sure, there would be hard times, but these moments could sustain me.

My commander, Lt. Col. Dennis McGuire, accepted the ceremonial flag that represented the transfer of authority from his predecessor, and the two colonels exchanged crisp salutes. Then Colonel McGuire shook hands with the deputy governor, his camouflaged sleeve mingling symbolically with the governor's baggy white blouse.

"You must have friends in order to make this work," Colonel McGuire said. "And I consider you all now my friends."

After my initial interaction with the director of information and culture, I wasn't in complete agreement, but I included the quote in my post-ceremony press release. I also highlighted the previous team: "The PRT facilitated more than one hundred projects worth more than $50 million supporting the areas of transportation, education, electricity, law and governance, health, agriculture, and water and sanitation." Though impressive, we were already learning that the numbers represented overzealous and unstainable activities. We had our work cut out for us.

I emailed the release to the Army brigade headquarters in the neighboring province, feeling a wave of satisfaction as I entered my signature block:

Lauren K. Johnson, 1 Lt., Usaf

Information Operations Officer

PRT Paktia

FOB Gardez

Then I sat back in my chair and stared at my two computer screens, and I realized I had no idea what I was supposed to do next.

Part Two

IMPORTANT *adjective*

Definition: Common

1. Marked by or indicative of significant worth or consequence: valuable in content or relationship.

2. Giving evidence of a feeling of self-importance.

Definition: in Military/War

1. As dictated by senior leaders and/or the United States government.

2. An event or activity, often of nebulous comprehension, which, though outcome and effects may be largely unknown, requires significant time and effort.

6

Outside the Wire

THE GAPING DOOR OF THE MILITARY VEHICLE looked like a tooth-less steel mouth, open wide in a bemused "Oh!" as if to say, "What the hell are *you* doing here?" I was asking myself the same question.

The engineers who designed these Mine Resistant-Ambush Protect-ed armored trucks (MRAPs) obviously hadn't done so with a five-foot-four occupant in mind. A fourteen-ton Humvee on steroids, the base of the door sat level with the nametag on my bulletproof vest. MRAPs were constructed for higher ground clearance to better deflect blasts from the increasing threat of Improvised Explosive Devices (IEDs), the roadside bombs responsible for the majority of military casualties in the Middle East. July 2009, my first full month in Afghanistan, had become the dead-liest month for American troops in the country since 2001. (In October, that record would be broken again en route to the deadliest year of the war, with more than double the casualties of 2008.) Two weeks earlier four U.S. soldiers were killed in an IED attack on a convoy of Humvees, the final straw that led our leadership to direct that only the RG-31 MRAP be used from that point forward.

Even MRAPs weren't infallible. Just weeks before our training group departed Camp Atterbury, Indiana, an MRAP from one of the current PRTs hit an IED, destroying the vehicle and killing two team members, including the PRT commander. If training had failed to communicate the seriousness of the situation we were about to enter, two Killed in Action certainly did. Passing through Bagram, we'd seen the gutted MRAP. I stood beside it, my heart in my throat, my eyes scanning the mangled metal. The truck looked like it had been through a shredder.

Today's convoy would be my first ride in an MRAP. In training, we only used Humvees. We practiced getting in, getting out, getting in and out quickly, getting in and out quickly with body armor, getting in and out quickly with body armor while upside down in a vehicle rollover simulator. With MRAPs, easy access didn't seem to be a priority. Some variants had foldout steps. The more primitive model in front of me had a two-rung makeshift ladder, which still only came down to my waist. I slid Annie, my rifle, gingerly along the metal floorboards inside the vehicle, grabbed the handles on each side of the door, and hoisted my boot to the bottom step. My arms strained with the effort. As my armor-clad chest cleared the opening the momentum carried me into a belly flop against the floor. Thankfully, Annie was the only witness.

I picked myself up—a benefit of being five-foot-four was that I could almost stand up completely inside—and chose the seat behind the driver. Two security forces soldiers would sit closest to the back door, better prepared to respond to a threat. My team was learning that threats lurked everywhere in Paktia Province. Even this simple route to meet government officials in Gardez City for what should be a peaceful handshake of a mission could quickly morph into combat. Just a few days earlier, on July 21, a gang of militants had attacked the governor's compound, the provincial intelligence headquarters, and the local police station, leaving five dead and four wounded. We were headed right for ground zero.

I put my Kevlar helmet and camera bag on top of the MRAP seat and climbed back out the door for the pre-mission briefing. Sleep clouded my mind and I felt disembodied, like I was watching from one of the qalat lookout towers as someone who looked like me marched around in body armor and prepared for an early morning convoy. Another sensation encroached on the grogginess, though, something I hadn't felt to this degree in Afghanistan: adrenaline. I'd spent my first three weeks flitting around a desk. Though I accepted a desk was where my job mostly required me to be, my body yearned for action. It was a twisted desire. I didn't wish for combat. I hadn't completely shaken the paranoia from my initial helicopter ride into FOB Gardez, but I wanted more than PowerPoint and meetings. I wanted to do something tangible. I wanted to shake hands and kiss babies and engage in the *Three Cups of Tea* work I'd boasted about to my parents. The promise of a mission off base sent anticipation zapping through my veins.

The rest of the convoy personnel formed a lopsided circle around the security forces platoon leader. The MRAP crews had been up for hours loading the vehicles, mounting weapons, and checking communications equipment. Their camouflage speckled with dirt and sweat. A few popped open Rip It energy drinks with dusty fingers. I tugged my hat down to shield my eyes. The sun came at me from all directions, slicing through the thin air, bouncing off the MRAPs lined up on one side and the dejected Humvees parked on the other, and radiating from the gravel under my feet.

Our security forces platoon leader lifted his hat, wiped his brow with his uniform sleeve, and squinted into the crowd. "Today's mission is to attend the Provincial Development Council meeting at the governor's compound in Gardez," he said. "I'm the convoy commander. Colonel McGuire is the mission commander." On the other side of the circle, our PRT commander nodded in acknowledgement.

Lt. Col. McGuire resembled nothing of the crusty, war-hardened military commanders of a Hollywood film. He was tall, thin, and bespectacled, with dirty blonde hair that was engaged in its own war against an onslaught of gray (by the end of the deployment, the latter would prove victorious). Friendly and approachable—"like a cool uncle," a teammate aptly described—I liked the commander immediately when we first met at Camp Atterbury. He had smiled and told me what an important job I had. Then he said he had spent most of his Air Force career stationed at Hurlburt Field as a special operations pilot. Colonel McGuire's colleagues now made up the base's leadership. His friends were my bosses.

"I was worried about having a lieutenant in the IO spot," he said, "but I've heard good things about you, L-T. It's a pleasure to have you on our team." I returned the colonel's smile, determined not to let him down.

In Gardez, the platoon leader reminded us of the "order of march," the lineup of vehicles and drivers. My MRAP was driven by Graham Bailey, a good-natured, tobacco-chewing sergeant who shaved his head but kept a well-groomed mustache. On a deployment to Iraq, Sergeant Bailey earned the nickname "IED Magnet" because his vehicle had hit roadside bombs five times. In Afghanistan, so far, he'd been explosion-free. I hoped today wouldn't be the day his luck changed.

Our travel would take place mostly on paved roads, which reduced the hazard of buried IEDs, but bombs could still be hidden in bushes, piles of trash, animal carcasses. We were trained to be alert for anything that didn't belong; it could be disguising a bomb. We'd also been taught to check culverts, the drains and pipes running under the road, which were perfect for concealing IEDs. On training convoys at Camp Atterbury, we stopped at each ditch and every pipe, sending a scouting team to look for wires. In Afghanistan, such thoroughness was impossible. If we stopped at every suspicious location, we would never reach our destination. Our sluggishness itself would make us a target.

In Afghanistan, convoys most often found IEDs by driving over them and blowing them up.

The previous night at our mission briefing our intelligence officer had warned us of specific threats. The first threat was serious but also an ongoing joke, in the caustic way of war zone humor: We should be on the lookout for white Toyota pickup trucks. Reports always mentioned potential weapons or attackers in a white Toyota pickup, and Gardez seemed to be a breeding ground for the vehicles. Like culverts and piles of trash, they were everywhere. We were also on alert for people in blue burqas, specifically with manly shoes or a manly walk. This had been briefed to all convoys since the deadly July 21 attack, where male suicide bombers disguised themselves in blue burqas. A news article I read reported, "Bits of the blue burqas could be seen on the bloodstained sidewalk and hanging from nearby trees hours after the attack."[4]

"Mount up!" The platoon leader hollered. "We roll out in five."

I locked eyes with Chris, who stood on the periphery of the now dissolving circle. He wasn't coming with us, but because his job included planning and troubleshooting every mission, he could always justify attending the briefings. I knew he was worried, sending me on my first convoy into the city while he stayed behind, waiting for the radio report that something had gone wrong. I held his gaze for a moment, his bright eyes serious under the shade of his hat. Then he slipped away between Humvees.

Back at my MRAP I managed to preserve my dignity in front of my teammates, climbing back into the vehicle with minimal difficulty. As I found my seat, the engine gargled to life, sending vibrations across the crew compartment and upsetting the fine Afghan dust. The dust never remained stagnant for long. Every step sent a plume rising around my boots. It hung in the air in a gritty fog, clinging to shirtsleeves, to hair, to lips, between teeth. Dust choked the belts of the treadmills at the base gym and had been responsible for the demise of many laptops. I blamed it for the nagging cough that grabbed me practically the minute I set foot in Afghanistan.

As other soldiers strapped in beside me, I swapped my hat for my helmet, careful not to disturb the hair bun that stuck out above my vest. I scrunched the bun tight every morning, but like the dust it never stayed put. Today, anticipating helmet-wear, I'd braided my hair before tying it up, like my mom used to do for me before soccer or softball games. With a carabineer clip, I secured my camera case to a metal ring on the wall, and then I fastened my seatbelt as snugly as possible around my metal-plated lap.

Our vehicles lurched forward, beginning the slow trek across the base to the main gate. I pulled a headset from the knot of wires above me. It fit lopsided over my helmet, but I could hear the chatter of the convoy. I flipped the switch that would restrict my comments to only my vehicle and pushed the white "talk" button.

"Hey guys," I said, "thanks for the ride!"

Sergeant Bailey's voice came crackling back. "Uh-oh, we better watch ourselves, L-T's up on comms!"

"Ah come on," I laughed. "You guys should know by now you don't need to censor yourselves around me."

These men and I had spent four months cramming our tired, sweaty bodies together in too small seats on buses and aircraft, bartering for the candy in combat meals, sharing stain remover and weapon-cleaning duties following particularly muddy training exercises. We'd celebrated promotions, birthdays, births of children, and discussed impending divorces. Together we'd outlined epic strategies for the Zombie apocalypse, a line of heated conversation that began when I posed the theory on a crowded Camp Atterbury bus that every guy has a Zombie Plan, and one that would continue throughout the deployment. I earned my credibility running in the fast group during morning training workouts and bringing back home-made cookies after the four-day break between Indiana and Afghanistan. The Army security forces team earned theirs making me feel welcome and safe. One minute they were in formation and shouting commands, the next they were telling dirty jokes or breaking into the chorus of "My Girl". They made me roll my eyes, and they made me laugh, but I never doubted their competence. I'd heard about the brotherhood of war, where you trusted your teammates with your life. With this group of National Guard soldiers, I understood the meaning.

Our convoy rolled by a tidy row of wooden barracks and onto the gravel lane that looped past the Helicopter Landing Zone on the right and an overgrown graveyard on the left. The graveyard was a unique facet of the base that both intrigued and unnerved me. Afghanistan bases were full of similar quirks. At Bagram, a relic from the Soviet occupation, thick rolls of concertina wire fenced off sections of the base and hung with signs that read, "DANGER! Mine area! Do not cross!" Down the road from the tran-sient lodging where we stayed while passing through lurked a boneyard of rusted tanks and aircraft, left behind after the Soviet withdrawal twen-ty-one years prior. Like an eerie drive-through museum, we watched out the bus windows exhibit after exhibit documenting the decaying remains of those who'd come before.

Beyond the Gardez graveyard, the convoy passed the FOB's second dining facility, a three-room industrial tent, and then entered a channel en-closed in high walls of HESCO barriers that would take us to the main gate. Just before the gate, we sputtered to a stop.

"Lock and load!"

The command rippled down the vehicles. Keeping Annie's long muz-zle pointed at the vehicle floor, I slapped the bottom of the magazine to make sure it was securely in place and yanked back the charging handle. The bolt sprang forward, pulling a round into the chamber with a satisfying click. Annie was ready to fire. I had practiced this process hundreds of times at training, with no bullets, with blanks, with live ammunition. A voice in my head reminded me that I was in Afghanistan now. This time it was real. I reached down to the holster strapped to my right thigh, wrestled out Janie and armed her, too. Between the two weapons and the extra magazines stuffed in pouches on my vest, I carried 225 rounds of ammunition. I looked much tougher than I felt.

The convoy started moving again, grunting forward to the inside gate of the base. The gunner of the first vehicle hollered over the rumble of the convoy: "Four vehicles, one civilian, twenty-two U.S., two local nationals!" The American soldiers guarding the gate waved us through, and we continued to the outer gate, manned by Afghan Security Guards whose long beards fell across their dark green camouflage. Then the gravel and HES-CO barriers ended at a concrete road. We were officially "outside the wire."

We turned left and slid cockeyed onto the road. There were no drawn lanes, but if there were we wouldn't have fit. A military convoy dominated Afghan roads. In one of the paradoxes of counterinsurgency operations, we were supposed to be winning hearts and minds, but we plowed through villages, parting traffic, disturbing cattle, and cracking pavement under our fourteen-ton vehicles. We were supposed to make locals feel safe, but we watched them from behind the double-plated glass windows of our armored vehicles, through ballistic sunglasses, under helmets we tightened with fireproof gloves. As I stared out the window at the world outside the gate, fear slithered under my body armor. Part of me still struggled to believe it, and another part couldn't yet reconcile how I'd come to be here, but off the FOB and away from overt American influence, it was clear that I was truly, undeniably in Afghanistan.

Growing up, I heard more tales of travels than war stories. Though I suppose in my family the two are linked. My grandparents were all globetrotters, with their adventurous spirits rooted in the military. For my dad's parents, Norm and Dot Johnson, the Air Force broke them free of poverty and simple, small-town Michigan life. Norm came of age just after World War II—angry, in fact, that the war had ended before he'd had a chance to contribute. When he couldn't earn enough working part time while attending college, he turned to the military. During the six-day train ride from his hometown outside Detroit to basic Training at Lackland Air Force Base in San Antonio, Texas, Grandpa saw more of the country than he ever had. He was earning more money than ever too, and he sent half of each pay check home to help his mother and three younger sisters.

Norm met my grandmother, Dorothy, on his two-week leave peri-od post-Basic Training. A farm girl, still in high school at the time, Dot's parents weren't thrilled about the older, military suiter who threatened to whisk her out of the Midwest. Her father had served stateside during World War I and seen the stressful and restricted lives military wives often led. Nevertheless, my grandparents married as soon as Norm finished his job training, after only five dates, and promptly relocated to North Carolina, where Norm instructed Korea-bound soldiers in radar maintenance.

Norm wasn't planning on making the military a career, but an as-signment to Italy with his young family changed his mind. Over the next twenty-six years, the Air Force took my grandparents to Greenland, Alas-ka, New Jersey, Germany, Oregon, Nevada, and California. My dad only remembers through stories learning to speak in a combination of English, Italian, and baby-talk, but he spent his middle school years in Germany and has fond memories of venturing to France for Boy Scout jamborees, explor-ing castles and old battlefields. Perhaps his father's Air Force adventures formed the foundation for my dad's love of travel as well.

My mom's parents, Jean and Jerry Home, grew up only a few miles apart outside Seattle but didn't meet until they were teenagers. Theirs is my favorite war story: During World War II, their older brothers served in the same Army unit, the Seventy Fifth Infantry—they actually shared a foxhole in the Battle of the Bulge—and their mothers planned a picnic by a nearby lake to introduce the families. Jerry wasn't enthused about meet-ing a girl, so as soon as they arrived he challenged Jean to a swimming race across the lake. He expected her to be intimidated, but she promptly agreed. Then she beat him.

Jerry was in Navy ROTC at the time. The following year, on his last mission before returning home, Jerry's brother was killed in action. Jerry was devastated. He wanted to quit ROTC, not to get out of the military, but to go fight. As it turned out, he didn't need to wait long; in February, 1945, Jerry's entire ROTC class commissioned six months early to join the invasion of Japan. Like my mom's fears for her deployment, Jerry thought his would be a suicide mission. He never found out. The U.S. dropped two atomic bombs and Japan surrendered. Even with the war ending, Jerry shortly received another set of orders to the Pacific Theater, based at Pearl

Harbor, Hawaii. Not wanting to leave Jean behind with nothing but nebulous hopes (and plenty of suitors), he proposed.

The Homes' travel origins were an inverse of sorts to the Johnsons'; military travel dictated their life trajectory, too, but in the opposite way. While on his Pearl Harbor assignment, Jerry spent thirty-five days at sea on a weather patrol. The ship offered no outside communication, so he couldn't speak with or even write to his new bride. Back on land, follow-on orders to Japan loomed likely, and the assignment would be unaccompanied. The threat of traveling to the other side of the world for potentially years without Jean drove my grandpa to the only major decision he ever made without consulting his wife: to resign his commission, leave active duty, and join the Navy reserves.

Travel began in earnest for the Homes after retirement. They joined a military retiree travel club and introduced Norm and Dot over a six-week motorhome tour of Australia and New Zealand. Mom's parents were exploring Turkey in 1990 when they heard about Saddam Hussein's invasion of Kuwait. As with all of us after 9/11, no one anticipated the effects rippling down to our family. Sometimes that's how it is with war; it creeps in slowly, low crawling through the brush and flanking you from behind. When you suddenly find yourself in the middle of a firefight, you wonder how you missed the warning shots.

I traced Grandma and Grandpa Johnson's travel stories through their basement. The room seemed a magical place: the plush carpet and bright orange corner chair, the cozy wood stove, the candy dishes featuring a rotating supply of gourmet chocolates. Most of all, despite the outdated wood paneling and chipping paint, I loved the walls. Covered with decorative plates from foreign places, the walls formed a scrapbook of my grandparents' travels. European cityscapes lined the center beam. Mountain ranges stretched above the sofa, and Australian wildlife frolicked around the windows. The plates provided a visual backdrop to the stories I loved and were my first glimpses of the world beyond the West Coast. I counted the plates; there were almost one hundred. I vowed to follow my grandparents' examples and collect hundreds of travel stories of my own.

By twenty-five I was off to a good start. I'd been to half the fifty states, plus Mexico and Canada. I'd swum in the Mediterranean off three different coasts, gotten lost in Westminster Abbey, and been kissed by a street artist on Rome's Spanish Steps. Building my own stash of travel collectibles, I added a shot glass for every trip.

Travel didn't lead me to the military, but it made for an appealing bonus. The Air Force sent me to school in Los Angeles, and then to a base in Florida, with forays to Colorado Springs, Washington, DC, South Dakota, and, though not on my bucket list, Montgomery, Alabama several times. Mali proved an unexpected delight; the way Italy had for Grandpa Johnson, the trip could have inspired a military career. When I learned I would be deploying to Paktia Province, a mountainous region in Southeastern Afghanistan, I was excited for the decorative plate-worthy scenery. In the convoy heading to Gardez City, though, nothing about the barren view outside my MRAP window inspired feelings of beauty or comfort. From the dusty landscape to the qalats along the roadway to the mountains in the distance, everything sulked in shades of brown. The only streak of color came from the clear blue sky, which melted into a brown haze at the horizon.

As our convoy rolled toward the city, pinpricks of color dotted the landscape. A child's red shirt. A garbage-filled ditch. The gaudy décor of a cargo *jingle truck* pulled (pushed?) off the road to let us pass. Lopsided billboards advertising personal hygiene and the upcoming presidential election. Children running alongside the convoy. Children throwing rocks at the convoy.

Downtown Gardez arrived with a jarring explosion of color. A neon green railing. A turquoise dome roof on a mud brick building. Under yellow, red, and orange umbrellas, a sidewalk market displaying green leafy vegetables, bright citrus fruits, and pink-skinned pomegranates. Bloody-red slabs of hanging meat buzzing with black flies. Boys in blue vests and red *topi* caps pushing pastel wheelbarrows heaping with nuts and grains. The images danced across the MRAP window like a children's flipbook, cartoonish and disjointed. Then we were in the traffic circle, where we were supposed to scan rooftops for potential threats. I craned my neck to look as the buildings whirled past in a billow of dust. Our convoy was flanked by mopeds and donkey-drawn carts, and white Toyota after white Toyota. Bearded men in Pashtun headscarves scurried down the narrow sidewalks, crisscrossed by women in blue burqas.

White Toyotas. Women in blue burqas. Women in blue burqas.

Then chaos faded as we pulled onto a side street and ambled to a stop beside the governor's compound. The complex, like the city itself, clamored with color. A grid of pale blue wrought iron fences, red rock walls, and concertina wire enclosed an olive green building with barred windows. A few spindly trees fanned with bright green leaves. *Oh god,* I thought. *Were those the trees hanging with blue fabric?*

"Dismount!" a voice yelled.

The two soldiers at the back of my MRAP responded quickly. The door *whooshed* open and they sprang out before I extricated myself from my seat belt and headset. I scooted to the doorway and waited for the sign that the perimeter was clear and it was safe to exit the vehicle. Through the open door I observed as the soldiers strolled a few paces in each direction, cocking their heads, watching and listening. I heard the squeal of downtown traffic, the rhythmic *thwank thwank* of boots on pavement, and my heartbeat, faster than normal, pulsing in my ears.

Sergeant Bailey popped his head around the back of the truck. "Come on out, L-T!" His voice sounded far away. I felt disembodied again. I watched Combat Barbie Lauren climb out of the vehicle and step onto the site of a recent massacre. Her boots hit the bloodstained sidewalk. She fell in confident step behind Sergeant Bailey.

I looked at my hands. My gloves wrapped around the grip and muzzle of my rifle, angling Annie at a "ready" forty-five degrees. How had they learned to do that? My body moved with an assurance I didn't feel. Yet there was something else, too, an excitement, that I *shouldn't* feel. It was as if I'd been spliced into two people: the Lauren who ducked behind barriers in paintball games, and the room-storming, rifle-toting Lauren from training exercises. But this wasn't an exercise. The rifle in my hands was real. I felt the weight of the vest against my chest, the helmet against my temples, the holster around my thigh, and I wondered, again, *What the hell am I doing here?*

7

Fear Smells Like Chai

FOR MOST OF ROTC, I DIDN'T THINK MUCH ABOUT WAR or politics. I did my schoolwork, shined my boots, and ironed my uniform. On weekends I collected bottle caps from Smirnoff Ice. I practiced marching tight squares around my dorm room and saluting my reflection in the mirror. The luster of my Hollywood dream school wore off quickly. The campus and its inhabitants were gorgeous, the Southern California weather perfect, the local beaches dazzling, but the atmosphere, for all its beauty, seemed flat and cold. Like a postcard, I could only stand back and admire. To compensate, I threw myself into the one place I felt comfortable. In ROTC I found the same easy camaraderie I'd enjoyed in the swimming pool and in that basement youth group, among other awkward teenagers, united in a common cause. I focused on being a model military cadet, on keeping my GPA up so I could make the Commander's List, on falling in love with a boy who looked especially handsome in his cadet uniform.

Every Friday, when ROTC classes took place, I put on my own carefully-pressed uniform and shoes so shiny I could see my reflection in the toes. If it was a Blues day, the pants were itchy polyester and the top flared at the waist in an attempt at femininity. On BDU days my Battle Dress Uniform matched the green and black fatigues my mom used to wear. Both outfits made me feel powerful. I was unique on campus, yet part of a community. And every time I put on my uniform, I felt connected to my mom.

The U.S. invaded Iraq the spring of my freshman year. Still, war seemed vague and far away. Politics wasn't a subject I consciously considered. Most of my knowledge came secondhand from arguments between my grandfathers. I identified as Republican because my family leaned that way. When an ROTC faculty member called CNN the "Clinton News Network," I found it funny and started repeating the phrase, though I didn't watch much news coverage, CNN or otherwise. I didn't have informed opinions about weapons of mass destruction or international oil reserves or what constituted an imminent threat to the United States, but I knew that I wanted Saddam Hussein gone. He was an evil dictator who tormented his people. He was the man who sent my mom to war.

When I called home, we said things like, "It's time to finish this once and for all," and "We'll get him this time." It was personal, and it was that simple. We even sang that old song:

Joy to the world, Saddam is dead!
We barbequed his head . . .

On the liberal arts campus around me, students drew body outlines in chalk on the sidewalks, giving them labels like *PREGNANT IRAQI WOMAN KILLED BY U.S. BOMB.* Mobs shouted about illegitimate President Bush and human rights and imperialism. Their fervor shocked me. I'd never witnessed protests before. The closest I'd come were the 1999 World Trade Organization riots in Seattle. I was a high school sophomore at the time, in the midst of finals and swim season, just twenty miles north, but it may as well have been another hemisphere. Now I listened to my college classmates prattle about social justice and inequity. Meanwhile, they wore designer clothing and drove expensive cars. When I participated in discussions, I offered dissenting views that often drew glares from around the room. I deemed my peers ignorant and hypocritical. I was the one in uniform. My mom had been to war. I thought that made me informed. I was too proud to realize that we were the same, my classmates and I: we knew everything and nothing.

In my uniform on Fridays, I took the long route to class, skirting around the angry gatherings. No one ever hassled me, and I never bothered them, but I didn't understand their anger. Attitudes in ROTC swung the opposite way; protests only stoked the fire. One day the whole detachment filed into the ROTC auditorium for a training briefing (we called briefing days Death by PowerPoint, an omen of things to come). At the end, a video flickered on the projection screen. The clip started slowly, with a few static patriotic scenes and Toby Keith's voice trilling the first notes of his post-9/11 anthem "Courtesy of the Red White and blue." The feed cut to a photo of flag-draped coffins. A chill shot down my body. Images of the crumbling twin towers melted into the Statue of Liberty and Uncle Sam. The music picked up, and the scenes came faster: waving flags, fighter jets peeling away from formation, targets locking, missiles firing, bombs dropping, explosions, explosions, explosions. Someone from the back of the room hollered "AIRPOWER!" and people cheered. My body pulsed with the music. My heart pounded. By the time Keith sang "We'll put a boot in your ass, it's the American way!" the whole room was cheering. More planes. More explosions. More cheering. I cheered, my face curling into a maniacal grin. My whole body swelled with emotion, and I realized for the first time that I was truly proud to be part of the military, to be, like my mom and my grandfathers before me, working toward something powerful and noble and greater than myself.

Seven years later as I followed Sergeant Bailey through the gate at the Paktia governor's compound, nothing resembling pride, power, or nobility found room in my mind. My heartbeat quickened when I stepped from one slab of concrete to the next, placing me officially on their turf. I reached up and removed my sunglasses, like the cultural advisors had instructed. Greeting the locals with unshielded eyes, they said, communicates friendliness and trust. Squinting at the governor's guards, I felt neither.

The soldiers around me exchanged cheery greetings.

"As-Salaam-Alaikum!"

"Wa-Alaikum-Salaam!"

As we veered around the inner wall, the guards fell in with our team, guiding us to the stone steps of the entry foyer, where more guards waited. The Army platoon leader hollered orders to his men. Some would stay outside and others would remain in the hallway while a few followed us into the meeting room, choreography the soldiers knew well.

Inside, the building transformed. Olive green gave way to white-tiled hallways flowing past wood-paneled offices fitted with large windows and commanding desks. We entered a light-filled atrium, where we were greeted by the familiar face of our government liaison, Dr. Raj. A lanky man, Dr.

Raj looked even more so in the baggy pants and tunic of his *shalwar kameez*. He kept his beard short, and his curly hair poked out around his *kufi* cap. If I chose to trust someone here, I thought, Dr. Raj would be a good candidate. He lacked the self-importance of many of the local men I'd met. He had kind eyes and a toothy smile, offset by a nervous air, like he didn't trust anyone either. In Afghanistan, this made for an appealing quality. Dr. Raj seemed genuine in his reception of me, like he saw me not just as an American or a woman, but as a human being.

Among my PRT teammates, my gender mattered little. I pulled my weight and did my job and carried my rifle with enough confidence to characterize me not quite as a badass, but at least as a competent soldier. Among locals, though, being a woman took on a new dimension. Most Afghan men were excited when they met with the PRT; we brought money and potential to this tiny province. But like the director of information and culture's cold reception, as the men approached me, looking more closely at my hands, my face, the hair bun protruding from under my helmet, many grew noticeably wary. Some slunk past my outstretched hand to the male soldier beside me. Others brushed by gently, just a hint at a handshake, a trace of a polite smile. A few bubbled over at the sight of me. At a recent meeting on base two men had pointed at me while they whispered and snickered. I asked Aamir if I'd done something wrong. He said, "I think they talk about how you look." For most men, I was either invisible, a formality, or an intriguing anomaly.

I knew my mom had experienced this too, in some form. When she spoke at school Veterans' Day events, she always mentioned how hard it was for women in Saudi Arabia and how, even as an American woman, her movements were restricted. For the first time I recognized how vulnerable and isolated she must have felt. I remembered her saying that even the Saudi hospital dining rooms were gender segregated. ("And the men got the good coffee!")

I began to wonder what else she hadn't said.

Dr. Raj smiled warmly as he welcomed us to the governor's compound. He escorted us across the atrium and down another hallway, stopping at an office on the left. "You can leave your things here," he said in clear, accented English. "I will lock the door."

I followed Colonel McGuire and the others into the room and watched as they took off their helmets and body armor, exposing sweat-darkened patches on their chests and hair stuck to their foreheads in wet clumps. My body yearned to escape the pressure of the metal plates, but my mind hesitated. The armor stifled but comforted me—a feeling similar, I suspected, to the love-hate relationship many Afghan women had with their burqas. Slowly, I unsnapped my chinstrap and lifted my helmet. I could almost feel steam radiating from my scalp. I set my helmet beside a bookshelf, then unwound my headscarf and camera from around my neck and laid them next to my helmet. Grabbing the flap on the front of my vest, I yanked upward, adding to the chorus of ripping Velcro and rattling ammo magazines. Under the flap, I tugged on the Velcro side straps. My body signed as the armor released its grip. Finally, I looped my thumbs under the shoulders and eased the heavy shell over my head, stopping briefly to wiggle it around my braided bun, which was by now hopelessly dislodged. Velcroing the armor to itself, I stood it next to the bookshelf and propped my helmet on top. In line with my teammates' armor, the display looked like a flock of post-apocalyptic scarecrows. I replaced my camera around my neck and draped my scarf over my disheveled hair, crossing it beneath my chin and flipping the ends over my shoulders.

Paktia Province remained one of the more traditional regions of Afghanistan. In progressive areas like Kabul and some northern provinces, local women dressed more freely. Many still wore headscarves, but not the all-encompassing burqas like Paktia women. As a sign of respect for local traditions, we PRT women covered our hair when we left base. I felt silly pairing rainbow stripes with my camouflage, but at least it hid the tangled mess of my bun.

Next to me Major Sandra London, our head medic, watched me fidgeting under the fringe, a concerned expression on her face. "I forgot a scarf!" she said. "Do you think that's OK?" She ran her hands nervously through her brown bob.

"I'm sure you'll be fine, ma'am," I said. I had no idea how the locals might react, but Major London was here to transfer a fleet of ambulances to the Department of Public Health. I figured the gift might ease the sting of her cultural faux pas. "They'll forgive you as long as they get the ambulances, right?" I shrugged hopefully.

"Honestly," she said, "they can be mad as long as they take those darn things off our hands."

"Everybody ready?" Colonel McGuire asked. He and Dr. Raj led our lightened procession back into the hallway. We passed a tiny bathroom with a porcelain hole in the floor. Not a bad option, if I needed it. Almost more than ambush, I feared having to pee on a mission. The guys could easily call Code Yellow and water an MRAP tire. As a woman, I had to loosen my body armor to reach my belt and undo my thigh holster to pull down my pants. Then I had to teeter under the extra weight in a ninja-like feat to keep from peeing on my boots. Our supply officer had ordered each of us seven PRT women a Female Urination Device, a plastic funnel attached to a tube. Most of us opted to go on missions dehydrated.

The governor's compound hallway ended at a set of large double doors. I didn't see hands opening the doors, though they must have been there. I only saw the heavy wood panels swing inward and felt their breeze wash over me with the sweet and sour tang of body odor and chai tea. From within the room, we must have looked like we were stepping onto a movie set: a wave of camouflage streaming through the dramatic doorway, backlit by white hallway tiles. Inside was certainly a Hollywood scene. The crisscrossed pattern of Persian rugs carpeted the stage, and long conference tables lined three walls. Extras sat at the tables. The casting call was strict: male, thirty to forty but looks older, tanned and leathery skin, bushy brown beard (length negotiable, henna dye optional), rail thin or moderately overweight, leery expression. Large windows framed in pink curtains provided natural lighting. The gust of the open doors sent rose-tinted shadows dancing across the white walls.

There was even a film crew here, the governor's personal media team touted by Major Rhodes. They went everywhere with him, she'd said, recording his meetings and activities to broadcast on TV in Gardez and on radio across the province. Our predecessors had used the media team as evidence that the governor understood the importance of communicating with his people, of his desire for transparency in government operations. The longer we were in Afghanistan, the more it would become clear that the team was, instead, the governor's way of controlling the flow of information. He was writer, director, editor, producer, and marketing manager—and he was far from my IO ally.

Our group proceeded to the outside of the tables and inched behind a row of seated extras, along a wall of windows. I imagined shrieking mortars and shattered glass, the wall bowing inward while we lunged for cover under the tables. The director would yell "Cut!" and makeup artists would rush in to paint blood across our faces and change us into ripped and soiled uniforms.

"I don't like sitting by the windows," someone whispered.

Colonel McGuire took a seat at the far end of the table, sending a dominoed wave down the line as we each sat in the next available chair. I felt painfully obvious with my bright scarf. Major London peered self-consciously from under her bangs. We sat in silence, reflecting the burn of the skeptical eyes around the room. We were the new guys, which meant those eyes saw a clean slate and possibilities. At training we'd been warned that the locals would have no reservations giving us a to-do list a mile long. The Afghans assumed we wouldn't know how to say no. As evidenced by our inherited PRT project list, the Afghans in this room had been right.

We were tracking more than one hundred construction projects worth more than $110 million throughout Paktia Province, funded by the PRT and built by local contractors hired by the PRT. They were worthy projects—schools, medical clinics, training centers—but more than we were equipped to handle. The PRT had three Air Force civil engineers, supplemented by one or two from the Army Corps of Engineers. In order to effectively oversee construction projects and provide quality control, engineers needed to visit every site as often as once a week. Paktia is only about the size of the state of New Hampshire. But to traverse New Hampshire, you don't need a four-vehicle convoy, a security team, and approval from regional headquarters. New Hampshire has paved roads where you can drive more than ten or twenty miles per hour. You don't need to plan ambush defense when passing through areas so dangerous that no Americans have entered since two U.S. soldiers were killed there two years ago. You don't need to avoid traveling at night, when the insurgent threat is greatest.

If construction sites were close together and weather and security cooperated, our engineers could visit three or four on one mission. Some sites in Paktia required such extensive travel that the mission convoy had to spend the night at one of the small American outposts scattered throughout the province. A few locations would prove too risky; in our nine months in Afghanistan, we would never visit those sites.

Here, at our team's first Provincial Development Council meeting, we didn't fully grasp how challenging construction management would be. We surveyed the Afghan government officials around the room, representing the provincial directorates for the ministries of education, economy, health, finance, agriculture, information and culture, and women's affairs. We sized them up, wondering if our hand-me-down profiles were accurate, wondering who was competent, who was sincere, and who was on insurgent payroll. Surely they were sizing us up too, tallying their mental wish lists, guessing our nerve. In our uniforms we all looked the same, except for Major London with her bangs and me with my rainbow scarf. We were the next in a long line of Americans who thought we knew best.

While we waited, we drank chai tea. The glass mug burned my hands when I took it from the gracious, bowing man who circled the tables with a serving tray. I had been told the tea was boiled excessively to eliminate waterborne bacteria. I set it aside to cool and watched the steam melt into the air. Then in a flurry of excitement the governor swept through the large wooden doors. He seemed to suck all the energy out of the room. While we held our collective breath, he pranced around the tables, shaking hands, and then stopped to curtsy in front of Colonel McGuire and say something that Dr. Raj translated. Then the governor sashayed to his seat at the head of the table, next to the flag representing the Government of the Independent Republic of Afghanistan, where a cup of tea, a microphone, and a voice recorder waited for him.

The governor was a congenial-looking man. His beard was clipped short and tinged with gray, matched almost exactly to the charcoal vest he wore over his blouse. Like any good politician, his smile was easy, and a bit unsettling. Thick eyebrows waggled up and down his expressive forehead. I watched his hands dart purposefully back and forth across the table, mesmerized by their constant motion.

The meeting began with a prayer. I didn't realize it was a prayer at first when a large bearded man, who I later discovered to be the spiritual advisor, stood and burst into song, a quivering, melodious warble, at once haunting and beautiful and bizarre. I didn't know if I should bow or clasp my hands. Afraid to look around for a cue, I sat in respectful silence, staring at my tea.

After the prayer, the governor said a few words in a resounding, inflection-filled voice. Then he turned the floor over to Colonel McGuire. At least I assumed that was what happened when Colonel McGuire began to speak. Then the governor spoke again. If I focused hard, I could hear the translation from one of the interpreters. But I had a job to do. Slowly, I pushed back my chair and slunk down the table, adjusting the settings on my camera. *I am the eyes of the American public.* I told myself. *I am a master communicator, a master photographer. Please don't trip!*

The skeptical eyes should have been on Colonel McGuire and the governor, but they followed me and my rainbow scarf past the end of the table. The governor's TV man glanced in my direction, and I willed him to keep his camera on my commander. I knelt down on one knee, trying to make myself small.

"They'll film you," Major Rhodes had warned me. "They like to take pictures of American women. One of our girls kept getting on the news. They were always taking her picture. We finally had to ask them to stop."

"That's . . . kinda creepy," was all I'd managed in response.

I snapped a picture of the governor smiling and nodding at Colonel McGuire, and one of the colonel gesturing to his deputy commander. He was introducing our team. When he got to me he motioned to the chair where I had been sitting a minute ago: "Our public information officer, Lt. Lauren Johnson." (I used this title publicly because it sounded less threatening than information operations, semantics being one of my IO tricks.) I waved awkwardly from the corner of the room, then retreated back to my viewfinder.

I would come to prefer Afghanistan through the filter of my camera. Without it, I was overwhelmed. Everywhere, activity and noise. Everywhere, potential threats. Through my lens, the landscape and the people softened. I'd never been uneasy with attention; I'd even been known to seek it. Yet here, the dual spotlight of "American" and "woman" burned too bright for comfort. I preferred to melt into the background and observe. As the meeting progressed, though, I couldn't be content kneeling on the floor. I needed to hear what was going on to accurately write up a summary for the storyboard PowerPoint slide I would send to brigade headquarters. I tiptoed back to my seat, where I sipped tea from my right hand and scribbled notes on the half of the interpreter's conversation I could catch with my left. From what I could tell, the meeting was a circus. Colonel McGuire would confirm later: The line directors listed nearly 500 projects they thought the province needed—from wells, to schools, to mountain highways and hydroelectric dams—identifying the PRT as the funding source for every single one.

I watched the heads of the directors bobbing up and down, the congregation raising their hands in a flourish of affirmative votes after each proposed initiative. I listened. I scribbled. I sipped. I remembered the windows behind me and had a flash of panic. I wondered if I would make it through the meeting without having to pee and panicked again. Then, suddenly it was over. The governor was standing and thanking everyone for the successful meeting. We were ushered back through the heavy doors, down the hall, and into an office with couches and a glass-topped coffee table. On one of the couches lounged the director of public health. The director was large, jovial, and notoriously incompetent. Probably a third of the meeting's propositions had come from him and included things that the province's primitive medical system couldn't support. As head medic, Major London worked closely with the director. When I entered the room, she smirked and rolled her eyes as if to say, *Here we go again!*

I couldn't look at Major London and not think of my mom, not just because she was a nurse, and not just for her freckled porcelain skin and short stick-straight hair or the fact that she was known in the PRT as "Mama London." Soft-spoken and mild-mannered, Major London emitted a soothing aura, even when she herself was frazzled. Of all the inexperienced first-time deployers at Camp Atterbury, Major London had been one of the most out of her element. Watching her, I imagined my mom preparing to deploy. I couldn't picture Mom holding a rifle. Mom's hands were gentle. They held mine when we crossed the street and cradled my broken arm when I fell off my bike right after Dad removed the training wheels. They cut the crust off my sandwiches and layered noodles for her special lasagna. I couldn't see Mom in a rustic combat hospital, breathing mechanically behind a gas mask as sweat and breath fogged up the eye shield, holding an IV needle in protective gloves like oven mitts. Yet my mom did those things. As training progressed, Major London's voice gained force. Her actions lost their timidity. By the end of the deployment, she would transform into a kindly take-no-shit huggable warrior, just like I envisioned my mom.

The ambulance handover was a legacy project from the former PRT. Major London had been communicating with the director of public health almost daily to finalize the arrangements, not an easy task if the frustrated grunts from her office across the hall in our qalat building were any indication. In theory, the ten ambulances were tools the province could legitimately use. In theory, they would be distributed to clinics across Paktia to increase medical transportation capability, to enable sick and injured citizens to get from isolated rural areas to Gardez City for proper care. But we couldn't control what happened next: Medical clinics were repurposed as government residences. Unfinished training centers were forsaken and schools abandoned, the cycle of functional-to-rubble accelerated by the harsh climate and lack of skilled maintainers. Our operations in Afghanistan were based largely on theory, and wishful thinking.

With the legwork done, the ambulance transfer happened quickly. I took pictures while the director and Major London signed the paperwork, and then everyone was suddenly standing again, ready to move outside for the official ribbon cutting ceremony. There was a flow to Afghan business conduct not unlike the "hurry up and wait" of military operations: *run, run, hurry! stop, wait . . . slooooooooow, not yet, OK go! hurry! slow down! wait . . . keep waiting, go NOW!* Back in Dr. Raj's office, my team collected our body armor, groaning as the familiar weight settled on our shoulders, and then rejoined our security detail in the entry foyer. If the morning had worn on the security forces soldiers, they didn't show it. They fell in step around us and led our procession back through the glass doors, across the courtyard, and through the wrought iron gate. Parked behind our MRAPs on the street sat a row of shiny white vans. A single Afghan National Policeman stood guard at the midpoint of the caravan. His gray uniform hung in sloppy wrinkles, and his pants flopped over his boots, but he held his rifle proudly across his chest. An Afghanistan flag patch clung to the sleeve over his skinny bicep. I skirted around the gathered crowd so just the policeman and the vans filled my viewfinder. The man straightened when he saw my camera. His chin lifted, and his face tightened into a dignified stare. I took the picture.

Around me, the Afghan officials spoke excitedly. *Sweet, look at those wheels!* I imagined them saying. *This is totally going to revolutionize medical transportation!* Colonel McGuire thanked them for their patience.

"I'm so happy to be able to finish what was started many months ago," he said, via Dr. Raj.

The governor thanked him in return, and then Colonel McGuire passed a handful of keys to the governor's assistant. I froze the scene with my camera.

Later in my storyboard PowerPoint slide I would write that the ambulance distribution "represents an important step in increasing healthcare capabilities in the province and connecting the people to their government through access to basic services. The inclusion of Afghan National Police escorts and security guards further served to garner increased support for local security forces." I would feature the photo of the policeman and the photo of the key exchange, faces alight with eagerness and relief, the hopeful instant before the ambulances were officially left to theory and wishful thinking. Images like this would always make it onto storyboards. They were evidence that relationships were intact, that progress was being made—if not tangible evidence, then evidence strongly-enough implied. For the PRT, these were the moments that would get us through the deployment: moments when we acknowledged our efforts and good intentions, when we tossed the ball down the field, believing that if they ran fast enough the Afghans could catch it, and maybe even keep going.

As I took my seat back in my MRAP, the long morning, the weight of my body armor, and a cool blast from the vehicle's ventilation system converged on my eyelids. I wasn't supposed to close my eyes. I had to stay alert to scan the landscape whirring past the window for anything suspicious, to keep my training readily accessible at the forefront of my brain. Just in case. I fought through the fog, telling myself I didn't deserve a nap. I had been gone for half a day. I had attended a meeting in a relatively safe location. Hundreds of missions every day sent thousands of soldiers around Afghanistan to do things more intense, more complex, more dangerous than I could even fathom. Those soldiers were probably working on an empty stomach. They would definitely need to stop to pee.

Our convoy thundered back through the market, still bustling with colorful activity, and around the traffic circle, past the lopsided billboards, white Toyotas, and women in blue burqas. We rumbled along the swath of brown, and then jostled as the wheels passed from concrete to gravel and we funneled through the HESCO channel leading to the FOB Gardez front gate. The soldier across from me unbuckled his seat belt. His shoulders lifted and then dropped with a sigh, as if he was checking off another day in his mental tally: *July 29. Mission complete. Still alive.*

I caught one last glimpse of Combat Barbie in the reflection of his sunglasses. Then I let out the breath I didn't realize I was holding and released the white-knuckled grip I didn't know I had on the buttstock of my rifle.

8

Waiting, too, is Hell

MORE THAN TWO DECADES AFTER MY MOM RETURNS from Saudi Arabia, three years after I return from Afghanistan, I sit cross-legged in my childhood bedroom next to a heaping Tupperware crate, a time capsule from 1991.

Yellowing newspaper clippings fan around me. "Fort Lawton Hospital Unit Called for Duty," "Rally, Yellow Ribbons to Show Troop Support," "War in the Gulf Hits Home," "Waiting, too, is Hell, Local Medics Learn."

A faux shooting range target fills a page over the face of Uncle Saddam.

A postcard advertises the Hard Rock Café, Kuwait location (opening soon). Others proclaim, beneath an American flag: "These Colors Don't Run," and beneath a camel: "Someone in Saudi Arabia Loves Me."

A card displays the "Official Desert Storm pin-up" (a camel). On a Valentine's Day card, palm trees curve into a heart around a heard of camels.

There are cards of folded construction paper, decorated with crooked hearts and loopy, careful printing. "Hello mommy I love you. I miss you a lot. I am having a good time at school." "Dear Mommy. Do you have any idea how long you are going to be over there? I miss you terribly. Hope you have a happy Valentine's Day. I love you." "Dear Mommy I wish you were home I love you Soooooo much I hope you get home soon XoXoXoXoXoX-oXo with lots of love from Lauren."

Glossy photos show Mom in her green and black camouflage. Other photos, from years later: the family on the deck of the aircraft carrier USS *Abraham Lincoln*, a tour arranged through Grandpa Home's Navy League chapter. My braces and permed hair place me in sixth or seventh grade. As I lay the photos on the carpet, I wonder why someone decided they belong in this box of Desert Storm relics. I wonder, as I study my wide, metal-toothed smile, how many scattered papers mark my own military legacy.

At the bottom of the crate, I discover pages and pages of creased letters. Mom's elegant half-cursive is so familiar. As I read, though, I'm struck by the familiarity of her words. Despite obvious differences in our decades-apart wartime correspondence—email wasn't an option in Desert Storm, operation-specific postcards and stationery appear to be an aspect of public affairs left in the nineties—the similarities to my own deployed messages are striking. In letters home, Mom and I both talked of using red-tinted flashlights (neither dwelling on the implications that we were targets for enemy fire). We griped about adjusting to the altitude and the restrictive blandness of our uniforms. We wrote of "interior decorating," of cards and photos taped to plywood walls in a makeshift wallpaper of home. We each acknowledged loneliness, but we put our situations in context. "We really must consider ourselves lucky," Mom wrote on January 22, 1991. "At least we have the facilities to use, we don't sleep in a tent, and the food at the hospital is excellent."

Food came up frequently. In 1991, the neighbor who watched my siblings and me after school wrote Mom about our weekly Wednesday dinners with her family. She said it was hard to find a meal everyone liked, but macaroni and cheese and hotdogs seemed to be a hit, and one time my dad picked up pizza. Mom wrote about eating dehydrated MREs (Meals, Ready-to-Eat) when she didn't have time for a hot meal, and about treating herself to ice cream after she and her roommate built a wardrobe for their unfurnished room. Shavonne gushed in a letter about the strawberry floats at her ninth birthday party. Dad learned how to use the Time Cook feature on the oven! A school mom said she was making us a casserole. Dad had ten meals in the freezer; maybe, Mom suggested, he could share some with her roommate's family?

From Afghanistan, I emailed to thank my family for the haul of care package treats: "The cookies and candy I force myself to share (I really don't want to come home 300 pounds) and my whole office is thankful!" I wrote a friend about the dessert Chris and I invented, Ooey Gooey Gardez: "We take a chocolate cupcake and heat it up, crush a vanilla caramel ice cream bar on top and add strawberry pieces. It's AWESOME! I look forward to it every night. We're thinking of pitching the idea to Ben and Jerry when we get back."

I commiserated with my college roommate, deployed elsewhere in Afghanistan, about non-dessert chow hall cuisine. "I can't even manage to go a freakin' day without eating red meat," I wrote once. "It's one of the five main food groups here. The other ones are fried food, potatoes, soggy vegetables, and ice cream."

She responded: "My food groups are surprisingly similar: soggy vegetables, dry meat, candy, under-ripe fruit, ice cream.

"Oh yeah, I forgot the under-ripe fruit," I wrote back. "I guess we have six food groups."

In food we all found common ground. We needed sustenance on this side of the world or that, at war and at home. Food was something missed, something to crave, either exciting or disappointing. It was a distraction from the chaos around us, and from other topics we'd rather not discuss.

Both Mom and I also wrote frequently of the small joys that, in the context of war, felt inordinately weighted. We relished the thrill of mail, as predictable as things got in a war zone, scheduled reminders that life existed outside the bubble of dust and camouflage. An endearing letter dated February 1, 1991 describes my mom's first encounter with camels (apparently they weren't as plentiful as the Desert Storm postcards suggested): "One day I saw three standing and another day I saw four walking along," Mom wrote. "They were fairly far away and out of a filthy bus window, so I didn't get a picture. But it was the highlight of my day—I'm definitely back to the very simple pleasures in my life!"

I smile at this version of my mom I know so well: sweet and sincere, curious and charming, compassionate to a fault.

But some of the letters reveal another woman. Within those same creased pages and that same familiar penmanship lives someone I've only just started to know. She's not the unfazed, infallible hero I saw as a seven-year-old, the vision I took with me to Afghanistan and back home into the aftermath. This woman is frightened and overwhelmed. "My letters home were pretty upbeat compared to how I was feeling," Mom admitted recently. But glimpses slipped in. Letters confess doubts about her ability to handle everything. She says she doesn't like walking on the compound after dark. In a letter to my dad, she concedes, "Sometimes the loneliness really gets to me." I struggle to recall a time I've ever seen my mom overtly lonely. I imagine her at night in her deployment bed, crying softly into her pillow, something I did many times in Afghanistan. I shake the image away and pick up the next letter.

Mom writes about taping her bedroom windows in case of explosions, of waiting for nightly scud missile attacks, for destruction and death. In between, she seeks refuge in music and reads letters from home over and over and over again. She decides she's "not cut out for combat." In one letter she predicts, "We will face much more difficult tasks as this war escalates, and I'm sure I will not be the same person when it is over."

I reach my brain back to identify a change after Mom returned, but I can't. On March 12, 1991, all I see is joy. In school carpools and classroom shifts and cutting the yellow ribbon off the big maple tree, all I see is pride. At Veterans' Day assembly after Veterans' Day assembly, all I see is strength. I wonder how I would perceive those events now, as an adult. Would I notice a catch in Mom's voice? A clenched jaw? A series of blinks to hold back tears? Would I shift anxiously in my seat, sensing that she doesn't want to be there? Would I acknowledge the truth in her words but also in the spaces between?

I ache for the woman who jumped from these letters right back into the flurry of Wife, Mother, Cook-to-order Chef, Taxi Driver, Schedule Master, Center of Gravity; who as a reservist lacked even the halfway house of a military base; who told me recently that she was never encouraged to talk to anyone about her experiences. I realize I've spent my life projecting my own emotions on all my post-Desert Storm memories. I saw the infallible hero that I wanted to see. I saw what I was allowed to see; because we needed her, and because she knew no other good option, Mom spent twenty years swallowing her trauma. Until I got back from Afghanistan. Until we started to peel away the scar tissue together.

9

War.ppt

IN AFGHANISTAN, I TRACKED TIME BY SUNDAYS. Every Sunday I took my malaria pill (though I had yet to see a mosquito; even bugs seemed repelled by Paktia's arid climate). And for an hour every Sunday, Chris and I took a break from war for song and fellowship. At the little white chapel, we joined a handful of our colleagues from the PRT and other base units. Then there was John. John wasn't his real name—most interpreters chose to go by American names to mask their identities as protection from insurgent retaliation. John pulled his alias from the Bible. He was a Christian who could only demonstrate his faith around us, the Americans. To maintain his cover, he still prayed to Allah five times a day. Even his wife believed him to be a devout Muslim. Solely on Sundays in the safety of the Gardez chapel could John truly be himself.

The chapel wasn't much, just a few rows of pews, a podium, and a projection screen, but it was far enough from the helicopter landing zone and the convoy staging area to provide the illusion of peace. Peace, with a gun rack.

"Doesn't it feel weird to bring a loaded weapon into church?" I whispered to Chris on our first visit.

He winked. "I thought you lived in the South."

True to his Italian heritage, Chris was Catholic. I called myself a Christian, though in the presence of John I felt I deserved a lesser title. I attended nondenominational services in Florida, plus a weekly Bible study a friend introduced me to almost exactly a year before I deployed. With the support of the youth group, I'd honored my middle school baptism through high school, and then fallen away—or stepped back—from religion in college, distracted by ironing, shining, and marching, writing papers and collecting bottle caps, falling in and out of love. Once in Florida I'd lunged back into faith when job stress and after-hours indulgence converged on my over-active conscience. The convergence felt dramatic, divine even, as though I crashed headlong back into religion, or it crashed into me, just when I needed it most. This time, I vowed not to let it go. I even branded myself with it, at ten p.m. on a Tuesday.

My housemate and I went to the tattoo parlor together. Within weeks we would both deploy, separately, to Afghanistan. We thought it profound to imprint ourselves with something permanent at the juncture before our lives shifted. A tattoo was a concrete fixture we could take with us. It was a reminder of our individuality, a visible declaration of who we were at this moment.

Later, we would discover it was also a marker of how much we would change.

That first Sunday at the Gardez chapel, the cross on my left forearm peeked out from under my uniform sleeve, and a tall blonde Army captain introduced himself as the Paktia chaplain. The chaplain had bright eyes and the Zen-like voice of a guided meditation exercise. He didn't strike me as someone who had been in a war zone for six months. After opening the service with a prayer, the chaplain bent over a laptop. He clicked a button, and music and static filled the small room. Bright block-letter lyrics danced across a projection screen. Around me, off-key voices joined the simple melody, one I'd learned in youth group that stuck with me even through my years without church:

> Lord, I lift Your name on high
> Lord, I love to sing Your praises

Wind rattled the chapel door. At every movement, Janie, my pistol, thunked against the hard pew. Chris nudged close on the other side, his singing pitchy but full. I closed my eyes. For the first time since arriving in Afghanistan, I felt something close to comfortable.

Weeks passed in little white malaria pills and the little white chapel. Hours upon inglorious hours trickled by hunched behind a desk or at a conference room table, punctuated by bursts of adrenaline and danger, like the mission to the governor's compound. Days bled into each other, a composite of monotony and frustration and a new shade of normal:

0630 hours: My alarm prodded me from a restless sleep, and I met Chris outside the HLZ, where the gravel road formed a one-third mile track around the graveyard. Chris and I had taken runs together at Camp Atterbury, in the twilight hour when the Indiana evening cooled and mosquitos still slept. We didn't talk, but our feet and breath found shared cadence. We'd easily clocked four miles at Atterbury. In Gardez, landing helicopters spit dirt and rocks over the HESCO barrier wall. Our feet slid over golf ball-sized gravel, and our lungs seized at the altitude and circulating dust. Every few steps a twinge shot through my left knee, nagging pain that arrived along with my body armor at Camp Atterbury. My marathon-running days already felt a lifetime ago.

0730 hours: Always ravenous by the time I showered, I met Chris at Olive Gardez for breakfast. Three times a day, I reminded myself to be thankful for hot meals. Still, after just a few weeks the menus began to blur together into mass-produced overcooked blandness. For a region where pigs were considered unclean, pork was served with surprising frequency. At breakfast, bacon and sausage steeped in a vat of grease or ham piled in gristled steaks. Potatoes also featured prominently at each meal, as hash browns or tots, fried, mashed, baked, chipped, wedged, or scalloped. Everything was seasoned with dust.

0800 hours: As a firm anti-morning person, I was surprised when my first few hours in the office proved to be my favorite time of day. In a place so full of noise and activity, I found respite in the interval before the dial turned to full blast. My Army IO colleagues, Nick and Jacob, were next door at their unit's Provincial Update Brief. Drew, the Agribusiness Development Team sergeant, immersed himself in headphones and photo editing. Across one office wall Sgt. Maria Rivera sang her good mornings. Over the other wall the engineers grunted theirs, classic rock crooning from their speakers.

I stretched and yawned, inhaling coffee and background noise as my laptops flickered to life. Around them, Major Rhodes' books still collected dust. The M&M's were gone, replaced by a rotating supply of care package candy. Along the desk shelves I'd taped photos of my family, my cats, my

Florida and Seattle friends. Except for the tangle of wires, my little corner cubicle was not so different from my desk in the public affairs office at Hurlburt Field.

Email remained the military's main communication channel, even in this remote, low-bandwidth corner of the world. I began the morning sifting through local, regional, and national news feeds that arrived in my inbox several times per day, pulling out headlines for the cultural advisors to include in radio scripts. Anything that highlighted the Afghan government or promoted a sense of nationalism, thus supporting our mission of "connecting people to their government," was radio gold. So was anything that might erode insurgent support: bombs intended for military or government targets that took out bazaars full of innocent people, martyrs' bodies left unburied to be devoured by dogs, children used as suicide bombers. The more grotesque the story, the more my stomach churned, the more excited my burgeoning IO brain became. I marked clips for Aamir and Rahim and forwarded them to headquarters and my fellow PRT IO officers. "Wow," I wrote once, "this is disturbing and disgusting . . . but something we can exploit!" I was learning to see information not just as a communications tool, but as a weapon.

Sometimes, I employed that weapon to defend the image of the U.S. military. Because we were the face of coalition forces in Paktia Province, the PRT got a lot of credit, but also a lot of blame. As the PRT IO officer, provincial messes fell partially to me to clean up. If a military operation damaged property, if Americans faced blame for an attack, if a contractor abandoned a construction site or a government official failed to deliver on a promise to his citizens, I issued Band-Aids in the form of words.

IO also served as front line of defense for insurgent propaganda. The Taliban were lightning-fast to pull the trigger of their information campaign, even without cause. A few stray bullets morphed into an epic firefight with air support, and always infidel casualties. Backfiring cars became deadly explosives. "According to a Taliban spokesperson," one report began, "face-to-face heavy fighting took place between the mojahedin of the Islamic Emirate and the joint enemy forces. Seven American and four soldiers of the mercenary Army were killed and four American and four internal soldiers were wounded in the face-to-face fighting which lasted for an hour." I knew these claims were exaggerated; if we'd suffered casualties, the operations center would be inundated with reports. I vetted the statements to get the real story. On this occasion, a convoy took small arms fire. No injuries, and no one killed in action.

Amidst the death and destruction, I also searched for stories that gave me hope. A class of local policemen graduated training. A severely injured Afghan girl made a full recovery in an American hospital. A new agricultural initiative would bring livelihood to a remote district. I regularly forwarded these positive stories to my parents.

"Thought you might enjoy this article about some of the GOOD THINGS happening in this area!" I wrote in July. "We have an agricultural team that works with the PRT in areas like forestry, water purification/ irrigation, and farming. Pretty cool stuff!"

My mom replied, with the enthusiasm I expected and craved: "What an awesome article! There is so much good going on over there, it makes me sick that most people never hear about it! I am asking everyone to pass on all the GOOD news!"

I didn't realize at the time that I'd made my parents targets of my information weapons; I was working to win their hearts and minds, too.

Seattle was twelve-and-a-half hours behind Afghanistan, half a world away in many respects. Every few days, I called home. Major Rhodes had let me in on a secret in the form of a phone in my office that could call back to the States, and I felt fortunate not to stand in line to sign out a "morale phone" for a thirty-minute block with strangers hovering impatiently and overhearing bits of my conversation. In exchange, I welcomed hovering colleagues overhearing and an unreliable connection that frequently dropped calls and never seemed to work on Wednesdays.

Excitement and relief always infused my parents' breathless greetings. "Helloooooo! How's our favorite out-of-area caller?"

"I'm good," I would say, "just tired and busy," an easy line I used even when it wasn't true. Like my mom's Desert Storm letters, our conversations rarely dipped below the surface. My parents asked about Chris, and I told them, cupping my hand over the receiver in a façade of privacy, that he was well (I would email later with more details). I thanked them for the latest haul of Twizzlers, books, and cards from Mom's weekly care packages. "I don't know if you intended the silly putty to be for us to give to the Afghan kids or keep for ourselves, but we're enjoying it in the office!"

My parents laughed. "Oh good!" Mom said. "It's kind of fun finding weird little things to send. The lady at the post office recognizes me now. Every time I'm in there she tells me she's praying for my daughter."

"That's very kind of her," I said. "I'll take all the prayers I can get!" Then, afraid emotion would sizzle through the phone line, I quickly changed the subject. I talked about my cool fort housing and the interpreter who somehow managed to grow roses in the gravel courtyard. I mentioned the goat that had taken up residence in the courtyard, named Skittles because of the rumor that a soldier had gotten her in a trade for a bag of candy, and the skittish feral cats that sometimes let me pet them. "There's one friendly guy," I said. "We call him Cheeto for some reason, even though he's black and white. He kept following me around the other day and actually followed me into my room! I wanted so badly to let him jump on my bed! How are my kitties?"

"Annabelle is on my lap," my mom said, and then her voice got sing-songy. "Do you want to say hi to your mommy?" I pictured Mom on the leather living room sofa, knitted blanket and black cat draped across her lap, lowering the receiver to Annabelle's fuzzy head. I could almost hear my dad rolling his eyes from the adjacent recliner.

Dad shared his thoughts on the subject: "They sure do poop a lot."

I craved non-feline news too. While at Camp Atterbury I'd learned in quick succession that I was going to be an aunt, and then an aunt times two: Shavonne and her husband were expecting twin girls. On my four days of leave after completing training, I'd flown to Seattle and kissed Shavonne's barely pregnant belly. Thereafter, I watched it grow through emailed photos. I wouldn't make the baby shower in August. I'd already missed the wedding of one of my best friends. While my family ate burgers and watched fireworks at the annual Johnson/Home Fourth of July gathering, I'd spent Independence Day in transient lodging at Bagram (thankfully without exploding projectiles). Next month, my brother would bring home a new girlfriend from college, and he'd celebrate his twenty-first birthday in September. The world seemed to have picked up speed since I'd deployed; in just a few weeks the landscape had changed. I hoped it would be recognizable when I returned.

I called my parents the night before every mission I took off base. I didn't tell them I was leaving the wire. I made sure to say "I love you."

1000 hours: Ten o'clock was marked by the scuffle of oversized boots and a series of baritone grumbles. I scrunched close to my desk to make room for Nick in his abutting chair.

"Good morning, boys!" I hollered. "How was the meeting?"

"Well, Larry," Nick said, "we learned two important things: Jack and Shit."

I laughed. In spite of my initial reservations, I'd quickly grown fond of both Army lieutenants. Individually, I had yet to find my IO groove. I'd been on the job long enough to confirm that I truly didn't know what I was doing. (I would describe IO to a Hurlburt colleague as "very broad and undefined, and includes a lot of meetings.") I was making things up as I went along but found comfort in the company of others doing the same. On my own, the clash between self-doubt and perfectionism might have paralyzed me. Nick and Jacob worked hard. They were smart. They were quirky in their own amusing, occasionally infuriating ways. Outliers on the spectrum of FOB personalities, they balanced each other out. Jacob, thoughtful and reserved, had aspirations of attending law school. Nick, a more traditional Army "grunt" was not thrilled to be stuck in an office or in a counterinsurgency mission; he said he'd joined the military to kill people.

Nick dropped into his chair with a thud and a sigh. He lifted his rifle sling over his head and laid the weapon gently at his feet, like a beloved pet. Jacob perched on the edge of Nick's desk. Drew removed his headphones, spun around, and stretched out his legs in the slow, casual way he did everything.

"Nothing much going on here this morning," I said. "Brigade called twice while you guys were gone."

"They sent a couple emails, too," Drew added.

Nick and Jacob both scoffed. Our military reporting headquarters, an Army brigade, was to the surrounding region what Nick and Jacob's Army unit was to Paktia: the umbrella unit and battlespace owner for the "P2K" area of Paktia, Paktika, and Khost provinces. The PRT didn't *technically* work for the brigade, just like we didn't *technically* report to Nick and Jacob's unit. Our official headquarters was at Bagram Air Base and oversaw activities for all twelve U.S. PRTs. However, since the FOB Gardez Army unit and the P2K brigade "owned" the battlespaces in which we operated, they became de facto bosses. Brigade staff officers pushed down regional guidance and taskings to their provincial counterparts. The brigade IO and PA officers were both Army majors, who, after Major Rhodes made the official introduction, were reintroduced to me by Nick and Jacob as Tweedle Dum and Tweedle Dumber. They had yet to disprove the nicknames.

When I said brigade called, Nick glowered at the phone, daring it to ring again. "Nothing urgent," I said, waiving my hand dismissively. "It's all in the emails. So, what's on the agenda for today?"

Nick shifted his glower to me. "We need to remake the IO campaign calendar."

"Again?" The calendar, detailing our plans for the next few months' radio programming, projects, and meetings, had been reformatted several times. None of the information changed, just the presentation of it, recalibrated around the impulses of the commanders.

"Yeah, the colonel doesn't like it," Nick said. "But I got it. I think I know what he wants."

"OK, "I said. "Seems like a ginormous waste of time, but good luck. We also need to finalize the topics for the IO Working Group"

"Fuck!" Nick said, loud enough to make me jump. "I fucking hate that thing."

"You're telling me," I said. "I have to lead it!" I'd hosted two working group meetings since taking over as PRT IO officer, trying to sound confident while introducing a few new ideas and soliciting feedback from a handful of attendees who ranged from distracted to downright bored.

"If it makes you feel better," Jacob said. "You've already made it way less painful than it was with Major Rhodes."

Nick and Drew mumbled in agreement.

"Well thanks, guys," I said. "Minimal torture is always the goal. I just really don't think anybody cares about IO right now with all the election stuff going on."

"I hate to break it to you, Larry, but nobody ever cares about IO."

"It's true, ma'am," Drew said. "For all the talk about IO being so important we get no funding and basically no guidance."

I sighed. I had quickly noticed that dynamic, but I hadn't given up blaming external factors like the learning curve of the new PRT, the impending Afghanistan presidential election, or the still missing-in-action Sgt. Bowe Bergdahl, for whom the official search would continue until mid-August, spanning thousands of square miles including Paktia Province. "Well," I said, "at least we'll have a pretty calendar."

"We fucking better," Nick snarled. He turned and spat a glob of brown goo into his dip cup.

"So, Lauren," Jacob said. "What's going on with the community ownership campaign? The colonel was asking."

The campaign was my first big idea, raising awareness about construction projects and training programs in each of Paktia's fourteen districts and the positive impact they would have on local citizens as a way of creating a sense of ownership. If local people were invested, we hoped, they would help promote security and accountability at construction sites. We would put the power in their hands by providing a hotline people could call to report things like security threats, bribery, or construction negligence, similar to the Fraud, Waste and Abuse advertisements the military employed. I was excited about the possibility of doing something impactful, but, I was learning, the road to impact was paved with logistical hurdles and bureaucracy.

"It's going," I said. "Aamir is researching vendors for the construction site billboards. Then we'll have to apply for funding. I drafted a basic template and a radio script, but I'm waiting on the stats for each district." I raised my voice to send it over the wall behind Nick and Jacob and over the musical strains of Journey. "The engineers haven't gotten those to me yet!"

After a second one of the engineers shouted back. "What? What haven't we given you?"

"The info on district-level construction projects!"

"Yeah, yeah, we're working on it! There's a lot of shit to go through!"

"Hi, Captain Wilson!" Sergeant Rivera's voice floated across the opposite wall.

"Hey Rivera!" the engineer hollered back.

Then from the Army first sergeant on the other side of the office: "OK, now everybody shut the fuck up!"

1200 hours: Chris and I met for lunch every day. Sometimes we trudged fifteen minutes past the HLZ and down the gravel walkway to eat at the second dining facility, the industrial tent, squeezing in hours of conversation along the way.

"What did you think the first time you met me?" he asked once.

"Tall, dark, and handsome," I said.

"Yeah, right."

"OK, medium, dark, and handsome. I liked your smile. And you seemed confident. Like you weren't overwhelmed by everything, which was impressive to me."

Chris chuckled. "I'm glad I seemed that way."

"What did you think when you met me?"

Chris cocked his head and eyed me, seriously, a dimple flashing in one cheek. "I thought you were cute. But you wore your helmet strap too tight."

Those walks to and from meals formed a condensed courtship. We covered frivolous first date banter, vented deployment frustrations, and discussed current events and politics. Chris was a rare military liberal. I typically shied away from political topics for fear of reaching beyond my knowledge, or, worse, offending someone, but even those charged conversations felt civil and thoughtful with Chris. As we talked, he became my outlet for deployment issues and my medium to the world beyond Afghanistan, beyond 2009. With him I could share not just my present, but also my past, and, I thought, maybe even my future.

I opened up about my dreams of becoming a writer. Chris taught me a few phrases in Italian. I talked about my childhood in swimming pools and heard about Chris's jockeying for attention in a large Italian American family and the impossible expectations of a tough-love father that Chris still fought against, years after his dad's death. Chris had followed his father, a Vietnam War veteran, into the military, like I had with my mom. Our stories weren't uncommon; children joining the "family business" make up a large percentage of military recruits.[5] Many of my Air Force friends had parents who served. Like Chris, sons often joined to prove something, to become, in one way or another, men. My own motivations weren't so clear cut. Chris seemed to take every step with purpose, and so I latched onto him as an anchor.

"I want to go to the places my dad went in the war," he told me on one of our walks, "in Vietnam and Cambodia." In my memory we're headed back from dinner. The sky is spackled orange and pink. Shadows carve sharp cheekbones into Chris's angular face and cast his expression wistful, then serious, then back again. "I want to walk in his footsteps and understand those places and what they meant to him. Help me understand him better. Maybe help me understand myself better too."

I in turn revealed pieces of myself, though I couldn't express with such precision how the military legacy had shaped me, too, or understand that I, too, was chasing family expectations, real or imagined: for success, excellence, and adventure. I couldn't yet understand that though I may not have enlisted to become a woman, the woman I most loved and admired had done the same. When you place someone on a pedestal, you inevitably end up worshipping at their feet.

1300 hours: Besides the dining facility, the far side of the base offered another attraction: the FOB Gardez mall. Chris and I often stopped there after lunch. Ours wasn't a mall like at Bagram, crowded with shops and fast food kiosks and selling brand name merchandise. If main bases had the Mall of America, Gardez had a rundown suburban strip mall, comprised of a string of storage connexes fashioned into storefronts. One connex had a crooked blue and yellow Best Buy sign nailed over the open front end. I laughed the first time I saw the sign and took a picture to send to my brother, who worked at a Best Buy in Tampa. ("Hey," I wrote, "did you know your company is outsourcing to Afghanistan?") The Afghan vendors stocked everything you could expect from an electronics store in an isolated pocket of a low-technology developing country: batteries, plug adapters, a few outdated small appliances, and a massive selection of two-dollar bootlegged DVDs.

In a time before widespread streaming services, DVDs were the most in-demand item. Movies offered a little shred of pop culture, a couple hours of mindlessness. "Best Buy" carried everything from Disney to westerns, rom-coms to slasher flicks, entire seasons and entire series of classic and contemporary American TV shows (with and without Chinese subtitles). "DVD quality!" the vendor always proclaimed when I picked up a disc. But if I asked him to test playback on the store's TV/DVD player: "Sorry, no, not working today. I fix tomorrow and you come back?" I learned to wait until after titles were released on video. Theater releases were often recorded on cellphones and featured fuzzy pictures, echoing dialogue, and bobbing silhouettes of fellow patrons who may or may not be coughing. A grainy version of *The Invention of Lying* transformed into *The Informant!* Halfway through. A disc masquerading as Kiera Knightly's *The Duchess* turned out to be footage of Afghan men performing a ceremonial dance (admittedly a decent quality recording).

Next door to "Best Buy" was "Walmart," which sold, among other novelty items, the soldier-favorite dip tobacco. A couple unnamed trinket shops followed, then the mall ended at "Armani," a connex piled with embroidered scarves and colorful fabric from which customers could order tailored blouses and pants. Besides the latest DVD titles, merchandise didn't change much, but flipping through discs or patterned fabric brought welcome relief from the monotony of daily life on the FOB.

1330 hours: Monotony reached its climax after lunch. Afternoons were packed with scheduled meetings, sometimes supplemented with impromptu meetings or meetings to plan meetings. We met for anti-corruption working groups, IO working groups, non-lethal targeting meetings, rule of law program planning, construction update briefs, the nightly Commander's Update Brief, and weekly Brigade Update Brief. Topics rotated, but conversations remained similar. We were learning the tangled web that tied all operational elements together and that kept us from reaching the heart of the issues. Subcontractors at PRT construction sites cut corners in order to save money to pay bribes to contractors. Contractors paid bribes to insurgents to ensure security. Insurgents took orders from Afghan government officials, who hid behind a barricade of red tape. Projects were left unfinished or were built so poorly that walls could literally be picked apart with a fingernail. The general population saw little progress and many broken promises. More mess to clean up. More information Band-Aids.

I hated spending hours in meetings, especially when they seemed to accomplish so little. I still expected my chance to relive a chapter of *Three Cups of Tea*, but Afghanistan was proving so much more complicated than Camp Atterbury or Major Rhodes or Greg Mortenson had prepared me for.

1800 hours: On either side of the FOB, dinner came in themed rotation: Velveeta enchiladas for Mexican night; Italian spaghetti or mini pizzas, soggy in the middle with burnt crusts; greasy undercooked yakisoba on Asian night; surf and turf, which sounded glamourous but never failed to disappoint—breaded shrimp for the surf, heavy on the bread, and charred turf, notorious for breaking our plastic utensils. Good old American food made appearances in buttered noodles, chicken nuggets, and a dish called Chipper Fish that we determined to be white fish smothered with Thousand Island dressing and topped with potato chip crumbles (just when I thought I'd encountered every possible potato concoction). Three times a week, salvation came in the form of commercial-sized tubs of ice cream.

"The food is getting old," I wrote in an email to a few friends, "but I live for those nights they have ice cream." In an echo of my mom's Desert Storm letters, I added: "Gotta take pleasure in the little things!"

1900 hours: On the administrative side of war, no day could be complete without filing reports. SITREPS (Situation Reports) went to Jacob, so he could compile a provincial IO report of Last 24/Next 24, what we had accomplished over the last day and what we planned to do the next. Sometimes he requested Last 24/Next 72, depending on the Army commander's mood. The PRT intelligence officer assembled a Daily Summary, to which I contributed an in-depth analysis of IO activities. The brigade commander also received daily reports with updates on Governance, Development, Rule of Law, and Information initiatives. Additionally, the PRT sergeant who served as our brigade liaison emailed regularly, though not predictably, requesting updates for the brigade commander. The commander wanted weekly reports, all filed on different days to keep us on our toes. Weekly IO SITREPS were logged as less concrete, more bullshitable Long-term Plans/Information Priorities. The Last 7/Next 7 days report helped prepare us for the weekly Brigade Update Brief. Every Thursday at the BUB, Nick, Jacob, and I took turns briefing as the lowest-ranking officers on the brass-studded conference call, none of us eager to open ourselves up to the virtual firing squad at brigade, made up of an ambitious commander who meant well but didn't understand the unique aspects of each province in his area of responsibility and favored a one-size-fits-all approach, and his IO and PA Yes Men, the Tweedles. Also weekly, we briefed Last 96/Next 96 hours at a teleconference with the Tweedles and the PRT and Army IO reps in Paktika and Khost provinces.

So lacking in battle was my "battle rhythm" that more than once I was tempted to write: *Last 24: Attended meetings and filed reports/Next 24: Attending meetings and filing reports.*

2100 hours: Finally, I emailed Chris next door in the operations center: "Done here! Movie?" Free time in a war zone is an exercise in choose-your-own-escapism. Sometimes I wrote letters or read. My *Daily Walk Bible* had quickly become a weekly walk. Movies just required less brainpower. And, always, I gravitated toward Chris.

I liked my IO colleagues and many of my teammates, but I didn't consider them friends. Nick and Jacob were more like business partners. Major London stood in as a mother figure. The engineers and intelligence officer were absorbed in their own demanding jobs and focused any extra energy on their families. I admired Sergeant Rivera and could always count on her for engaging, insightful, often hilarious conversation, but with military fraternization rules prohibiting personal relationships between officers and enlisted personnel, I was wary of getting too close. Of course, the same rules applied to my relationship with Chris, a superior officer of the opposite sex. I'd always been a staunch rule follower. Yet in an environment governed so strictly, deprived of so much, I decided some rules could be bent.

I needed a subject for my emotional investment, and I chose Chris. Looking back, I wonder if I might have been better off, during and after the deployment, leaving room for other people. But that was how I operated, by diving into things: swimming then running, ROTC then public affairs, religion and relationships. I had trouble doing anything without letting it consume me.

2130 hours: Chris and I met nearly every night in the small USO building, a quick walk beyond the qalat, furnished with bookshelves, a stash of board games, a PlayStation, and a Ping-Pong table. We favored the corner sectioned off as a theater, where we could burrow into beanbag chairs, make out and hold hands, and, for two hours, almost feel normal—if we tuned out the video games and Ping-Pong in the background, if we didn't jump every time footfalls approached the curtain door, if we didn't look down at our camouflaged uniforms or boots, if the movie was only a moderately grainy bootlegged copy streaming from the failing old projector.

10

Ballots & Bullets
& Kebabs

AUGUST 2009: MICHAEL JACKSON'S DEATH was ruled a homicide. Chris Brown was sentenced to five years' probation for assaulting Rihanna. A massive Typhoon devastated Taiwan, killing 698 people and causing $3.3 billion in damage. North Korea pardoned two American journalists who had been arrested for illegal entry into the country and sentenced to twelve years in prison. Black Eyed Peas' "I Gotta Feeling" continued a fourteen-week run at number one on the Billboard Hot 100. Jaycee Lee Dugard was found alive after spending nearly twenty years as hostage of her kidnapper.

I was not aware of any of these events. In August 2009 in Afghanistan, everything revolved around the country's second democratic presidential election. The August 20 election was billed as one of the most strategic events in the Afghanistan conflict, with democratic implications throughout the Middle East. After the international community's heavy-handed assistance with the 2004 election, 2009 also marked the first time the process would be Afghan-led.

"Remember: The Afghans are in the lead," the FOB Gardez Army unit commander reminded us at each nightly election meeting. The slogan would become a refrain for meetings, conversations, public messaging, and psyches over the next eight months. Just a few weeks into my deployment, it didn't yet sound like a broken record. For an Afghan-led process though, I noticed Americans devoted a lot of time and resources preparing for the election.

The election hijacked our daily schedules with planning meetings, security meetings, shows-of-force convoys, and before/during/after campaign preparation. Every evening, the operations center conference room bulged with PRT and Army leadership, plus our representatives from the U.S. Department of State and U.S. Agency for International Development, our developing world election experts. Sometimes, when logistical planning didn't delve into the classified realm, Afghan government and security officials joined us for afternoon meetings, bringing with them an entourage of scribes and interpreters. I sat in a squeaky folding chair in the back, watching conversation ricochet between bearded Afghans in bright vests and clean-shaven Americans in camouflage. I felt like a tennis rookie at the Wimbledon final; the rules and jargon escaped me but faces and inflections on both sides communicated a spectrum of excitement, appreciation, annoyance, skepticism, and distrust. The Afghans argued that they had the knowledge, training, and resources to do everything on their own. But of course they were grateful for the hundreds of prepackaged meals and thousands of water bottles we would supply, for the "presence patrols" and ballot transport security leading up to the election, and for the Election Day stand-by security our personnel would provide. The American mentors remained obliging, but impatience swelled in the tightness of their jawlines, the color of their cheeks.

I jotted a few bullet points in my notebook. I scrutinized bearded faces, looking for identifying quirks to log their images in my own cognitive PowerPoint bible: an especially bushy mustache, a mole on the left cheek, a beard trimmed to a sharp V. A few chairs down, Chris watched the proceedings. Like me, he came mostly to observe. Unlike me, Chris had a refined poker face, cultivated through frequent family disagreements and military diplomatic assignments around the world. When we talked after these meetings, he would tell me he'd been bored, that he was reciting Italian nursery rhymes in his head, or that he'd been frustrated or he really had to pee, but his face always remained attentively fixed on the front of the room. Frown lines twitched across his brow, and his head cocked slightly to the left as he took notes.

When my mind drifted, I observed the room itself. I counted the framed portraits on the opposite wall, under the sign "Fallen Comrades of Paktia Province," and studied the proud, stoic faces of the seventeen young soldiers. Each of us had taken a portrait like that at training, a head-shot in front of the American flag. A "just in case" photo. I'd smiled in mine.

After one of the joint U.S.-Afghan election meetings, I made a story-board documenting the session for brigade headquarters. On a tidy Pow-erPoint slide, I arranged a few photos of important-looking Afghan men addressing the crowd and an analysis that Colonel McGuire and our De-partment of State representative helped compile. "Afghan National Secu-rity Forces personnel vocally debated concerns and discussed ideas," we wrote. "In the end, the commission successfully consolidated the number of polling sites in the province from 212 to 195, or by 8%. In the two most 'high risk' areas, polling site numbers were decreased by one third," and "local security forces verified they are equipped for and capable of provid-ing security for those areas."

Internally, we were less optimistic. With less than a month to the election, only a small percentage of sites had been visited by Afghan Na-tional Security Forces (ANSF), and insurgent activity kept escalating. District-level election field officers complained about poor security, point-ing fingers at government officials. Government officials and ANSF point-ed back. Within ANSF, the Afghan National Police and Afghan National Army pointed at each other.

We weren't the only ones filtering the message. Among talking points pushed down from high-level U.S. officials: "All of the Afghan institutions involved are pulling their share. The Afghan Ministry of Interior, Minis-try of Defense, and National Directorate of Security are working coun-trywide, coordinating effectively across their offices and with the inter-national community, ISAF, and coalition forces to plan for the security challenges faced."

Like our local ANSF, President Hamid Karzai and his staff pro-claimed self-sufficiency in election security, even though the elections had been delayed four months, to August 20, to allow for additional inter-national military assistance. All told, the international community's elec-tion-related financial support was estimated at nearly $500 million.[6]

In Paktia, as costs mounted and Election Day crept closer, we doubted the disparate officials and security forces would figure out a way to get along, let alone resolve security-related issues. In short, we expected a shit show.

In early August, a week after my first convoy mission to Gardez, I returned to the city to discuss the election with provincial leadership. Election posters hung everywhere, dangling from traffic lights, slapped on street signs, taped in crooked rows on the brick walls surrounding the governor's compound and the police headquarters across the street. The incumbent President Karzai featured overwhelmingly as subject, with the occasional ad for his main rival, former Minister of Foreign Affairs Abdullah Abdullah. Karzai was of the Pashtun ethnic group and the heavy favorite in Pashtun areas like Paktia. The president appointed the Provincial governors, who appointed their provincial staff. The men we met at the governor's compound were eager to keep their jobs.

The meeting was short, full of chai tea, handshaking, and reassuring nods.

Yes, we are ready.

The election will be good.

Insha'Allah.

The nonchalance aggravated me. At FOB Gardez, we lived and breathed elections. August 20 had even invaded my dreams. Here at the governor's compound, everyone seemed more interested in lunch. The governor invited us to join him for the meal at his guest house. I hadn't yet tasted the local fare, and my empty stomach growled expectantly, momentarily displacing my annoyance. The security forces team didn't share its enthusiasm. They grumbled as I heaved myself into the back of my MRAP.

"That's a fucking brilliant idea. Let's change the mission to go schmooze at the governor's house."

"Why the fuck do we even have a mission plan?"

I buckled in quickly and busied myself reviewing the photos on my camera. I was excited to eat at the governor's house, but I knew the security forces soldiers wouldn't be dining with us. They would be munching on granola bars and tobacco while they secured this new, unfamiliar location.

They would be radioing Chris at the operations center to alert him of the changes and planning a new route back to base. For them, each deviation brought danger. What if this was a trap? What if insurgents were watching as we inched through the alleyway behind the governor's house, knowing there was only one way out?

At the same time, as PRT commander, Colonel McGuire couldn't easily have justified telling the governor no. Our team was only here for a few months. Building relationships takes time, and doing everything else takes relationships. Every missed opportunity set us back. Colonel McGuire held a deck of cards of American manpower and resources, and he couldn't afford not to play a hand when he had the chance. I was grateful to be at the center of the deck, where I didn't feel the pressure of either end.

The governor's guest house was near the compound, but only accessible through narrow, winding streets. Local children popped out from behind mud brick walls to gawk as our vehicles lumbered around corners. The kids were cute, with shaggy hair and wide, curious eyes. I was supposed to look at everyone as a threat. We'd seen increased reporting of children being used as suicide bombers. Still, I couldn't help smiling at the kids from under my helmet and ballistic sunglasses.

The convoy squeezed into the back alley behind the guest house, and we dismounted. Guards lurked like gargoyles around the premises. They guided us through a gate in a brick wall and along a walkway with a view of the grounds. The house, though a humble two-story by American standards, loomed castle-like among Afghan qalats and shanties. The garden contained more green than all of Gardez. I was impressed, which I assumed was the intended effect. We stepped into a marbled foyer, where several pairs of shoes lined the doorway. Afghan custom dictated removing one's shoes when entering a home, but we were generously obliged to remain in our boots. This must have been a time-honored understanding, all the better to make a quick exit if necessary. Whatever the reason, I was glad to limit the number of exposed sweaty socks.

Off the main hallway, our escort led us into an elegant parlor where a handful of men from the meeting perched on a rainbow of richly upholstered couches, sipping tea. They stood to greet us as we entered, cupping our outstretched right hands in both of theirs.

"As-Salaam-Alaikum!"

"Wa-Alaikum-Salaam!"

We peeled off our body armor and squished together in a hodgepodge of couch cushions, camouflage, and *salwar kameez*. An attendant placed a teacup in each set of empty hands. I sipped mine slowly. After the morning at the governor's compound, I was approaching borrowed bladder time. Thankfully, before long the Afghans stood up. There must have been a cue, had I missed it? I felt like I was doing a foreign language remix of the hokey pokey: sit down, stand up, move to the doorway, look around wondering where everyone left their teacups, gather at the stairs.

At the top of the staircase, the crowd snaked into an assembly line of hand washing. I delighted at the sight of the familiar ritual. I'd heard Afghan meals were communal and eaten without silverware. The thought of grabbing rice with hands that had been sliding across the dusty MRAP interior, gripping Annie's oily rifle stock, and fingering my grimy body armor, after other dusty, sweaty patrons had all taken handfuls, was less than appealing. When my turn came, I held my hands over a ceramic basin. The attendant lifted his pitcher, letting a thin stream of water dribble out, and I rubbed my hands together vigorously for about two-and-a-half seconds until the dribble stopped. I looked hopefully to the attendant. Then I cursed my spoiled western sensibilities and blotted my hands lightly on what seemed to be the cleanest corner of the towel next to the basin.

The dining room had barely enough room for the long table and chairs but glowed cheery and bright in the afternoon sun. A colorful display of fruit adorned the table. Near the end of the line and with the seats nearly full, I chose the first open chair, next to a man I recognized from photos as the chief of police, General Asim. The general appeared, as his PowerPoint bible pictures suggested, a strange blend of regal and goofy. Taller than most Afghans I'd met, he had the ragdoll manner of a gangly teenager and a belly determined to wiggle its way over his belt. His long face, framed by bushy silver eyebrows and a matching mustache, sagged and wrinkled like his baggy police uniform. As his biography promised, General Asim was exceedingly friendly. If I'd known the secrets he was hiding, I wouldn't have found him so endearing.

"Hello! Hello!" he chimed when I approached. He smiled, revealing a set of crooked yellow teeth. "Sit! Sit!" I sat. "I am General Asim."

"Very nice to meet you, sir." We shook hands. I imagined germs leaping back and forth between our palms. "I'm Lauren Johnson. I'm the public information officer, Major Rhodes' replacement."

"Oh yes, nice lady."

"Yes."

"Welcome to Gardez!"

"Thank you."

General Asim turned to the other end of the table, where the governor and Colonel McGuire sat. I noticed our government liaison, Dr. Raj, had taken the chair to my left. He smiled warmly. "Hello again, ma'am."

"Hi, Dr. Raj," I said. "Glad you could join us!"

Across the table camouflage and *salwar kameez* shuffled closer together to make room for more chairs, and the final guests took their seats. The doors closed, and the governor, through his interpreter, welcomed us to his guest house: "This is a meal to represent our friendship as we work together to bring peace and prosperity to Paktia." Next to me, General Asim nodded enthusiastically. "Now, let us not talk about work. Please, eat!"

Multi-language conversation enveloped the table as tray-toting men brought steaming plates of kebabs, bowls of rice, and stacks of fluffy naan flatbread. Naan was famous among American troops; one of my friends blamed it for a ten-pound weight gain on his deployment. I had been anxious to taste the bread. As if he could read my thoughts, General Asim flopped a piece onto my plate.

"Uh, thank you." I stammered.

"Yes?" He held a rice bowl, which, blessedly, had a serving spoon.

"Yes, thank you!" The general plopped a heaping spoonful on top of my bread and handed me the bowl to pass to Dr. Raj. Next came the kebabs. "Oh, just one—" Two skewers landed in front of me. "Thank you."

The food smelled savory and fresh, scents forgotten at Olive Gardez. I rubbed my hands together in anticipation and said, to no one in particular, "This looks amazing!" I ripped a wedge from the naan and used it to scoop up some rice and a hunk of meat. Then I froze. Could I eat with my left hand, the hand considered unclean in Muslim culture? And if not, how would I manage to not shove food up my nose with my right? Hands poised, stomach rumbling, I looked frantically around the table, where everyone ate contentedly. Where were the cultural advisors when I needed them? I was about to confess my dilemma to Dr. Raj when I noticed General Asim happily shoveling food into his mouth with his left hand. A piece of rice dangled from his mustache.

I giggled into my plate and took a bite. The naan, moist and doughy, practically melted in my mouth. The rice was sweetened with plump raisins, and I tasted saffron and pepper. The meat, probably goat, was course and gristly, but richer in flavor than anything on the FOB menu. My tongue hadn't been so excited in months. Around the table pleasant conversation started and stopped. When my plate was empty, I sat back and sighed, wiping my fingers discretely on my uniform pants. I didn't see General Asim's arm until it was too late.

"Oh, no thank you, I'm fi—" *Plop.* "I'm really not hun—" *Thunk.* A kebab joined the fresh mountain of rice on my plate. General Asim grinned at me. "Thank you," I said. He nodded and resumed eating.

Chipping away at the new pile in front of me, I felt my stomach pinching against the waist of my uniform pants. But I couldn't stop. Leaving food on my plate would be rude. Plus, the meal was too good! I wanted to shove fistfuls into my cargo pockets to share with Chris. Using my naan, I blotted the last crumbs and watched as General Asim made another lunge for the rice bowl. This time I was prepared. I snatched a handful of grapes from a basket in front of Dr. Raj. The general seemed satisfied with the substitution. The grapes were tiny, like the not-quite-ripe ones I'd throw out from bags back home. Tentatively, I popped one in my mouth. It was firm and bursting with flavor. I quickly finished the bunch and, despite the protests of my top button, grabbed another.

"These grapes are delicious!" I said to Dr. Raj, because I had to tell someone.

He beamed. "Really? You like them?"

"They're the best grapes I've ever had!"

"They are Afghanistan grapes."

I reached for another bunch. "They're really, really good."

"If you would like I could bring you some," he offered. "On the base."

"Really? I mean, you don't have to. But if you wanted to sometime that would be nice. I'll share them with everyone so they can taste how delicious they are!"

Dr. Raj nodded and said, seriously, "I will bring you some. Every day."

I laughed. "Well you don't have to do that. Maybe like once a week."

Between meetings on and off base, I drafted radio messages with Aamir and Rahim to counter anti-election propaganda. We got reports of threatening "night letters" delivered to houses warning citizens not to vote. *Do not support the infidel puppet government. We will cut off voters' fingers. Voters will be tortured. Polling sites will be blown up.* Military channels picked up the feed from an insurgent radio network broadcasting similar messages. Before the location could be tracked or the network jammed, the signal would disappear, only to surface later at another location on a different network. We suspected a broadcasting center in the back of a truck, makeshift but effective.

Our messages played from stationary radio towers on American outposts. *You have the power to change your future! Afghan Security Forces are well trained and will keep voters safe! Your government is working to make a better life for all the people of Paktia!* The signals faded into valleys and bounced off walls of mountains. Pockets of Paktia were unreachable.

In the weeks leading up to the election, the PRT planned a series of government outreach missions to transport provincial leadership to outlying districts to meet their constituents, one of our most direct means of "connecting the people to their government." Paktia's roads were poor and dangerous—if roads existed at all—so officials rarely left the bubble of Gardez unless we transported them by military convoy or helicopter. Many citizens had never seen their government representatives.

The first government outreach mission targeted the district of Chamkani, an agricultural region at the northern tip of the province where the PRT sponsored several ongoing construction projects. I was assigned to the mission, and I armed myself with information weapons. As part of my new Community Ownership Campaign, I made a poster with photos of the main projects in the district, against a backdrop of the nation's flag and under the headline, "Your government is developing Chamkani district to bring peace and stability to the people of Chamkani." (Technically the projects were funded and overseen by the PRT or USAID, but we didn't broadcast that. Remember: The Afghans are in the lead!) Beneath the photos I listed the cost and the estimated number of people each project would impact.

Aamir told me that some people could read and that they would read to other people. People would understand, he said; they were hungry for information. I was hungry for a chance to provide it. The Community Ownership Campaign gave me my first real sense of purpose in Afghanistan. Maybe I wouldn't be building schools like in *Three Cups of Tea*, but I could help make people aware of and invested in the schools and other development projects happening in their communities. I could look into a man's eyes and give him tangible evidence of progress. I envisioned passing out flyers and watching faces light up with joy and hope. People would wave over friends and point excitedly at photos of medical clinics and district centers. Parents would tell their children that they could go to school next year; that their brother or sister would get the medicine they need. I wanted desperately to trust in American good intentions, to believe the promises we made on behalf of the Afghan government: security, education, healthcare, rule of law, all in exchange for ink-stained fingers on Election Day. I made for a perfect military apostle, easily gobbling up three big cups of Kool-Aid.

The afternoon before the Chamkani mission, I threw up. I set my computer to print one hundred copies of the flyer, and then ran to the bathroom just in time for my bowels to explode. I had to steady myself on the handrail on the way back to my office.

"You look terrible," Nick said.

"I feel terrible," I said. "I think I have food poisoning." I hated to blame the governor's kebabs or the delicious micrograpes, but my body was clearly rebelling. Most everyone got "the crud" in Afghanistan, ranging from respiratory problems to digestive issues brought on by dust, altitude, toxins, exhaustion, stress, and/or local food. My sinuses had been angry since touching down at Bagram, and I'd hoped that was the worst of it. As the printer spit out flyers, I stumbled to the bathroom again.

Major London gave me an anti-nausea pill and told me to get some rest. I slept. I woke to my room spinning around me, my Eeyore pajamas soaked with sweat. Outside I tripped, then crawled to the bathroom. My whole body retched and shook. I crawled back to my room. By the time I woke up, the Chamkani mission team had returned. Chris had been on the mission, and he came straight to my room from the helicopter.

"How are you feeling?" he asked when I opened the door. My appearance answered his question. I sat down on the doorstep while he talked. "I'm sorry you missed it," he said. "It was really cool. There was a huge *shura* (a community meeting) with hundreds of people. It was standing room only! I took lots of pictures for your storyboard. They fed us too. It was really good."

"BEWARE THE FOOD!" My voice was like something out of *Tales from the Crypt*.

"I actually think you might have the flu," Chris said. "Apparently Captain Jenner—you know, the Army ops guy? He had it a few days ago, and a couple other people have gotten sick."

"Well tell Captain Jenner he sucks."

Chris laughed. "Can I get you anything?"

I shook my head, slowly, not wanting to test my equilibrium. "How'd the Community Ownership flyers go over?"

His face melted into a frown. "We couldn't pass them out."

"What do you mean?"

"There was a PSYOP guy there," Chris said, a military psychological operations officer. "He looked at them and said we couldn't pass them out because they were blank on the back, and people could write messages on them and turn them into propaganda."

Whatever energy I had mustered to get out of bed left in a long sigh. "Well, that's good to know," I said. "Too bad I killed a tree first."

"We can probably print stuff on the back and still use them," Chris said.

"Next time we're in Chamkani before the election."

"Yeah . . ."

"OK," I said. "Thanks for trying. I'm going to sleep some more."

The next day I felt better long enough to make a storyboard with the photos and information Chris provided and to notice Nick was sick. "It's all your fault, Larry!" he wheezed, with none of his usual gruffness. I alternated days in my office and in bed. Chris got sick. I made two-sided Community Ownership flyers for an upcoming mission to another district. One of the PRT medics got sick. Everyone recovered, but I kept throwing up.

"I think I'm allergic to Afghanistan," I whined to Major London.

She handed me another pill. "I'm worried you might be really dehydrated," she said. "If this doesn't work we might have to send you to Salerno." FOB Salerno, in neighboring Khost Province, was the main base in the region and home to brigade headquarters. I imagined the Tweedles greeting my helicopter and escorting me to the clinic, pestering me about ongoing projects and unanswered emails. I didn't know what the new medication was, and I didn't care. I would probably have eaten camel spider eggs if there was a chance they'd heal me.

Perpetual sickness was not a new development. As a child, illness was cyclical: cold, sinus infection, ear infection, bronchitis, repeat. Multiple rounds of antibiotics gave a few weeks' reprieve. Allergies carved dark purple crescents beneath my eyes. I've always been a connoisseur of the not-so-common cold, the kind that morphs into co-infections or conjunctivitis. As I got older, bouts of sickness spread themselves out more generously, but their intensity held. I marveled at people whose illness barely registered in their demeanor and those who could bounce back quickly. I always looked as awful as I felt, complete with raw red nose, puffy eyes, and ghostly pallor. Sickness was the one thing that stalled my search for perfection, the only thing that overpowered my incessant need to say yes, to work harder, to do everything and be the best at all of it. I let my mom swaddle me in blankets and feed me chicken noodle soup. I leaned into her soft reminders to not worry about anything, just rest; the world will be there when you're better. My Afghan illness left me aching for Mom's healing touch. Blessedly, her deployment proxy came through, and Major London's pill worked.

As the election neared, the provincial chairman of the Independent Election Commission joined us at a few meetings. A handsome young man with just the stubble of a beard, he impressed me initially, exuding eagerness, confidence, and ambition. He seemed relaxed, despite the daunting task of ensuring polling site preparation and leading voter education efforts across the province. With access to my own limited share of communications resources, I thought maybe I could assist with education.

I couldn't imagine an election without months of highly-publicized campaigning, without nationally-televised speeches and debates, with no news websites, papers, magazines, and broadcasts breaking down the major issues, no mud-slinging advertisements, celebrity endorsements, or *Saturday Night Live* impersonations. I couldn't picture an election ballot with thirty-eight candidates for president and more than one hundred vying for seats on the local council, each denoted with their photograph and a unique symbol so they could be identified by an eighty percent illiterate electorate. I couldn't fathom the chairman's task of traveling to outlying areas on rough unpaved roads, through hostile territory, in the face of direct insurgent threats, to not only inform the local populace of the voting process and the location of their closest polling site, but also to possibly alert them that there even was an election, and what the election meant to them—if it meant anything; it was impossible to know. I just knew the election meant everything to coalition forces.

And I knew the energetic young chairman in front of me could probably use some support. I'd arranged to meet with him prior to our evening election meeting. We sat on a bench in the qalat courtyard, sucking in the fresh air before the windowless conference room took us hostage.

"Thank you for meeting with me," I said. Aamir translated. "I just wanted to let you know that the PRT is here to help in any way we can with the election. We can put messages on our radios, and we have people at outposts who can talk to citizens in those areas. Is there anything we can help you with?"

The chairman spoke for a minute, animating his Pashtu with vigorous nods and hand gestures. Aamir turned to me and shrugged. "He said the job is done. He has been everywhere and everyone knows what to do."

"Oh. Um, OK. That's good." I searched the chairman's earnest face. Could he possibly be telling the truth? Could he really have accomplished that monumental task in such a short time and lived to talk about it so enthusiastically? There were areas in Paktia where American troops hadn't been in years because the locations were too dangerous and inaccessible. But the chairman was a local. Travel could be easier for locals. It could also be harder. Either way, I didn't feel right challenging him.

"OK," I said. "Well, please let us know if there's anything we can do for you." I shook the chairman's hand, then he said something to Aamir.

"He asks if you can do him a favor?" Aamir said.

"I can try," I said, cautiously.

I watched their faces as the two men talked. The discussion seemed serious. Finally, Aamir turned to me. "He wants to know if you can get him a special powder for working out."

"A special . . . what?"

"To make him stronger at the gym. He says American soldiers use powders to put in their drinks that help them get strong."

In the face of a pivotal international strategic event, the local man in charge wanted nothing more than protein powder. I tried to keep my expression blank. "I'll see what I can do."

On August 20, election day, I woke early, my heart pounding me out of a nightmare I couldn't remember. I'd half expected to be startled awake by the whistle of incoming mortars or the pop of automatic weapons. I heard the buzz of my fan. Footsteps on gravel. A muddled conversation. Grimly aware that election violence might shatter the FOB's fragile peace, I'd laid out my body armor the night before, prepared for groggy, late-night grabbing. Now, my vest and helmet sat idly on the floor, camouflaged with extra pinks and blues in the light from my scarf-draped window.

Outside, the sky was clear. I walked to the bathroom, then to my office, looking up every few steps. Surely any second a rocket would slice through the blue. I ate Cheerios at my desk. I checked my email. I wished my colleagues Happy Election Day with false cheer. They returned anxious greetings. I stared from my phone to my laptops. They stared back.

The PRT had no planned missions; we were standing by in case we were needed as a Quick Reaction Force, on alert to provide mobile security and first aid. A convoy of trucks waited in the qalat parking lot. Security Forces soldiers lounged nearby, playing cards, smoking, and sipping Rip It energy drinks, or resting on pillows of body armor.

The Afghan government had ordered an Election Day media blackout. No polling site attacks or insurgent intimidation would be broadcast. Publicized violence could discourage potential voters, and low turnout could undermine the election's credibility. Censorship in the name of democracy (the paradox didn't strike me at the time). We could communicate through official military channels. So far, official channels into my office remained silent. "We're just playing the waiting game," I emailed Chris next door at the operations center. "I feel utterly useless."

There was nothing to do but hope that there continue to be nothing to do.

After a while I wandered to the operations center, glancing up on the way. The sky was still blue. I walked past the conference room to the command and control center. I'd only been through this room in passing, repelled by the dim lighting, the mass of technological equipment, and the general air of agitation. Today, the command center swelled with people. Regular inhabitants manned their desks, fidgeting with nervous energy. I said a quick hi to Chris and Jacob in the next room and then joined the crowd of visitors standing along the command center's back wall, tracing their gaze to two screens showing video surveillance of downtown Gardez and a town to the north.

Following last-minute security adjustments, around 170 polling sites opened across Paktia.[7] Afghan National Army, Afghan National Police, and Afghan Border Patrolmen were theoretically providing security and would theoretically send periodic updates, but we didn't really expect to hear anything unless something went wrong. Every time a phone rang or a radio crackled, the room froze with tension. Cue the scene of Tarantino carnage.

Usually, it was nothing. Then:

A polling site attack in the north. Minimal damage. Voters scattered and then started coming back.

Nothing.

Nothing.

Two suicide bombers on a motorcycle. They didn't reach their target. Possibly taken out by Afghan National Army.

Nothing.

Reports of lines at polling stations! And women voters!

Nothing.

Nothing.

Nothing.

The more time that passed without reports of a significant attack, the more nervous we got. I scurried back and forth to my office to check my phone and email. The sky stayed blue; it seemed almost mocking: *Come on, insurgents. Is that all you've got?*

Nothing.

Nothing.

Then it was six o'clock and the polling sites closed. Notifications of minor incidents trickled in. Elsewhere in the country, there were reports of extreme violence. Voters were hanged in Kandahar. Rockets rained down on Helmand. Somehow, Paktia had made it through Election Day relatively unscathed.

The danger wasn't over yet. For several days, the ballots would be kept at the polling sites for counting. Sites remained vulnerable, especially at night; insurgents were known to attack under the cover of darkness. Then the ballots would need to be transported across difficult and dangerous terrain to a long-term storage facility in Gardez. There were still a million opportunities for disaster.

Afghan security forces were tired. They weren't used to working overtime, and their pay didn't account for it. With the Islamic month of Ramadan fast approaching, many had planned to travel as soon as the election ended. Some still did. Daily reports from the Army teams monitoring the sites showed Afghan security personnel numbers dwindling.

I didn't mention desertion in the op-ed I wrote a week after the election. I didn't corroborate reports of registration fraud, low turnout, ballot box tampering, or voter intimidation. My article had to be approved by my chain of command and would never be published with that information. It wasn't my job to embarrass Afghan security forces or to endorse rumors. My job was to discuss the election from my boots-on-the-ground perspective, the perspective directed by the military—and, of course, to highlight military talking points whenever possible. Though doubts and frustrations had begun to creep in, they weren't yet strong enough to overtake my PA brain. At the time, my prevailing feeling was pride.

I wrote about the challenges of coordinating such a massive effort and lauded the hard work on both sides. Because I was supposed to, and because in my post-election glee I forgot to be skeptical, I reminded readers that the election had been an Afghan-led process. I commended the success of the Afghan security forces and the bravery of the voters. I acknowledged, "The election wasn't perfect," but it was, I declared, a victory for democracy. "And more importantly, it was a victory of hope."

I published a similar commentary in my new blog. I'd had the blog idea for a while; just one more medium to broadcast PRT activities, I'd told Colonel McGuire. I thought we were the best thing no one knew about—*I* didn't even know about PRTs until I volunteered to serve on one—and I wanted to showcase our mission to the whole world (or at least to my mom and my Facebook friends). The election seemed like a powerful place to start.

The day after my op-ed published, Ramadan observance began. Votes were still being tallied. Some sites had been almost completely abandoned by Afghan security personnel. Allegations of fraud emerged, widespread and severe enough to threaten the election's legitimacy.

On September 1, an article for the independent nonprofit research organization Afghan Analysts Network questioned the integrity of the elections, and also my op-ed. Author Thomas Ruttig had also been in Paktia during the election, but he emphatically stated that the elections I wrote about "were quite different" from what he witnessed. "Lt. Johnson saw an outright 'success,'" he wrote. "Although she concedes that the run-up to the elections 'was not an easy road' and E-Day itself did not pass 'without incident.' There were 'more than 80 attacks' across the province, she reports. 'But damage was minimal. In the battle of fear the enemy suffered a decisive loss.' For her, the international media talked down the electoral 'success' and 'fraud, corruption and low voter turnout' were just 'rumors.' I am sorry but this is plain propaganda."

I didn't see Ruttig's article until several months later, in April 2010, when I was back in Florida. Reading Ruttig's words, I felt a surge of anger, not at Ruttig, but at myself. "I am sorry but this is plain propaganda," he wrote. In April 2010, I agreed.

I wouldn't have agreed in September 2009, at least not completely. In hindsight, I struggle to separate in-the-moment pride and relief from the cloud of cynicism and doubt that built over the rest of the deployment. The cloud certainly started gathering in September. In the wake of the election, the UN-backed Electoral Complaints Commission (ECC) received thousands of complaints and flagged tens of thousands of questionable ballots. Recounts and audits were ordered for suspect polling stations, including many in Paktia. All the while my information operations colleagues and I followed orders to "aggressively pursue media engagements" with Afghan security forces, government officials, and election officers "highlighting transparency and legitimacy of the election process." Even to my PA brain, at best this sounded like an oxymoron, at worst an outright lie.

Nevertheless, I complied. My post-election reporting notes that during this time my IO colleagues and I "prepared talking points for/interviewed security officials and government officials highlighting high turnout and good security and thanking citizens for their participation." We also "created handbills congratulating citizens on election success and security forces on good security."

On September 16, the Independent Election Commission announced that incumbent President Hamid Karzai had received 54.4% of the votes, but the results would not be official until approved by the ECC. Two weeks later, Deputy UN Envoy to Afghanistan Peter Galbraith was removed from his position after alleging the UN Special Representative to Afghanistan had downplayed election fraud in order to maintain relations with Karzai.

Then it was October, and the international community urged Karzai to develop a power-sharing agreement with his closest rival, Abdullah Abdullah, to unite supporters and end the election. If fraud brought Karzai below the fifty percent threshold, the two candidates would be forced into a runoff. Within weeks, winter weather would arrive, blocking mountain passes for ballot transport. On October 12 an ECC member resigned, blaming foreigners for "improper interference" in the fraud investigations.

Finally, on October 21, two months after Election Day, the final certified results were released. No candidate had secured the required fifty percent of the votes. There would be a runoff. We would repeat the process all over again.

"You know, although the process was messy, I'm pleased to say that the final outcome was determined in accordance with Afghan law."
—President Barack Obama, November 2, 2009, regarding the Afghanistan Presidential and Provincial Council Elections

Part Three

COMMUNICATION *noun*

Definition: Common

1. A process by which information is exchanged between individuals through a common system of symbols, signs, or behavior; also: exchange of information.

2. A technique for expressing ideas effectively (as in speech).

3. A message that is given to someone: a letter, telephone call, etc.

Definition: in Military/War

1. A one-sided exchange; i.e. an order.

2. Jargon specific to a single unit or entity, often foreign to outsiders.

3. A lengthy dialogue, written or oral, intended to confuse or overwhelm, which can be made less lengthy, though not less convoluted, with acronym usage.

4. Information effectively transferred in only one direction, usually down; lateral communication or communication "up the chain" will likely not be acknowledged or attempted, respectively.

5. As in reports, information relayed in multiple formats, multiple times, for the same audience.

6. Perfunctory phrases which capture a version of the truth, though not the whole story.

7. Strategy; words wielded to elicit a specific response.

8. Anything on a PowerPoint slide.

see also HOOAH

11

Glimpses

A MEMORY OF MY MOM: We were all at Grandma and Grandpa Home's house on the Puget Sound a few years after Desert Storm. The weather must have been cold and wintery, because we weren't outside. The Puget Sound house was made for outside: collecting clams and mussels, wading into tide flats, canoeing down the creek under the bridge, tossing horse-shoes on the lawn. This time we sat around the high-ceilinged living room. Someone popped in a videotape, and the TV burst to life with an old news broadcast. On the screen we saw two-year-old Matt in his puffy red and black coat, coiling his tiny hands around the chain link fence at McChord Air Force Base on March 12, 1991. The recording didn't get very far before Mom started crying.

She scolded herself, dabbing at her eyes. "I don't know why I get so emotional."

I was used to seeing Mom cry. As a child, her tears didn't surprise or upset me. I even found comfort in them; we were linked through our open displays of emotion. I never connected the dots between Mom's tears and her deployment, though. I didn't notice a shift between before and after. She remained the same strong soldier-mom who cried sometimes because she cared so much about everyone.

Mom admits that she tried to keep the post-deployment tears hidden. She cried in her bedroom, in the shower, after she dropped us off at school. Yet at my grandparents' house or on what must have been many other pub-lic occasions, our family didn't accept the invitation to reflect. We paused to hug, to pass the tissues, but not to gently pry, to start to peel away the layers beneath the tears. Like politics or racism, we spoke of war in vague, safe terms, leaving room for ignorance and barriers to grow.

The first time I saw my dad cry came years after Mom's deployment. We were watching the movie *Forrest Gump*. In one scene, Forrest, played by Tom Hanks, recovers in a military hospital from a bullet wound received in the Vietnam War ("directly in the buttocks"). His reluctant friend, Gary Sinise as Lieutenant Dan, has been in the neighboring bed, but when Forrest pulls back the curtain the Lieutenant isn't there. In his place lies a man in a full body cast. He looks like a mummy.

At the sight of the casted man on TV, my dad started crying. Not silent tears, but gulping, wailing sobs. Shavonne and I, preteens at the time, sat at the foot of the couch, stunned. We were accustomed to Mom's emotions, but Dad was the opposite. An engineer by trade and manner, he looked to logic, rather than feelings, as his guide. While Mom scooted quickly across the cushions and held our crying father, Shavonne and I looked at each other, hoping for an indication of how we were supposed to react. In an unspoken agreement, we both got up and left the room. We didn't know what else to do, so we started laughing, our nervous tittering merging with Dad's weeping down the hall.

At the time I made out muttered snippets about knee surgery and a war vet in a body cast. Much later I would get the full story: In 1970, after blowing out his knee, my seventeen-year-old dad spent a week in the orthopedic wing of Madigan Army Medical Center. The Vietnam War was in full swing. On the bed to one side of Dad's lay a war patient, a boy just two years older than him in a full body cast. On the other side another young soldier was being treated for a spinal injury. He had a neck traction collar and a bolt through his head. Later still, after my own military service ended, I would learn that my dad had received a college Army ROTC scholarship. Following his hospital stay, he turned the scholarship down.

My brain spun with the revelation. How different would Dad's life have been had he joined the military? Would he have survived Vietnam? Would he and Mom have stayed together? Would his service have dissuaded her from joining? Grandpa Home's brother was killed in World War II and his soon-to-be-wife's brother came home in a full body cast like the one Dad saw; a shrapnel-severed artery would leave permanent leg damage. Still, Grandpa joined the Navy during wartime. Even without Dad serving,

Mom had friends who deployed to Vietnam and a friend whose older brother died there, but she enlisted in that era. Shavonne, Matt, and I all saw Mom go to war. I was the one most overtly affected, yet I alone went on to serve.

In the face of trauma, what drives people to react in such opposing ways? Surely Dad's stoicism would have served him well in the Army, but it was Mom with her cellophane emotions who followed that path. My siblings inherited Dad's interiority, his rational engineering brain. Did that arm them against the patriotic swell of 9/11, whereas something programmed in my emotional landscape came alive? Mom and I share a caretaking instinct that verges on extreme, a desire to sponge up everyone else's pain. Why was the military, notoriously closed off to vulnerability, the recipient of our care?

Regardless of the reasons behind all the family decisions that conspired to bring me here, how altered would my life be if one person had chosen differently?

In Afghanistan, as the election saga raged on and evidence of corruption mounted, as I continued to follow orders to paint the results with a rose-colored palate, a feeling started brewing inside me. I didn't identify the feeling right away, just like I couldn't name it all those years ago when I watched my dad cry. It was the same feeling I first encountered when Mom deployed, and one I experienced over and over in middle and high school.

My mom recalls times I came home from school in tears. I'd learned a friend had a drug-dealing mom. Another, the youngest of several children, was often ignored. There was the girl with the gorgeous house on the water but whose workaholic parents were never there, so she rebelled with alcohol and crazy parties. I cried to my mom because for the first time I recognized our family bubble, the wholesome vault of my upbringing. Outside that bubble was shit. Big, fat, smelly piles of shit. With the exception of Mom's deployment, I'd never had to walk through it before. I knew I had no bearing on my friends' situations. I could offer at most a carpool, an afterschool hangout, a mom-for-a-day cheering from the stands. Then they would go home and things would remain unchanged. There would always be shit piles. I couldn't un-see them, and I couldn't keep others from stepping in them.

I couldn't prevent Mom from deploying. I couldn't stop Dad's crying. I couldn't make the Afghan election legitimate; all I could do was pretend it had been, tell people it had been, and prepare myself to keep pretending, while that feeling—helplessness—festered beneath the surface.

Shortly after the August 20 election, the International Security Assistance Force commander, General Stanley McCrystal, issued a bleak assessment of the Afghanistan war. The report, leaked to the *Washington Post*, echoed much of what we said in meetings, or, as in my case, growing doubts we kept to ourselves. "Although considerable effort and sacrifice have resulted in some progress," McChrystal wrote, "many indicators suggest the overall situation is deteriorating. We face not only a resilient and growing insurgency; there is also a crisis of confidence among Afghans—in both their government and the international community—that undermines our credibility and emboldens the insurgents." Failure to turn the tides within the next twelve months, he said, "risks an outcome where defeating the insurgency is no longer possible." We would be in Afghanistan for seven of those twelve months.

McChrystal requested sending as many as 40,000 additional troops to the region. *Go big or go home,* I thought. Even from our tiny corner of the country, even through my PA goggles, mounting evidence revealed the precarious state of the war. In fall 2009, Iraq still had roughly double the troop strength of Afghanistan. Iraq was going well. The equation made sense:

What are we going to do? Win the war!

When are we going to do it? Now!

How are we going to do it? With 40,000 more troops!

Though grim, McChrystal's assessment felt validating. Finally, Afghanistan would get the attention it deserved.

Then in October President Obama put the troop request on hold while the administration debated the way forward.

Afghanistan had a way of balancing things out. Just like every little victory seemed swallowed by defeat, so, too, were negatives tempered by a glimpse at the opposite.

I got a glimpse one sunny late September afternoon from under my headscarf. Sitting in a Gardez City schoolhouse, I felt awkward and itchy. I couldn't get the scarf to drape gracefully over my shoulders like the Afghan women around me. My hair bun bulged against the fabric, and the frill kept sticking to the Velcro on my uniform. The other women didn't care. They appreciated the cultural gesture and told me I looked beautiful. The Afghan women were all radiant, dressed in bright flowing fabric with faces made up to emphasize angular features and dark, kohl-lined eyes. This was the first time I'd met with local women, the first time I'd seen them without their burqas and the first they'd seen me without my body armor. The air of the small classroom buzzed with excitement and curiosity. Unlike government meetings, conversation here wasn't a requirement; it was a desire.

The thin walls of the four-room schoolhouse did little to cover the din of downtown Gardez: passing mopeds, rustling gravel, an occasional military helicopter, and the growl of our own waiting vehicles. The city sounded remarkably like FOB Gardez. The women around me didn't appear to mind. They laughed and chatted animatedly, obviously thrilled by the company. Had they been with each other like this before, expressive, open, vulnerable? With a rainbow of bright headscarves, the room held more color than I'd yet seen in Afghanistan.

The class would begin soon. These sixty women, teachers of all ages, formed the latest cohort in a PRT-sponsored civics training course discussing constitutional law, government structure, and women's and children's rights, lessons not included in the formal Afghan education system. In theory, sharing information with educators, specifically women, allowed them to pass the knowledge on to their students and children. As with most American initiatives in Afghanistan, our intentions were noble. Unlike many activities, however, civics training classes were met overwhelmingly with enthusiasm and hope. Local teachers received personal invitations to the classes, but word-of-mouth pushed attendance beyond the target audience. Classes were usually standing-room-only. Women went home gushing about the lessons and returned the following day with sisters in tow. Still, success didn't come without resistance. In one of the most dangerous and conservative districts of the province, men refused to allow their wives and daughters to attend the training. "We will go," they said, "and tell our women what we learn."

Sergeant Rivera supervised the PRT's Afghan legal advisor, who coordinated the civics training classes. He stopped by the office frequently, often bringing gifts or treats from the local bazaar. Tall and rail thin, he had both the gawkiness and spastic energy of an adolescent boy. He seemed too young and immature to have a title like "legal advisor," but his good nature made him impossible not to like. Then Sergeant Rivera told me that the legal advisor had received death threats warning him to stop the civics training classes. He was determined to continue. He knew threats meant the work was important. As I had with John, the Christian interpreter, I wondered if I myself, when it really mattered, could believe in anything so strongly.

If this Gardez classroom served as any indication, students hadn't been deterred by threats either. Stuffed into the small room, Americans and Afghans angled our chairs so we could better talk to each other, though "talk" is a generous term for what I was doing. At pre-deployment training we learned a few basic Pashtu phrases, but they focused on security. I could tell people to "Stop!" "Put your hands up!" or "Don't move!" but I didn't know how to communicate cordially. I fumbled through the few greetings I knew and then resorted to shrugging and shaking my head sheepishly. The women around me smiled. They seemed genuinely touched by my feeble attempts. An older woman with deep wrinkles etched into her brow patted my hand. "Thank you," she said. "Thank you. Thank you." I didn't know why she was thanking me, but I wanted her to keep her calloused hand on mine. Her hand, her eyes, her smile could have belonged to one of my grandmothers.

Across the room Sergeant Rivera gabbed admirably in broken Pashtu. She had told me that she longed to be able to walk off base with our female interpreter, Leila. "I wish I could just put on local clothes and wander through the villages and talk to people as equals," she mused, "not as a soldier or an American." Leila was an American citizen but a Paktia native. Sergeant Rivera and Leila had the same olive skin, dark eyes, and thick black hair. Sergeant Rivera could blend in. Even without my uniform, pale skin, or light hair, I knew I never could. As much as I told myself I wanted to be unguarded here, I couldn't turn off my paranoia. I wanted to embrace the idea of connecting as equals but also keep myself at arm's distance, ready to retreat into the safety of my armor or behind my camera lens. The old women's hand was the first Afghan touch that didn't feel like an invasion. Like the America I served, despite my best intentions, I'd started putting up walls.

Near Sergeant Rivera, a young Afghan woman raised her hand. I was tickled to see that the gesture stretched across cultures. The instructor translated her question, looking at Sergeant Rivera while he spoke. "She wants to know why you have come to Afghanistan," he said. "Why do you leave your children to come be here with us?"

Sergeant Rivera regarded the woman for a long moment. "Mothers are mothers everywhere," she finally said. "As mothers we don't work for ourselves. We work to make a better future for our children." Her voice cracked on the last word. Sergeant Rivera spoke of her children constantly. Her son had started middle school this month, and her daughter just lost her first tooth.

I couldn't fathom deploying with a family at home. Leaving had been difficult enough as a single girl with three cats. Recently in a phone call my mom let slip that it was harder for her having me deployed than when she was deployed herself. "I've decided being on this side of a deployment is worse!" she said, her voice a notch higher than normal. I heard her take a deep breath before she continued, more carefully. "It was horrible for me when I was getting ready to go, but once I was over there at least I knew I was OK. I worry about you all the time!" When Mom deployed, she left behind a husband and three small children. She had no idea how long she would be away. She thought it was a suicide mission. Yet she found it harder having me gone. That phone call was the closest I'd come to crying to my parents. I said something like, "Well, from what I remember when you were gone, that side of the deployment *was* pretty rough." Later, back in my qalat room, I pressed my face into my pillow and wailed. Listening to Sergeant Rivera, my eyes brimmed again with tears. I thought of Shavonne and the twins I wouldn't meet for several months. I thought of homecoming celebrations at Hurlburt Field where soldiers were introduced to new babies for the first time, or reintroduced to toddlers who didn't recognize the strange, camouflaged person prying them from Mommy's or Daddy's arms. I thought of March 12, 1991.

When the instructor translated Sergeant Rivera's response, the women around me nodded. Fierceness blazed in their eyes. Our gaps in language, culture, and history were vast, but somehow I knew we understood each other, these women, Sergeant Rivera, and I.

"We are very grateful for you being here," the instructor said.

As class started, Sergeant Rivera and I moved to the back of the room to observe. I gave her a hug. "That was amazing," I said.

"I know," she said. "I love them. I wish women could run Afghanistan. We'd all be so much better off."

Though unable to follow the lessons, I watched the students eagerly watching the instructor. They nodded. They laughed and issued animated responses. I snapped a few pictures, careful not to capture any of the women's faces, as the instructor requested. I found myself smiling more than I had in a long time.

When the session ended, two young women pulled me aside, speaking in English much better than my Pashtu.

"Teacher say you are a writer," one said.

"Well, I like to write," I said. "Hopefully someday I will be a writer."

"You will be."

I blushed, wishing I shared her confidence.

"We are writers too," the other woman said. "We want to write about our country."

"That's wonderful!" I said. Prior to the deployment, I had read all the Afghanistan literature I could find. Many of the books lined the shelf of my room back on FOB Gardez: books by journalists, memoirs by soldiers and diplomats, cultural analyses, historical textbooks. Missing were Afghan voices, and certainly Afghan women. "I hope to read your writing someday," I said.

The women were twenty-two and twenty-four and unmarried, surprising in a place where the average bride was around sixteen. They wanted to have careers, they told me; then they would think about family. Me too, I replied.

We giggled, like girls anywhere would. Then they put on their burqas and I put on my body armor, forgetting to be grateful that one day soon I would take mine off for good.

12

The Truth, the Whole Truth, & Nothing but the Truth

AMERICAN TROOPS IN AFGHANISTAN LOSING HEART, say army chaplains." I read the *Times* of London late September headline from my IO PowerPoint slide, grimacing as if it tasted bitter in my mouth, and then looked around the PRT conference room at my teammates. I paused dramatically, wanting the words to make an impact. "Obviously," I said, "from the title alone you can see why brigade is upset."

Upset was an understatement. The article had nothing to do with Paktia, at least not directly, but for the second time in as many weeks brigade thought the media had manipulated "high-risk" statements made by careless troops to paint a negative picture of U.S. operations in Afghanistan.

"The many soldiers who come to see us have a sense of futility and anger about being here," one chaplain said in the article. "They are really in a state of depression and despair and just want to get back to their families," and, "they feel they are risking their lives for progress that's hard to discern."

After seeing the article, the Tweedles had called together all PA and IO officers from Paktia, Paktika, and Khost to remind us that our job was to present a positive outlook. "WE control the message!" the PA Tweedle kept repeating. I pictured him slamming his fist on his desk for emphasis, his IO colleague sitting nearby, nodding like a bobble head doll. As directed, I'd instructed all PRT personal in effective media interaction and how to push command messages to promote positive, or at least neutral coverage, like I'd trained airmen countless times as director of media relations at Hurlburt Field and as the loan PA officer during the training mission in Mali. The words and messages flowed almost automatically from my well-trained mouth.

"I know we've been through media training," I said now to the PRT conference room. "And I don't want to beat everyone over the head with it, but this is a good reminder of how damaging these types of high-risk comments can be." Across the room, Chris doodled in his notebook. Others urged me with their eyes to finish up; dinner awaited. "So," I concluded, "before you say anything to the media or to other sources that could potentially take advantage of what you're saying, ask yourself: How would the enemy react to your comments? And how would your family, friends, and Americans react? If you ever have any questions about what's appropriate, you can always talk to me."

After the meeting we spilled out into the qalat courtyard and scurred en mass toward Olive Gardez. One of the civil engineers, Capt. Eli Wilson, caught me in the doorway. "Hey Lauren, do you have a minute?"

"Of course," I said. Then to Chris, "Would you mind saving me a seat?" Remembering we were in public, I added a delayed, "Sir?"

Chris smirked. "Will do. See you at the O-G."

I turned to Eli. The two of us didn't always get along. Eli wasn't shy with his opinions, which sometimes ground against my nonconfrontational nature. Still, we bonded over our affinity for triathlons and craft beer. Eli's wife also served as an Air Force civil engineer and was deployed with a different PRT elsewhere in Afghanistan. She'd been one of the first people I met at Camp Atterbury, her sweet, bubbly presence infusing much-needed warmth into the women's barracks. During our Indiana training, Chris and I had passed the Wilson couple holding hands on evening walks, and we joined them for dinner in Indianapolis after our last training day. From Afghanistan, Eli spoke to his wife almost every night on an office phone. I couldn't help but appreciate the fragments of conversation that seeped through the thin half wall separating our workspaces. He could be moody and short-tempered, but Eli's eyes lit up at the mention of his wife, and on the phone his voice dripped with affectionate coos. Now in the qalat courtyard, he looked disturbed.

"Everything OK?" I asked.

Eli's face and hands twisted in sync. "I just have to ask," he said. "About that article. Was the chaplains' talking to the media really that bad? They were truthful. They were standing up for their troops. Honestly, I think some of those same things." Eli looked directly at me now. His cheeks burned pink. He wasn't just disturbed; he was angry.

I'd seen Eli fired up plenty of times, but never over IO issues. Like most, he acknowledged the importance of IO but acted more or less ambivalent about the actual goings-on of my job. The challenge startled me, so I defaulted to one of my standard lines. "You have to realize you give up a bit of your freedom of speech when you're in the military," I said. "When you say something in uniform, it can be interpreted as something all people in uniform believe. If you're discontent, there are proper channels for addressing it. Not the media."

"And what if those channels don't work?" Eli countered. "Do you really think this is the first time someone's said they're not sure about this mission? It's just the first time we're hearing about it because it's in the news. Why is that a bad thing?"

I felt my mouth open, then close. No good response came out. Eli's face had turned thoughtful. As I met his gaze, I realized I agreed with him. Grappling with the elections, McChrystal's assessment, the fogginess of my own job description, I was beginning to relate to some of the sentiments in the article too. PRT missions had recently discovered buried explosives on three different school properties. An attack just a few days earlier had killed eight U.S. soldiers and two Afghan security officers at an outpost north of Paktia—an outpost slated for closure but kept open for bureaucratic reasons. I'd confessed to my college roommate that Afghanistan increasingly left me feeling bi-polar. I got giddy over ice cream in the dining hall, a particularly juicy Taliban mistake, or a compliment from Chris. In between, each bit of bad news and every negative interaction sent me spiraling. I snapped at Chris or withdrew to my room, hugged my Walmart pillow and cried, or I laced up my sneakers and ran until my knee throbbed with pain. Round and round I tumbled, like in the Humvee rollover simulator from training. The more I spun the harder it was to find my way out.

But I didn't want to admit that to Eli. Agreeing would go against my PA training, which still clung tightly to my intentions. It would also mean

openly accepting discouragement for myself. Too much deployment remained to willingly take on that weight. So, like a good public affairs officer, I gave a non-answer. "I mean, there's so much negative information out
there already," I said. "We don't need to put out any more."

We needed feel-good stories: the American public, the locals, me. The
headlines filling my email inbox overwhelmed me with bad news, and reports around the region weren't much better. Suicide bombings. Civilian
casualties. Corruption. Billions of dollars with little to show for it. The election runoff saga continued. A senior State Department representative became the first U.S. official to resign in protest over the war in Afghanistan,
writing bluntly in his letter of resignation, "I fail to see the value or the
worth in continued U.S. casualties or expenditures of resources in support
of the Afghan government in what is, truly, a 35-year [sic] old civil war."[8]
Though several years had passed, the Abu Ghraib Iraqi prisoner abuse
scandal still festered in the public psyche. Reports of abuse at the military
prison at Afghanistan's Bagram Air Base had also surfaced.

A local Bagram detainee presented a chance to add a positive narra-
tive. The detainee had been at Bagram Prison for several months but was
now deathly ill and had been offered a compassionate release to spend his
final days with his family near Gardez. The story packed the warm-fuzzies
we were looking for: *See how merciful the Americans are, taking an old man
home to his loved ones!*

My job was to exploit our compassion, to work with the Gardez coalition forces radio station DJs to interview the prisoner about the kind treatment he'd received at Bagram and his gratitude to be going home. Usually,
radio scripts came from coalition forces. The detainee could give a firsthand
account, a local man speaking directly to other locals. He was an ally in our
information war. I knew the interview offered an important opportunity,
but my mind went wild imagining all the terrible actions that must have led
to the man's capture. *See how merciful the Americans are, taking an old man
home to his loved ones! Never mind the soldiers he killed with homemade bombs
or through weapons smuggling . . .*

I fumed as I approached the holding room, a vacant apartment in the
PRT qalat, unable to get the image of the base's memorial wall out of my

head, the portraits of the seventeen soldiers killed on local missions. I imagined the prisoner, a composite of mug shots of the U.S, government's most wanted terrorists, with a similar wall of portraits at his home, and, like a movie mobster, throwing darts at each successive face. Target eliminated. Maniacal laugh.

The detainee's handler, a young Army soldier, greeted the Afghan DJ and me when we entered. The prisoner didn't move from where he hunched in a sagging corner chair. He wasn't the threatening figure I'd pictured but an old man. When I sat across from him, next to the tall, slim DJ, the prisoner slowly raised his head. He looked ancient, though appearances could be deceiving in Afghanistan. The skin of the man's face folded into deep, dirty crevices. His long beard crawled gray and matted down his chest. A filthy, ripped tunic hung loosely on his scrawny frame, which seemed even smaller in contrast to the armored guard. The detainee's blindfold had been removed, but his frail wrists were bound together, and he rubbed them, trance-like, over and over, as the long end of the zip tie brushed against his knees. His body shook with raspy coughs that left him keeled over and wheezing. He didn't acknowledge me. When he spoke he focused on a spot below the DJ's chin, but I could see blankness in his eyes. He looked like Afghanistan outside the FOB Gardez gate: parched, ravaged, forgotten. He looked like a man who had given up. And all I felt was pity.

By the time Aamir finished translating the detainee's interview, I had put the man's blank eyes out of my mind. My public affairs alter ego regained control. Drew, the Agribusiness Development Team public affairs sergeant, oversaw the radio DJs, so he reviewed the transcript first. When he finished he stormed into the IO office, more agitated than I'd ever seen him, waving the printed pages in front of him.

"I don't know why the DJ asked him about why he was captured," Drew said. "We told him not to ask that." He shook his head and lifted his arms in exasperation. The papers flapped in his hand.

"What was the answer?" I took the paper and skimmed the first page. Under the question it read: *I don't know why they took me.* I scowled. "Yeah, that's not something we want to broadcast."

"I know," Drew said. "And he asked the same question again at the end!" He pointed to the second answer: *I don't know.* "Why would he ask that twice?"

I sighed. "Can they edit those questions out for the radio broadcast?"

"Yeah," Drew said, "that's what I asked them to do."

Only after the radio spot ran did guilt start to scratch at my resolve. We earned a small victory in the fight for hearts and minds, a positive news story straight from the source: *I was treated well at Bagram. I'm thankful to be going home. END.*

No one would miss the extra question, omitted twice.

That evening, I wrote a blog post about the detainee. I didn't include the deleted lines. I talked about my anger and how it quickly morphed into pity. I said that the detainee spoke kindly of his treatment at Bagram. I wrote about the exhaustion and resignation in his eyes. But then I added that his eyes "were also thankful."

I don't know if it was a conscious lie. The detainee did mention he was thankful to be going home; maybe I took creative liberty and applied the sentiment to his appearance. I could call it self-preservation, what the military refers to as CYA, or Cover Your Ass. Controlled speech was a way of life, especially in public affairs. Deployment blogs had been shut down over controversial comments. Mostly, though, I simply wanted that line to be true. I wanted my loyal blog readers (my family and Facebook friends) to fully benefit from this "good news story." More importantly, I needed the line to be true for myself.

Barely a month had passed since I started my blog, but I only wrote one more post after that night. A battle was raging in my brain between public affairs policy and individual expression. I wanted to do what I'd always done and purge my mixed emotions into writing so I could make them tangible, sort through them, and regain a sense of control. I wanted to tell the world (or at least my family and Facebook friends) not just how good, but how bad and ugly, how extremely complicated this war could be. Yet somehow my brain recognized that talking wasn't so simple anymore. Ultimately, the forces settled on a draw. I wouldn't keep personally broadcasting PA-friendly messages, but I wouldn't spill my guts either. I would just stop writing altogether.

13

Potempkin Village

I SHOULD HAVE TAKEN THE MORTAR DRILL as a warning sign that I was headed for what the military called a Charlie Foxtrot—a clusterfuck. Huddled in a shallow bunker, my head vibrated with the shrieks of the siren signaling an incoming attack. The concrete wall pressed against my back, and body heat seeped from the security forces soldiers squished on either side. I hugged my legs into my chest to leave more room for my taller teammates sitting across from me. Our armor waited in our vehicles. Without it, we had more room in the concrete cave. But we were also more exposed. My mind ticked through a wheel of logical feelings: fear, panic, anger, hope. I settled on annoyance.

Our convoy was late to depart back to FOB Gardez. We'd been about to load the vehicles when this drill began. We didn't have mortar drills at FOB Gardez. Though only about a mile away, the base wasn't attacked with the frequency of our neighbors here at FOB Lightning, which housed American military units as well as an Afghan National Army battalion, making for a two-for-one target. FOB Gardez also lacked security infrastructure. We had a few concrete tunnel bunkers like the one I sat in now, but nowhere near enough to shelter all FOB personnel. I couldn't identify the bunker closest to the qalat. Maybe the one by the gym? Surely too far to run, unprotected, in an instance of imminent danger. I wondered if the qalat itself was supposed to serve as our "hardened structure." The qalat with the crumbling passageway and the corner tower that visibly melted when it rained.

Sitting in the grimy FOB Lightning bunker, I knew I should be relieved that this didn't happen to us regularly. Quality of life was a trade-off. FOB Lightning had superior facilities and paved roads. The dining hall boasted a full salad bar with healthy green lettuce, juicy chunks of sliced fruit, pasta salad, and potato salad (the one form of potatoes that hadn't made an appearance at FOB Gardez). The FOB Lightning gym had solid walls and working treadmills. Their internet wasn't just reliable, it was fast. But they got mortared.

Even with the proximity, getting to FOB Lightning still required a four-vehicle convoy and full security detail. This supposedly short mission had already sucked up more resources than the PRT could easily spare. As the mission commander, the reason for us being here, responsibility for delays would fall on me. Today wasn't a life-or-death mission by any means, despite our current bunkered state, but it carried bureaucratic importance. We were fulfilling a leadership directive. Unlike many directives, I saw true value in this mission, which helped ease the knotting in my stomach. I was conducting a site survey of FOB Lightning to identify a good location to train government officials in media interaction. Brigade had pushed down the mandate, and I jumped at the chance. Flimsy though the local media infrastructure was, Paktia leaders needed the training. In the three months I'd been in Gardez, the chief of police had made several erroneous statements to the press following security incidents. The PRT's mission to help legitimize the Afghan government couldn't be accomplished with uniformed officials running their mouths; winning hearts and minds required their communications savvy. Plus, after months of discontent in hearing talk about information operations being "the most important" focus in Afghanistan but getting little support or guidance, I felt this mission represented a shift.

Running a province-wide training program for government officials was no small task. I could have been intimidated by the responsibility— perhaps I should have been—but amid the floundering uncertainty of IO, I snatched at something familiar. Media relations formed a large part of my job back at Hurlburt Field. I knew how to teach subject matter experts to build credibility with the media, plan for crisis communication, and effectively respond to public concerns. In press conferences and high-profile interviews with outlets like CNN and the *New York Times*, I'd seen the training pay off. As this mortar drill hinted, though, media training in Afghanistan would be more complicated. I'd initially requested to host the class at the governor's compound, but the governor himself vetoed the idea, afraid that the event would make him a target. I tried not to dwell on his insinuations.

I knew my uniform painted me a target in Afghanistan. FOB Gardez was a target. Our MRAPs were slow-moving, fourteen-ton targets. Preparedness, alertness, smart decision making, competence, the fact that I spent most of my time on base; all these things could help me get back home alive. Ultimately though, as in all wars, survival was a crapshoot.

My mom dealt with the unknowns of her deployment by writing letters to the family saying goodbye. "Just in case" letters are common practice among deploying servicemembers. You see the tradition in movies: dying soldiers shakily hand over crinkled, blood-soaked pages to the medic or chaplain or whoever is nearest in the final moments. They utter something like, "Tell my wife I love her," and I always cry.

When Mom deployed, Dad tucked her letters away, out of sight but never out of mind, until she got back and neither of them wanted to think about what could have happened. To this day, the letters remain unopened. Before I deployed and while in Afghanistan, I thought about what could happen to me frequently, but I never wrote a letter. I meant to. I started one during training in Indiana. It seemed like something that should be handwritten, but the only paper I had came from my reporter's notebook, which was warped and dirty from being scrunched in my cargo pocket, or the backs of PowerPoint slide printouts. Once, I began typing on my laptop:

Dear Mom and Dad,

If you're reading this, it means I'm dead.

I didn't know how to continue. *I'm sorry? Please don't cry? Remember me as a badass?* And what was I supposed to do when I finished, email my parents under the subject header "Don't read this unless I die"? My reservations were excuses, of course. Most "just in case" pre-deployment practices didn't bother me. I made a will: my parents would get back their hand-me-down furniture, Dad would continue to tolerate my cats, Shavonne and Matt could pick through my extensive DVD collection. After I got my tattoo, I updated my military records to reflect the cross on my left forearm. In the event I was missing in action, injured, or killed, the symbol could help identify me. Holding up my branded arm for the records manager to examine, I felt proud, as if having a unique marking made me more legitimate. The smiling-in-front-of-the-flag stock photo I took at Camp Atterbury I viewed as a formality, like armfuls of immunizations or reams of paperwork, merely another box to check on the way to war.

The concept of a farewell letter was the one thing that struck me as too morbid. I knew I could die. If I ever forgot, there was always another casualty announcement in my inbox, the seventeen fallen comrades' portraits on the conference room wall, or the Paktia governor to remind me. I never considered how much heavier that knowledge would be with a spouse and young children at home. The thought might have paralyzed me. I just made sure to tell my family I loved them every time I called. I told them I was well and happy-as-could-be-expected and honored to work with the PRT. I let the words hang in the air and the unspoken flutter in between. Even when they didn't ring true, I stuck to my lines like public affairs talking points:

I'm tired but good.

I miss you, but I'm really glad I'm here. We're doing so many amazing things.

It's so cool to be changing people's lives.

In times of evasion, I was glad I hadn't written a letter. I wanted my parents to trust in the rose-tinted version of my war. I needed them to. But it's one thing to speak dishonestly. It's another to put it in ink.

The mortar drill proved to be just a minor, dusty inconvenience. I secured a media training location at FOB Lightning, not one I'd visited but a theater that the soldier in charge of facilities assured me would be sufficient for our needs. At last, after a month of preparation, we were almost ready.

When the media training planning first began, the brigade PA Tweedle introduced me to a Marine captain in Kabul who ran something I'd never heard of called a GMIC, a Government Media Information Center. The GMIC provided the type of training we needed and also hoped someday to establish a regional center in Paktia. I delighted at the connection and gave the Tweedle a rare mark in the "Pro" column on the scoresheet I kept in my head. The Marine captain brought resources and expertise, swooping in like a knight in shining body armor. While she prepared curriculum and kept the Tweedle appeased, I threw myself into logistics. I coordinated flights and lodging for the captain and her team, worked with Chris to secure interpreters and convoy transportation to and from FOB Lightning, and arranged stipends and catered lunches for the attendees. The director of information and culture for once seemed pleased with my partnership. Government officials and Afghan National Army leaders from thirteen Paktia districts committed to attend. Those same entities who finger-pointed at each other during the election meetings would come together to create a unified voice for Paktia.

In my eager brain, desperately clinging to idealism, media training evolved into a test. Here was my chance to prove myself worthy and capable of the big, important job in the big, complicated war. So, too, would the event be a test for this war, this place, to prove their worth to me. Finally, I thought, I would get my *Three Cups of Tea* moment.

Then, just a few days before the scheduled training, the Marine captain sent an email. Paktia's media training went against the GMIC's policy, she said. The center usually only hosted training in Kabul until after a regional center had been established. "Now, with this said," the captain wrote, "I have talked them into doing this training in Paktia Province."

I reread the email. Then I read it again. My gut reacted with a mix of gratitude and incompetence. *I went about this the wrong way, but the captain pulled strings to make it possible; how thoughtful!* But then . . . *wait a minute* . . . The PA Tweedle had referred me to the GMIC. Why was I being shamed for a working relationship dictated by someone else? Or for breaking protocol that hadn't been communicated? The captain copied the Tweedle on her message. Based on previous interactions, I assumed he wouldn't read beyond gratitude and incompetence. I scoffed audibly, shoved my chair back from my desk—ignoring Nick's cursing when it rammed into his back—and slammed my laptop shut. I needed to run.

Like all electronics, the FOB Gardez gym treadmills were embroiled in a fight against the powder-fine Afghan dust. Only one treadmill was winning, and only by a slim margin. Its belt hung loose on the gears. The smooth rhythm—*vrump vrump vrump vrump*—was interrupted every few footfalls with a short, sticky *veep!* that pitched me into stutter-steps. Still, it beat running outside. Chris and I gave up our morning graveyard routine after a handful of ankle-rolling, rotor-wash-sputtering jogs. Between my sore knee and the temperamental gym equipment, I'd mostly been settling for the stationary bike. Today, I laced up my sneakers, set my iPod for the loudest, angriest playlist I had, and jumped on the treadmill, ready to pound out my frustrations. *Vrump vrump vrump vrump veep! Vrump vrump vrump vrump veep!*

Why the condescension in the captain's email? Why were these issues just being voiced now, after nearly a month of working together? It was as if I'd landed at the center of an internal information operations campaign between the Marine captain and the PA Tweedle. I'd been pointed in a direction and bulldozed my way through, only to learn I'd tread on forbidden ground. Suddenly, I felt a wave of guilt. I was employing equally warped logic with the Afghans and the international public, I realized. They were my targets, literally the subjects of what we called "non-lethal targeting." In everything I did and said, I sought to influence their beliefs and actions.

I never completely bought into the idea that public affairs dealt strictly in facts. Every sound bite, base tour, presentation, and newspaper article, no matter how benign, aimed to elicit a particular response. The military wanted to educate people about our cutting-edge technology, best-in-the-world training, and well-rounded airmen who could root out Taliban sleeper cells one day and rescue kittens from trees the next. We wanted to build understanding and support for our mission and assure the public that we were good stewards of their taxpayer dollars—and, of course, their uniformed sons and daughters. Like any public relations or marketing department, everything we touched was peppered with influence. It was a seasoning, not a main ingredient. I was comfortable with that subtle level of persuasion. I didn't even think about it; it was simply part of my job. Moreover, I'd always believed that our technology, training, and airmen were as amazing as my messages claimed.

Now, though, the claims were starting to feel exaggerated, the efforts sleazy. As the treadmill sputtered under my feet, I thought back to my conversation with Eli over *The Times* of London article and to the omitted lines from the detainee's interview transcript. Jacob, Nick and I had recently hosted a reporter at FOB Gardez who had previously written an article that, though not untrue, brigade considered to be overwhelmingly negative about American military activity in a nearby province. We had been ordered to babysit the reporter, to take shifts to watch her twenty-four hours a day, including sitting outside her barracks while she slept. We didn't go quite that far, but we did choose her missions selectively to expose her to only the most favorable, low-risk information. My overly optimistic story-boards gave the same positive spin I promoted in my media lectures to the PRT staff, and those lectures were not unlike the training I was preparing for Afghan officials.

Whereas the captain's tone may not have been intended how it was received, my actions were deliberate. Maybe I really was the Minister of Propaganda, as the PRT communications sergeant liked to joke. Maybe this was some kind of IO karma.

The treadmill's squeaky circuit seemed to mock me: *Vrump vrump vrump vrump veep! Vrump vrump vrump vrump veep! This will not go well! You suck at I-O!*

I shook the doubts out of my head. *No.* This training was good and necessary. My work here was good and necessary. We just needed to sort out the miscommunications. In her email, the captain emphasized, again, that the training must be an Afghan-led process. This was a "very sensitive topic," she said, with the professional reputation of the GMIC at stake. The director of information and culture spoke with the cultural advisors nearly every day. The list of attendees had come almost entirely from them. At the director's request, I arranged a condensed two-day course as opposed to the GMICs standard three, since officials worried about the time away from work.

I'd been coordinating with the director of information and culture be-cause that's who the PRT always worked with for communication matters. Now, the captain asked that all correspondence go through the governor's spokesperson. In several meetings with the director, the governor's media team, and the governor himself, I had never met or even heard about a spokesperson. He wasn't listed in Major Rhodes' PowerPoint bible. How was I just learning about him now, and from a Marine captain based in Kabul?

I'd also, almost by accident, discovered another new resource. While recruiting the local Afghan National Army (ANA) commander for the training, I stumbled upon a public affairs mentoring team based at FOB Lightning with the ANA. Another U.S. military group worked right down the street advising Afghan communication officials. We shared a bat-tlespace and a mission, but somehow we'd never spoken. It was too late for the mentoring team to be involved with the media training planning, but they promised to have someone at the event. At least that was something, I thought.

Vrump vrump vrump vrump veep!

Four days later, on October 8, I celebrated my twenty-sixth birthday with the ambassador's visit to Gardez.

If we'd thought the elections were an all-consuming vortex of time and energy, hosting the U.S. ambassador to Afghanistan took preparatory mania up another notch. As a PA officer, I frequently dabbled in the dog and pony show military genre, the drop everything/roll out the red carpet/put on your happy face act to impress a distinguished visitor whose the-oretical purpose was to observe average everyday operations. I despised these events.

Everyone at FOB Gardez knew of the ambassador, a retired Army general who helped shape current policies in Afghanistan. We heard him mentioned in news broadcasts and saw him smiling from chain of com-mand portraits. His name appeared often in my email bulletins. Yet he was to us like President Obama or Santa Claus, a vague figure of mythical proportions whose job affected us but was so vast and so far removed that we regarded him only with detached interest. In October 2009, we learned more than we cared to know about the ambassador.

The ambassador brought specific demands. On his October 8 visit, he wanted to walk around Gardez City with no body armor as a way of showing the locals he felt safe. Ensuring his safety, however, required a robust security detail and a fleet of military vehicles—none of which could be visible. In a war zone, even in the quiet moments when you almost let yourself believe you're free from danger, you acknowledge that security is mostly an illusion. For the ambassador, we flipped the notion on its head: our security mission was to *create* an illusion. All other activities, including the impending media training, took a back seat. We cleared our schedules. We recalled vehicles and personnel from combat outposts, which meant, with a day's worth of travel to and from FOB Gardez, a several-day delay in local operations. Base leadership and security personnel formed a think tank to coordinate the ambassador's schedule and invisible protection.

For our part, the PRT would take him to our prize construction project, an education center in Gardez. The ambassador would witness the epitome, perhaps the only provincial example, of premier Afghan engineering. We wouldn't show him the projects with poorly-built walls he could kick over. He wouldn't see the vacant site where a school had been contracted but had been built elsewhere on a bribe. He certainly wouldn't tour the PRT-funded hydroelectrical dam just north of Gardez, which was nearly complete and signed off for by U.S. engineers but was neither operational nor safe. These things, like the ambassador's security, would remain in the shadows.

At the time, I didn't question our strategy—to turn our information weapons on our own government leadership. Though I hated the pageantry, I dove into preparing for the ambassador's visit with the same fervor as any job requirement. Instead of finalizing media training logistics or continuing election runoff planning, I designed place cards for the conference room table and compiled provincial history for a briefing booklet. An entire day went to Googling and printing chain of command portraits and taking unofficial official government photos of the PRT Department of State and U.S. Agency for International Development representatives (they stood against a white office wall while the tall PRT intelligence officer stood to the side, dangling an American flag that kept twitching as he giggled). I dug 8x10 frames out of a storage connex and hung the framed photos on the PRT conference room wall. Jacob scribbled "Operation Potempkin Village" on the whiteboard above Nick's desk, next to a quote from their commander along the lines of, "The ambassador would not be pleased to hear that resources were being diverted for his visit."

October 8 came, but the ambassador never did. Called away for something more important, he sent his second-in-command and his wife.

Three days later, around five thirty the evening before media training began, I got a call from FOB Lightning. The Marine captain's smooth, cheery voice clashed with the sharp tone of the woman who introduced herself as the Air Force sergeant in charge of the PA mentoring team.

"Hello ladies!" I prattled. "It's so great to hear your voices! Is everything good to go at Lightning?"

Everything was not good to go. The theater I'd reserved was small and dingy, they said, not ideal for the training. I tried to stay upbeat as we debated whether to move forward. On one hand, we had invested countless man-hours and resources. The attendees had rearranged their schedules. Last-minute changes in Afghanistan weren't like last-minute changes in the U.S. At home, a series of phone calls, an email, a notification to the facility manager warranted annoyance but got the job done. The event would be rescheduled, and people would attend. Disgruntled feelings would fade. In Afghanistan, alert systems were unreliable and potential ripples into perceptions even more so. Canceling in the eleventh hour could be more damaging to local U.S.-Afghan relations than proceeding with problematic conditions. The attendees were government officials on whom the PRT and PA mentoring team relied for our missions. We had worked over the last several months to cultivate relationships, and teams before us had worked for collective years. We decided to continue as planned.

14

F*#K

THE MORNING OF MEDIA TRAINING, a convoy dropped me off at FOB Lightning along with an interpreter. I found the Marine captain waiting outside the reserved theater, almost unrecognizable as a military officer in a flowing brown skirt, white blouse, and peach headscarf. The captain had advised me to wear civilian clothes too, to "reduce the perception of receiving solely military PA training." Since the only civilian clothes I had were Eeyore pajamas, I opted for my uniform.

"Good morning, ma'am!" I said. "Are we good to go?"

"Dr. Fahim is working to set up the presentation," the captain said, referencing a tall, well-dressed Afghan man huddled inside by a stack of electronic equipment. "Hopefully it will work."

I peered around her into the dimly lit theater, a room not much larger than the IO office with three rows of folding chairs across the back. "Well," I said, "it's cozy!" I'd spent the last few days grasping for silver linings and could feel my optimism wearing thin.

The training was scheduled for eight o'clock. As my watch ticked toward eight fifteen, I tried not to worry; the Afghan government didn't pride itself on punctuality. By eight thirty I was biting my nails. I called Aamir, who was standing by to help with coordination.

"They are on their way, ma'am," he said.

I left the captain to prepare the facility and took the interpreter to meet attendees at the arrival gate. The short walk was long enough to build up a nervous sweat, which intensified when I saw no government officials waiting at the U.S.-manned base entrance, just a petite, serious-looking Air Force sergeant with brown hair pulled into a tight bun and a fixed grimace beneath her glasses. I recognized the name on her uniform as that of the PA mentoring team sergeant.

"Good morning!" I called. "It's great to finally meet you!"

The sergeant matched a skeptical greeting with a skeptical salute. She seemed to regard me as one teetering on the brink of failure. I couldn't blame her; cynicism made a logical default setting in Afghanistan and likely hadn't been appeased in our limited interactions. It wasn't appeased at 8:40, when Aamir called and said the government officials were having trouble getting on base. I had sent an access list to the FOB Lightning operations center and been assured attendees would be pre-approved, but apparently bad blood between the Afghan National Army and the government had thrown a monkey wrench in our plan—the same bad blood I hoped this training might help dilute.

The word "fuck" hung on my lips. It had been creeping into my dialogue the last few months, proving its versatility to capture myriad deployment-related feelings. I gritted my teeth to keep frustration from registering on my face. The PA sergeant volunteered to go to the base's outer gate to vouch for the attendees. I barely had time to bite my nails before she returned, alone.

"They're saying the officials were already let on base," she said.

I called Aamir. "No ma'am," he said. "They are still waiting outside."

Fuck fuck fuck fuck fuck, I thought. "OK," I said into the phone. "We're going out to meet them now." I hung up, and Aamir immediately called back.

"I'm sorry to confuse, ma'am. The officials are on base now."

"Oh, OK, great!" I said. "Thank you!"

The U.S. and Afghan gates were separated by a long, zigzagging HESCO barrier corridor. The sergeant, interpreter, and I wound our way past the American checkpoint. Technically, we were off base. Technically, we should have been wearing body armor. The region seemed to grow more dangerous by the day. This would become the deadliest month of the deadliest year so far in Operation Enduring Freedom. The day of the Ambassador's would-be visit, a suicide bomber in Kabul killed seventeen and wounded more than seventy people. Over the last week, the death toll from multiple attacks in Pakistan had topped one hundred. The mortar drill and brief stint in the bunker a few days prior shot across my mind as we snaked through the corridor. I pushed the thoughts away. This was a time for poise, not paranoia. A solitary figure walked in our direction, eventually revealing himself to be the director of information and culture. Visibly upset, he spoke to the interpreter in hurried, harsh phrases. His eye lasers burned hotter than usual.

"He said only he is on base," the interpreter said. "Eleven more people wait outside."

Fuck fuck fuck fuck fuck, I thought. We started jogging toward the outer gate, where I saw a gaggle of men gesturing wildly back and forth with a guard. I ran my hand across my sweaty face.

"As-Salaam-Alaikum!" I greeted the men as we approached. "I'm so, so sorry for the problem." I turned to the guard. "These men need to come on base now. They are all government officials attending training. All their names were cleared." I attempted to match the director's assertive tone, but my voice wobbled with building emotion. I hated how small and unassured I felt. I straightened my shoulders and fixed the guard with what I hoped was a commanding glare.

The interpreter translated. The guard considered me. He glanced from me to the men, to a fellow guard behind him. He hollered at the other guard, who hollered back. Finally, he nodded and said something to the interpreter.

"He says they can come in now," the interpreter said.

"They need to get on base tomorrow too," I said. "If we bring them a list of names, can they guarantee everyone will be able to get on base again tomorrow?" The interpreter translated, and the guard nodded again. I wasn't sure I believed him, but sometimes trust isn't a choice.

"OK," I said, a bit too cheerily. "Let's go!"

The officials followed us through the HESCO maze, talking among themselves. Though I couldn't understand the words, I could hear their agitation. At the inner gate, the American guards insisted on agitating the men further, giving each a body search and confiscating all cell phones. On FOB Gardez, government members were almost always exempt from these practices. Perhaps it was the expectation of a less-than-cordial reception that had led several officials to boycott the media training for not taking place at the governor's compound, a fact Aamir had alerted me to earlier this morning. I wondered if now would be an appropriate time to teach my Afghan partners about the versatility of the word "fuck."

We were an hour late by the time we arrived at the theater. The door was propped open, and a projection flashed on the screen. I heaved a sigh of relief. Then I saw the captain. Her headscarf hung disheveled around her sweaty face. She shook her head as she approached.

"This isn't going to work," she said. "We can't get our laptop hooked up. And I really don't think the room's big enough. They won't be comfortable." She gestured to the group behind me. The officials' chatter had stopped. I felt their eyes boring into my back.

Fuck fuck fuck fuck fuck, I thought. "OK," I said. "So what do we do? Should we cancel the training? Maybe we can find something else for tomorrow and do a condensed version?"

"I think it's best to cancel," the captain said. "I'd rather cancel than scrounge things together and not have it go smoothly. I don't want it to look unprofessional. If we're going to do this, we need to do it right or it's a waste of everyone's time." I didn't want to concede that this morning alone had looked unprofessional and been a waste of everyone's time. The captain continued: "I'll have Dr. Fahim explain to these guys and see what they think." She nodded toward the government officials. I could sense that they could sense that the news was bad.

I turned around and shaped my mouth into something resembling a smile. No one smiled back. As the GMIC trainer addressed the crowd, I stepped inside to give them space and to get away from the glowers. The theater smelled like stagnant rainwater. Before my eyes could adjust to the dim lighting, the PA sergeant charged up behind me.

"Lieutenant Johnson," she sneered. I turned around to a face even angrier than her voice. "This event is a disaster. You have made all of us look bad. We work with some of these people on a daily basis, and because of your poor planning, all of our relationships are damaged. You've undone a lot of hard work today."

I was stunned. I didn't disagree with the sergeant. In fact, I shared her concerns, but having them flung in my face with such bitterness from someone I'd only just met caught me off guard. As an enlisted airman too, the sergeant should have shown respect for my officer's rank, if not for me myself. My instinct was to defend myself, to tell her how many hours and how much hope I'd poured into this event. Mostly, I wanted to cry.

"I'm so, so sorry," I stuttered. "This definitely didn't go how we were hoping. We've been planning for a month, and I thought everything was squared away, but obviously not." I flailed my arms, as if grand hand gestures could express my remorse. "I accept complete responsibility, and we're going to do everything we can to smooth things over." The sergeant didn't look convinced. I wasn't either. "I'm really sorry we had to meet under these circumstances," I said. "I hope we can work together again in the future."

"I just hope you haven't done too much damage today," the sergeant said, storming away.

I turned to the muddy wall of the theater and started crying, hating myself for it. Tears were evidence of my weakness, as good as admitting I'd failed. This was all too complicated, too much for me to handle. I'd made a terrible mistake. This wasn't *Three Cups of Tea;* it was a different book, in an entirely different genre. *What the* fuck *am I doing here?*

The Marine captain walked up behind me. I took a shuttering breath. "It's going to be OK, Lauren," she said. It was the only time in our interactions she'd used my first name, and somehow it comforted me enough to stop the tears. "Dr. Fahim explained everything to the guys and walked them back to the gate. They took it OK. They'll get over it." She shrugged. I envied her nonchalance.

The captain decided she should go one step further and make a personal appearance at the governor's compound to apologize. "It's just a good gesture," she said. I didn't even think about protesting her offer to clean up my mess. Clearly, I was in no state to talk to anyone. And I was suddenly very, very tired. Aamir agreed to drive the captain to the governor's compound. Sitting in the back of his blue sedan, scarf pulled tight around her face, the captain looked at ease, more comfortable than I thought I could ever feel on my deployment, and I envied her for that too.

Pacing outside the American gate as I waited for the PRT convoy to pick me up, I prepared for shouting matches over my incompetence. I could deal with shouting; I'd been yelled at before. What made the tears well again under my sunglasses was concern that the PA mentoring team sergeant was right. I imagined relationships destroyed. Months and years wasted. Whatever confidence I'd inspired with Colonel McGuire, the brigade commander, the Tweedles, gone. The GMIC and the mentoring team would never work with the PRT again. I took a deep breath and repeated my old public affairs mantra: *My job isn't life or death.* "Right, Janie?" I said out loud, rubbing my hand along my pistol's firm, steadying grip.

The shouting match never materialized. At the next evening's Brigade Update Brief, rather than angry, the brigade commander seemed confused. "So, this was media training, but for the Afghans?" The commander's voice crackled across the speakerphone in the operations center conference room.

"Yes, sir," I said. "To help them communicate in a unified manner and better respond in a crisis." I stood alone in the center of the room talking into the speakerphone, hating the spotlight.

"And how long was this supposed to be?" The commander asked. "Just the one day?"

"It was planned for two, sir. Originally three, but the Kabul training team adjusted their curriculum at the director of information and culture's request."

"Kabul?" the commander said. "I didn't realize people had flown in from Kabul. This was a big deal."

"Yes, sir, it was." I apologized and mumbled something about establishing a working relationship with the GMIC to continue the initiative in the future.

The commander admonished the room to do a better job supporting the others and coordinating on missions, and then he dismissed me with a brusque, "Lesson learned. These things happen."

Later that evening Chris and I climbed up to the qalat tower. The sun had set, and stars started to materialize in the darkening sky. With no light pollution for miles, the Afghanistan night sky seemed to hold entire galaxies. I liked to lean back over the tower's railing and get lost in them, a mesmerizing kaleidoscope of pinpricked light. Tonight, I propped my elbows on the railing and dropped my head into my hands.

"Well, that was a shitty event," I grumbled.

"I'm sorry," Chris said. "I should have supported the mission more."

"It's not your fault," I said. "It's all just a big. Fucking. Mess." The tears came again, and I let Chris wrap me in a long hug. Colonel McGuire and the FOB Gardez Army unit commander had both apologized after the meeting too, and while I appreciated the sentiment, apologies felt wrong. Part of me wanted a shouting match. The muted response didn't match the weight the media training carried in my mind. Hadn't I just failed this big, important test? Even so, I couldn't identify where exactly I'd messed up. Had I trusted myself with too large a task? Should I have coordinated more with my supervisors? Asked for help? Somehow conducted a second site survey at FOB Lightning in the thick of the ambassador's visit? How could I troubleshoot issues I didn't know existed?

At the same time, how had the brigade commander been so unaware? The directive had come from brigade in the first place, and the plans had been in my reports for a month, all the BUBs and CUBs and SITREPS and daily/bi-daily/weekly updates. As an official brigade tasking, the training had been monitored on Chris's PRT operations tracker too. I'd worked with the Department of State representative and with Army contacts at each of Paktia's five combat outposts to finalize the attendee list. I'd coordinated with pay agents, air transport, security, intelligence, convoy operations, and the mission commanders for the days I planned to hitch rides back and forth to FOB Lightning. The PA Tweedle had been included on all email communications, and I had called him as soon as I got back to FOB Gardez after canceling the training. Wasn't he responsible for keeping his boss informed? Between the lack of coordination at brigade and the mysterious GMIC that had pounced on the tasking even though it went against protocol, the crossed lines of communication were worse than the tangle of network wires winding through my office. And what about the PA mentoring team at FOB Lightning—how had we not known to pool our resources earlier? I addressed these issues in the Lessons Learned section of my media training After Action Report. The formal, emotionless language did little to communicate, or alleviate, my frustration:

1. GMIC operating procedures should be made clear upfront and followed by requesting units in order to establish effective working relationships and put minimal strain on both organizations.

2. A disconnect between IO and PAO elements at FOB Gardez and FOB Lightning was identified. Team IO reps and the PA mentoring team do not currently coordinate operations even though they work with many of the same Afghan partners in the same battlespace.

3. A disconnect among government media personnel was also identified. Team Paktia's government POC is the director of information and culture, while the PAMT works mainly with the Governor's Spokesperson.

The media training directive itself represented another persistent problem: duplication of effort. The Department of State was disseminating a similar media training request down to the PRTs, and the U.S. Agency for International Development had recently completed an iteration of journalism training in Paktia, both programs I didn't learn about until after my event. When we finally all got on the same page, I joked, "So many options, so little time!"

Our USAID representative was more frank. "We should probably have sat down to figure out how these programs could have been better integrated from the start," he said.

He was right. Still, surely at some level above us the money-allocators and goal-setters were talking to each other? These national initiatives must have been conducted previously, or at least been discussed and brainstormed and contingency-planned?

We were all familiar with the saying that Afghanistan wasn't a nine-year war; it was nine one-year wars. We fought fresh campaigns every year with the rotation of units and the influx of new leadership bringing different philosophies and priorities. *Spend, spend, spend!* Then *Stop spending! Account for all money!* Our team was preparing to conduct a massive province-wide survey to measure the future impact of our work and the actions of the Afghan government. Questions like: *Is your way of life better than it was at the start of Karzai's government? Who do you think is most responsible for improvements in your village? Who do you think is most responsible for the decline in services in your village? Do you consider yourself to be a supporter of the Government of the Independent Republic of Afghanistan?* The focus was *future* measurements because no baseline existed. Besides daily interactions, which were colored by politics and fear, we had no way of knowing if perceptions had changed since the beginning of our deployment—or since the beginning of Operation Enduring Freedom. We tallied Measures of Performance—numbers of schools built, millions of dollars spent, frequency of insurgent attacks—but not Measures of Effectiveness. For nine years, we had been pouring in time, money, and American lives lives with little measurable evidence of what, if any, lasting impact resulted.

Beyond nine one-year wars, I realized, efforts in each of Afghanistan's twenty-six individual provinces seemed more or less autonomous. Maybe we were actually fighting iterations of twenty-six separate one-year wars. And at province-level, maybe individual units, like our PRT and the PA mentoring team, were fighting separate wars too; and even within units, segments like the Department of State and USAID were entrenched in related but independent efforts. We'd witnessed in development projects how military, government agencies, and non-governmental organizations were essentially doing the same thing in isolated bubbles, mitigating everyone's effectiveness, not to mention multiplying expenses. How many different wars were we actually fighting?

And when it came to my war, the war of information, how could we expect to educate the Afghans on effective communication—let alone out-IO the Taliban—when we ourselves did it so poorly?

"Despite the frustration and missed training opportunity, the gathering, as well as a separate meeting coordinated between the GMIC trainers, the director of information and culture and the governor's spokesperson, served as an orientation to GMIC's capabilities, introduced key players, and helped pave the way for future actions."

—my media training After Action Report

INTERMISSION:
Mid-Tour Leave

REDUNDANCY *noun*

Definition: Common

1. The state or quality of being redundant; superfluity; unnecessariness. Also: a case or instance of this.

2. Excess; abundance.

3. The condition of having more elements or components than the minimum necessary in order to store or convey a given amount of information.

4. The deliberate duplication of parts in a system so that its function is not impaired in the event of a malfunction or failure. Also: an instance of this; a deliberately duplicated part.

5. The condition of being surplus to an organization's staffing requirements.

Definition: in Military/War

1. Contingency planning; preparation for accident, natural disaster, or other incident of negative effect. Hopefully unneeded.

2. The use of back-up systems (and back-up back-up systems); additional weaponry.

3. Organizational inclination for repetition (in reporting, regulating, etc.), esp. of a tedious or unproductive nature.

4. October to December 2009.

15

The Doldrums

AFGHANISTAN IS AN ACCORDION MEMORY. The beginning moved so quickly, yet so layered, in its pacing. Everything was fresh and new and chaotic. Each witnessing felt profound because it was the first, experienced with the intensity only culture shock and danger can elicit. Then came the jolting blow when expectations and reality first clashed.

At the time, through the frantic fog of my brain, I couldn't have expected recollection in those first few hectic weeks. Yet when I pieced together a timeline from emails and storyboards, there they were, front-loaded flashes of clarity: the faces and quirks of my new colleagues, firehose turnover from Major Rhodes, stargazing with Chris, my initial missions, elections, the detainee, the ambassador who never came, and the media training that never happened. My mind must have parceled the events out, given them order. So much so condensed defies the logic of time. Moments get caught in the accordion's folds.

After Election Day, the PRT kept busy making up for lost time and squeezing in activities before winter weather ended the construction season. That nagging itch to do something propelled me to escape from the FOB while escape remained possible. Though paranoia still clung to my nerves, getting off the tiny base was always refreshing in a backward way I didn't understand, as if in moving toward danger I could justify my paranoia and also prove that I was doing the exceptional, meaningful things I'd signed up to do. I volunteered for any mission that could warrant my presence. The survey of progress on a retaining wall to keep farmlands from spring flooding? I could easily turn that into a PowerPoint storyboard. The launch of a nutritional supplement program to combat childhood malnutrition? A storyboard, plus photos of cute kids!

Of course, storyboards could never capture the whole scene. Even the news article I wrote didn't do justice to the palpable hope of the civics training class in Gardez. A storyboard couldn't express my relief at the nutritional supplement launch, where, in a humble village medical clinic, political pretenses and duplicity for once seemed absent. I photographed a handsome male nurse with a tidy beard as he pulled a wooden spoon through the thick "Strong Foods" mixture as PRT medics instructed. His face alternated between deep focus and bubbling delight, like a child baking cookies for the first time. The nurse's joy came through in the photo, but the image didn't communicate the genuine buzz of excitement that filled the room, and filled me.

One of my favorite pictures from the deployment never made it onto a storyboard. Taken at the Strong Foods launch, the photo holds no evidence of American capacity-building or Afghans "in the lead," just the shy smile of a shaggy-haired girl with a smudge of flour on her nose. The photo doesn't reveal my inexplicable attachment to the girl or my overwhelming desire to take her with me, to introduce her to my soon-to-be-born twin nieces, to give her a safe home. The image can't show how, in a way I hadn't been able to with other Afghan children, I let myself believe that this child already had a safe home. Isolation and insignificance would protect the village from violence. The girl's school wouldn't be bombed. She wouldn't be doused with acid on her way to class. She wouldn't be paraded around in makeup and bedazzled dresses at puberty, a last feeding frenzy for suitors before she went under a burqa. Her father wouldn't marry her off as a teenager to a much older man, subject to house arrest and domestic violence. As our MRAPs pulled away and the children ran after us through swirls of dust, I let myself believe this girl would be happy.

While photos and storyboards couldn't capture all the positives, I simply didn't document the moments that seemed to squeeze out hope.

In the most unstable district of the province, we were finally seeing improvements, thanks in large part to an influential elder. Then the elder went missing. He was found a few days later along a roadside, in pieces.

Around the same time, Colonel McGuire fired an Afghan employee, our engineering liaison, for selling confidential contracting information.

Then he fired two more local workers for stockpiling cell phones, batteries, and wiring—three main ingredients for homemade bombs—in an old, condemned FOB latrine.

We uncovered a corruption scheme that wound through the province and up to several high-level government officials, including the chief of police, General Asim—the man who'd piled kebabs and rice on my plate at the governor's guest house—and the governor himself. The following July, the WikiLeaks release of the Afghan War Logs would reveal the scheme in vivid details: bribes, coercion, money laundering involving U.S. funds. Some of the leaked cables would mention PRT members. But for us in the winter of 2009, the corrupt officials were untouchable. We couldn't have them arrested or expelled, and we couldn't confront them. We could send complaints up the chain of command where they would eventually, theoretically, land with someone who had authority to act. Meanwhile, we continued business as usual so as not to upset working relationships. My IO colleagues and I even enlisted the governor to read an anti-corruption public service announcement on the radio advising Afghans to report any instances of fraud, waste, or abuse to government authorities.

The governor had come to represent all Afghan men for me. Certainly, my perception was skewed by the echelon of most men I encountered, those in leadership positions, and by the nature of our interactions, with money and power at stake. Still, in my generalizing I could have pictured the aimable government liaison, Dr. Raj, who, true to his word, delivered regular platters of delicious Afghan micro-grapes to me on the FOB. Aamir and Rahim could have been my model, two of the kindest and most dedicated people I'd ever met. After the arrests of the three Afghan PRT employees, I couldn't help but regard local colleagues more skeptically. Even so, I could have pictured the gentle nurse who helped launch the Strong Foods program, or any number of kindly men who waved as our vehicles drove through the villages, or even the old, tired detainee with blank eyes. Instead, my mind conjured a terrible stereotype in the form of the governor. I envisioned him reclining in a chaise lounge in his lavish guest house while servants fanned him with olive branches and fed him hunks of bloody goat meat. Chained by the governor's side

153

I imagined his wife, like Princess Leia as Jabba the Hut's prisoner in *Star Wars*, only she would be wearing a burqa, not a gold bikini.

My storyboard on the groundbreaking for an expansion of the Gardez Women's Development Center didn't include a quote from Sergeant Rivera seething over the director of women's affairs. The director was Paktia's only female line director, and as such the most influential woman in the province. "She's so two-faced!" Sergeant Rivera snarled over dinner the night before the mission. "I hate that she's the one with that kind of power." Usually a beacon of positivity, Sergeant Rivera's anger surprised me. She stabbed her frustrations into her enchilada with a plastic fork. "She could do so much for the women here, but she's only out for her own gain."

At the groundbreaking event, I noticed the director didn't wear status like her male counterparts. Her small frame hunched over a walking stick. Thick glasses magnified the wear in her eyes, the crinkles at the corners that flowed into the deep cervices of her face. If Sergeant Rivera was right about the director, I thought, at least greed had aged her.

I didn't write these observations in my notebook. I took notes as the director led us on a tour of the small existing Women's Development Center, explaining that they planned to use the new classrooms for training sessions in subjects like sewing and typing, and for women's rights and legal advisement. A poster on one wall caught my attention. It was large and bright with cartoon-like figures and a message that I hoped was lost in translation; it seemed to say, "Don't set your wife on fire."

Moving into October, my accordion memory stretches, and slows. Days felt longer yet less filled, or equally filled but less profound. Somewhere between paranoia and complacency, I had established a routine: Eat, sleep, work, repeat. Intermittent gym time. Church and malaria pill on Sundays. Needing Chris. Increasingly, fighting with Chris. As stress weighed heavier on each of us, I responded with gushing emotion. Chris countered with insecurity, offended when I gave time to anyone or anything else. I wanted him to be exactly how he'd been at the start of the deployment, when I'd been inspired to email my mom: "He is so understanding and level-headed—he's my rock out here." It was an unfair expectation; I myself wasn't the same as I'd been a few months prior. I admitted as much in an email to my college roommate. "It's both easy and hard to really get to know people," I wrote. "I feel like I know people here very well just by virtue of living/eating/working/sleeping with them and being through all these ups and downs together. But at the same time, I know I'M not 100 percent myself here, so I'm sure other people aren't either. I've come to the conclusion that situations like this bring out the best and worst in people."

Chris remained my rock, ever tolerant of my emotional pendulum, and I served a similar purpose for him. But our relationship had absorbed elements from our occasional Ping-Pong tournaments. We volleyed our doubts and frustrations off each other, and they bounced back and forth, back and forth, gaining speed and power. We were living a new relationship at warp speed, and in a war zone. Heightened emotions matched the extreme backdrop of our courtship. Flashes of anger and jealousy made me wonder what lurked beneath Chris's levelheaded exterior. My own undercurrent boiled with neediness and resentment.

Despite Chris's aid, my breakdown after the failed media training hit my resolve like the first crack in the qalat tower nearest my room. After that initial fissure, the cracks quickly spiderwebbed. Soon they would threaten collapse. Like my mom, I did my best not to cry in public. I let tears mingle with the sweat and condensation in the gym tent, or trickle down the mildew-stained shower curtain, or leave wet splotches on my Walmart pillowcase. Some mornings I woke before my alarm and lay still for a long time, watching the scarf-filtered colors shift across the ceiling, scanning the photos and cards taped to the blue plywood wall, and I tried to remember what home felt like.

In November, we passed the bittersweet milestone of Halfway, excited to have made it this far but depressed that we still had an equal distance to go, feeling blessed to not have suffered any serious casualties but worried that we were biding our time. Here, in the doldrums of the deployment, my memories blend together. I look back at mission storyboards and see a collage of copy and paste: different locations, varying government officials and tribal leaders, but the same concerns voiced, the same promises made, the same public affairs-friendly spin in the analysis:

"The leaders in attendance were proactive, intuitive, and relatively successful in mediating local issues—they took an important step in moving from talk to action and further extending the reach of the government to a historically disenfranchised region . . ."

"[This mission] represented an important step in connecting the people to their government in an area which has traditionally suffered from a lack of government presence . . ."

"The PRT and international partners will continue to work with the Government of the Independent Republic of Afghanistan to bring peace and stability to the province . . ."

The lines sounded like our radio PSAs: interchangeable, hollow, restrained.

The timeline thins from October to December 2009 due to poor weather, holidays, and mid-tour leave. In the thick of a stalemate, it makes sense for time to drag. More than external factors, though, the change happened inward. Where initially I vacillated wildly between hope and elation and disappointment and frustration, in the wake of dampened expectations, I found balance in a leveled monotone. My brain ascribes this three-month period less meaning. A haze surrounds the few moments that do emerge, the space between the accordion notes where meaning is found, or lost.

Most standout memories are outliers, the highs and lows flanking the daily flatness, the surreal interjecting the routine. I remember in scattered snapshots, like those from mom's deployment:

The season's first snowfall and the impromptu snowball fight that broke out in the qalat courtyard between PRT and Army colleagues and several Afghan employees who outmatched us in speed and accuracy.

A heard of dogs that had gathered on base, casually shot one night for population control.

An email from my brother on October 25 with the subject line: "Congrats, Aunt!" and frolicking around the office announcing to everyone that the babies had arrived, a drunken smile plastered on my face. Later, the smile faded into a deep ache for not being there.

The arrival of a new non-military threat, and a rare instance where the rest of the world seemed united with us in daily fear. Though H1N1 incited panic in Afghanistan as early as May 2009, when officials quarantined the country's only pig, a resident of the Kabul Zoo, fear really set in after the virus killed eleven Afghans in October and November. We couldn't know that H1N1 would never reach Gardez. Yet, other than Major London, who had to calm Paktia's director of public health, on FOB Gardez we were oddly complacent. In competition with other concerns and priorities, to me, at least, the virus felt otherworldly, too normal to affect us in our strange little corner of the world. The threat seemed almost comical: Soldier Survives Six Months in Afghanistan, Succumbs to Flu.

More international news arrived, this time of a shooting rampage at Fort Hood, Texas, where an Army major killed thirteen people and injured more than thirty others in an apparent act of religious extremism. Then came the realization that violence had spread to America too.

I remember a Halloween package from my mom and hanging a skeleton decoration on the IO office door. The skeleton became an office mascot, a meager version of ventriloquist Jeff Dunham's Achmed the Dead Terrorist, scull replaced with a printout of Achmed's turbaned head, "I KILL YOU" scrawled across a speech bubble. He would get new attire to mark each holiday.

When we learned the election runoff would never happen, I remember overwhelming relief. In the face of what he saw as hopeless corruption, Karzai's rival conceded. Logistically, it was the best news we'd heard in months. Yet, as I highlighted the "Election Runoff" folder on my computer desktop and dragged it to the folder marked "Archive," something twisted around my joy, something more complex that I couldn't define. One part frustration. One part well-that-was-a-lot-of-hard-work-for-nothing. A sprinkling of what's-the-point. A dash of hopelessness.

Early November marked my first mention of leaving the military when my four-year contract ended. "I'm getting pretty sick of this bureaucratic bullshit," I wrote in an email to a Hurlburt friend. "I'm 90% sure I'm getting out."

November also brought a surprisingly happy Thanksgiving, complete with a feast prepared by PRT chefs in the Olive Gardez kitchen, which had been recently closed for manning shortages.

In December at the remaining dining facility, what felt like the whole of the FOB crowded around two TVs to watch as, halfway around the world at West Point, President Obama turned the nation's attention to Afghanistan. He announced he would send an additional 30,000 troops. No one in the dining facility looked surprised. Save for mumbles of "It's about time," no one appeared excited or disappointed. For me, in the three months since General McChrystal's request for 40,000 troops, reality had set in. The fingers of the surge would barely touch us in Paktia. After the election planning chaos, the polling site desertion, and the uptick in violence nationwide, the idea that we could start handing over security to Afghan forces by 2011 seemed ridiculous, with or without 30,000 more troops.

With December, too, came the opportunity for mid-tour leave: two weeks of vacation and a plane ticket anywhere I wanted to go. I had a chance to go home for Christmas, my favorite holiday and one I'd never spent away from family. I decided not to. I told my parents I didn't want to deal with the odyssey of getting to and from the West Coast—through Bagram, then Kuwait, then Germany, to the Eastern Seaboard, probably another stopover somewhere in the Midwest, and then finally, after several days of exhausting travel, to Seattle. People often returned more tired than when they left, I said. I also told my parents I was eager to spend time with Chris as a "regular" couple. Plus, I said, I wanted to take advantage of the chance to see a new part of the world, that Bavaria's castles, museums, and, after several months of forced sobriety, beer, were too appealing to pass up.

I didn't admit that I couldn't bear more goodbyes. Pre-Indiana had been difficult, but predictably so, and tempered by the promise of the coming adventure. Three months of training let us all ease into my leaving. The quick trip to Seattle before deploying still proved more sweet than bitter and was met on the other end with anticipation: the destination, the fulfillment of duty, and the ultimate return; when next I saw my family, I would be home for good. Leave from Afghanistan was different. Whatever joy I would feel at a reunion would be tainted by the knowledge that I would be leaving again. I might be able to handle the frenzied, wistful, not-quite-Christmas, but I didn't know how to respond to the *how's the deployment going* questions. I couldn't even answer that question for myself in any satisfying way. I could deflect with half-truths on the phone, but could I manage face-to-face? I imagined my parents' worry spilling out over me, and I didn't trust I could clean it back up without breaking down myself. I had to keep the mess internal, I reasoned, for my sake and for theirs. The excitement and optimism I'd left everyone with needed preserving. If something were to happen to me, I didn't want my family to blame the military or go crying to reporters that I'd died for something I didn't fully believe or understand. At the core, my decision not to go home wasn't just about protecting myself or my family. A dutiful public affairs officer, I was also protecting the military's image.

My parents said they understood. Shavonne's twins were too young to really enjoy the holidays anyway. Next year would be better. My parents didn't know that Grandpa Johnson would soon be fighting a war of his own, against cancer. They couldn't know I'd be missing his last Christmas.

Leave came and went in a series of culture shocks, a blur of Bavarian food and drink, and scenery so stunning it was as though I'd jumped inside one of my grandparents' decorative plates. I remember the warmth of *Glühwein* seeping through my stomach to my brain. Following a taste of absinthe, I remember nothing, though from pictures I appear to have enjoyed myself. Chris and I bought new coats and shoes, attempting to blend in. I let my hair down from its tight bun for the first time in months and laughed at the way it tickled the back of my neck and blew across my face. We ate too much, relishing the freshness and flavor that got lost somewhere between production and Gardez. We wore goofy Santa hats, like tourists would, and took photos to prove we were having fun. We tried not to talk about Afghanistan but found we didn't have much else to discuss. Talk often led to *Glühwein*-fueled blowups. It was as if neither of us remembered how to be normal. Or maybe our normals weren't compatible. Maybe Afghanistan was the glue that held our relationship together.

Our first evening in Nuremberg, Germany, after a day browsing the enchanting glitz of one of the world's largest Christmas markets, Chris and I ducked into a small café off the main square. I'd taken an instant liking to German food—the rich sauces, fresh herbs, juicy brats nestled in crusty bread and doused with mustard so spicy it, like the *Glühwein*, seemed to warm me from the inside out. The café emanated unpretentious charm, with stone walls, wide-beamed hardwood floors, and cozy candlelit tables. Smells from the kitchen prickled my nose with expectation. My stomach growled. It was approaching eight o'clock, well past closing time at the Gardez dining facility. *Glühwein* tugged at my brain. The host did not smile. He didn't even acknowledge our shivering figures in the doorway. After a few minutes of me grumbling and squirming like a child on the verge of a tantrum, Chris approached the host. Chris had spent time in Germany and could speak the language conversationally. He said something to the host, who issued a response that sounded equal parts gruff and bored. Chris came back looking resigned.

"They're done serving for the night," he said.

"They let us stand here for five minutes without telling us that?"

Chris shrugged. "That's kind of how things work in Germany. Customer service is different here." His defense irritated me more than it should have. I wanted anything not in Afghanistan to be perfect, simply because it wasn't Afghanistan. "Let's just find something else," Chris said. "There are plenty of restaurants around here."

A block away lively music and zesty aromas beckoned us into a Spanish tapas bar. Chris greeted the host in Spanish. The man's face lit up, and the two chatted back and forth, gesturing excitedly and laughing at something the host said. Usually I found Chris's language skills sexy. Though my Italian lessons weren't producing much more success than my bumbling Pashtu, I was content to just listen to the smooth rhythms of Chris's voice. Now it irked me. Fellow patrons jabbered in German and Spanish and other languages I couldn't identify. The décor and the music were loud. The food smelled good, but distinctly foreign. All at once, in this Spanish restaurant in Germany, on leave from Afghanistan, every fiber of my being yearned for home. I shouted at Chris to order me something and excused myself to the bathroom, where I huddled in a stall and cried.

Two weeks jostled by in a similar cycle of beauty, adventure, exhaustion, and tears. I wanted to share this magical experience with this man I felt so strongly about, because it *was* magical, or should have been, or at least it wasn't Afghanistan; and I *did* love this man, or I thought I did, or I needed to. But I also wanted to let the hot shower run over me until my knees turned red and numb and I couldn't hear anything but the water. Then I wanted to curl up under the fluffy hotel comforter and read. Then I wanted to sleep. And sleep. And sleep.

We hit seven cities in three countries and then spent Christmas Eve at an airport hotel back in Germany before beginning our return trip: Christmas morning flight to Kuwait, twenty-four-hour standby at Ali Al Salem Air Base, C-130 to Bagram and a three-day layover before catching a helicopter ride to Gardez. Bagram, already sprawling when our team first arrived in Afghanistan six months prior, had grown exponentially in preparation for the troop surge. I felt lost and overwhelmed among the mass of uniformed humanity and annoyed by the very un-war zone feel of a walled metropolis with concert venues, YMCA-sized gyms, fast food kiosks, and seven dining halls, at least one of which had a review page on the travel website TripAdvisor. Unwittingly, I had adjusted to the deprivation in Gardez. I found myself anxious to be back on our tiny, familiar FOB.

Chris and I arrived in Gardez just before the new year. With our return comes another memory shift, this time into a mounting crescendo. Nick and Jacob's Army unit had been replaced by a new unit, bringing new IO colleagues, Markus and Alex. Brigade, too, would shortly change over. In the midst of the transition, we were hit with a series of sharp, elongated punches as the timeline seemed to stretch and fold into itself.

Winter in Operation Enduring Freedom was traditionally referred to as the quiet season, because heavy snowfall restricted insurgent movement throughout Afghanistan and blocked transit routes from Pakistan. In winter 2009-2010, however, the troop surge and an expanded drone strike program in Pakistan pushed insurgent operations back across the border, into our backyard. A few days before I returned from leave, a suicide bomber attacked a government building in downtown Gardez. Six people were killed. The FOB jumped to high alert and stayed there as the shocks kept coming. This was what we'd been waiting for, what we'd been dreading.

The last ten weeks of the deployment just make short columns on my timeline spreadsheet, but my brain gives them weight. January bled into February, which swelled far beyond its twenty-eight days, marked by shrill, staccato beats. The headlines would haunt me for years to come:

Seven CIA Agents Killed
Bodies Found Gagged, Bound
Afghan protesters condemn U.S.-led civilian killings

Suicide Bomber Strikes U.S. Base
Information Cover-up

Then the deployment was over. The end came at once fast like the beginning and blurred like the middle; a quick flick of the conductor's baton, and the music stopped. The vibrations continued.

Part Four

TRUTH *noun*

Definition: Common

1. The character of being, or disposition to be, true to a person, principle, cause, etc.; faithfulness, fidelity, loyalty, constancy, steadfast allegiance.

2. Disposition to speak or act truly or without deceit; truthfulness, veracity, sincerity.

3. Conformity with fact; agreement with reality; accuracy, correctness, verity (of statement or thought).

4. Absence of deceit, pretense, or counterfeit.

5. Conduct in accordance with the divine standard; spirituality of life and behavior.

6. The fact or facts; the actual state of the case; the matter or circumstance as it really is.

Definition: in Military/War

error: entry not found

16

The Quiet Season

THE FIRST BIG EVENT OF THE QUIET SEASON sent shock waves that still shook me more than three years later.

In spring 2013, an Army friend and I sat stiffly in a nearly-empty Boston theater for an afternoon showing of *Zero Dark Thirty*, the Oscar-winning account of the CIA's search for Osama bin Laden. We were clearly the only military veterans in the small audience. No one else laughed at the vulgar trash talk of Jessica Chastain's brash CIA character. My friend drew disapproving looks when he snorted into our popcorn during the scene of the SEAL Team Six raid on bin Laden's compound. "They would never yell so loud at a breach," he chortled. (Since my only exposure to raids remained the faux village pink paint incident at pre-deployment training four years prior, I took his word for it.)

Our whispers were mostly positive. We appreciated the plot's slow boil, less action movie than a behind-the-scenes look at intelligence-gathering and the bureaucratic obstacle course of progress. I settled into passive engagement, letting myself relax and enjoy the movie. Then, an hour in, my brain snapped to attention at the mention of Camp Chapman.

"Holy shit!" I whispered more loudly than intended. A middle-aged woman two rows up shot me a glare. "That's where the Khost PRT worked!" Khost Province, adjacent to Paktia, also served as home to the Tweedles and brigade headquarters.

A heading flashed across the screen: CAMP CHAPMAN, Khost, Afghanistan. The background looked familiar, not because I'd been to Camp Chapman; the closest I'd come was brigade headquarters at nearby FOB Salerno for a weekend regional IO conference. The movie scenery was familiar in the way of any small Afghanistan base: brown sectioned off with HESCO barriers, a smattering of military vehicles, connexes in tidy rows, hulking olive drab industrial tents. Add a qalat, take away the two short paved roads, and it could have been FOB Gardez.

In the movie a CIA team prepared to meet with an informant, a Jordanian doctor with inside al-Qaeda access. He could be their big break. He could lead them to bin Laden.

The camera panned to more footage of Camp Chapman. An American flag twitched on a guard tower with chipping white paint. We heard the roar of an approaching aircraft overhead. Then a date: December 30, 2009, two days after I returned to Gardez from mid-tour leave.

My body reacted before my brain could process the connection. I knew this scene. I'd run through imagined versions more times than I wanted to count. But I hadn't witnessed it until now. My body trembled. Tears sprang to my eyes. I didn't wipe them away; I couldn't. I was frozen.

It happened as I knew it would. Of course, in real life, there would be no swell of music as the informant's car pulls up. That swell happens internally—a wave of joy, a flutter of anxiousness, the thrilling relief of *oh my God this is actually happening.*

The dialogue, too, felt familiar, as if I'd observed this conversation in another life:

"Let me set the tone, then I'll turn it over to you . . ."

"We'll cover the basics then get into the nitty gritty . . ."

"I'll introduce you, you introduce the team . . ."

Of course, we'll never know the exact words exchanged as the operatives waited. We can only imagine them leaning on HESCO barriers, squinting against dust and desert sun as a Humvee grumbles by. We'll never watch the real car weave through the concrete gate barriers, just its approximation: not a white Toyota, but still the kind of old rusted sedan that litters Afghanistan's streets. Perhaps there was no yelling for the informant to remove his hand from his pocket, no cry of "Allahu Akbar". Certainly there was a flash of light, a plume of smoke, a sickening *boom* before the world fell silent.

* * *

DECEMBER 30, 2009

There was a briefing. Or a mass email. Or a phone call. Or a round of whispered reports.

A suicide bomber blew himself up outside the FOB Chapman gym.

I don't remember how I heard, but I remember how the news struck me. "Struck" is a good word for it. Stunned to paralysis for a moment, I swear my heart actually stopped, as if my entire system suddenly flipped off. When it switched back on an instant later I crawled back to functioning, like the florescent lights of my elementary school gym, flickering, crackling, slowly brightening in arbitrary sequence. I don't know when I became fully functioning again, or if I did at all before the deployment ended. A murkiness settled around my brain, my heart.

My first thoughts flew to my friends, the Khost PRT IO officer and a few other contacts based at Chapman. Their communications would probably be shut down in the wake of the attack, a standard precaution I knew about from exercises at Hurlburt Field. Somehow they quickly replied to my emails. They were all rattled, but fine. That knowledge made space in my head for those who weren't fine. Seven CIA agents were killed and six others wounded, making Camp Chapman one of the most lethal attacks in CIA history. Seven people dead. Seven men and women, gone in an instant. I didn't know them. I wouldn't recognize their faces. But I superimposed their portraits onto the Fallen Comrades wall in the operations center conference room. Seven frames would add an entire row. The wall grew in my mind like a family tree, each photo sprouting branches to mothers and fathers, sons and daughters, brothers and sisters. The room wasn't big enough to hold every shattered life.

At FOB Gardez, all local nationals were temporarily kicked off base, including the cultural advisors, the PRT interpreters, the Gardez radio DJs, and others who not only worked but also lived on the FOB. I pictured Aamir's kind round face crinkling in confusion, Rahim's puppy dog eyes watering, the legal advisor hunching his scrawny frame in shame. I knew these men. I trusted them. Or at least I thought I did. The CIA trusted the Chapman informant too. He'd been vetted. He was exempted from front gate searches, like many of our Paktia colleagues. So more than feeling sorry for the Gardez employees, I felt relieved.

For Aamir and Rahim and other FOB residents, the ban ended quickly. Commuting workers remained barred for several days. Too consumed in my own fear, I didn't worry how they might fair with lost wages. Though still crammed with soldiers and contractors, the base seemed lifeless. The FOB Gardez mall shuttered, leaving a ghost town of abandoned connexes. We wore body armor outside hardened structures. What constituted a "hardened structure" was open to interpretation—the qalat, perhaps, with its dripping mud walls and crumbling tower, or the plywood operations center or PRT office building. Like most, I limited movement as much as possible. I stockpiled cereal cups and energy bars and ate breakfast at my desk. Instead of enjoying the walk to dinner with Chris, I shuffled quickly in my armor and scarfed down a scoop of the day's entrée, barely tasting and not caring what I ate. My eyes flitted around the tent, meeting other nervous faces. Around the FOB I stared down every Afghan, scrutinized every twitch, every errant glance, certain someone was about to explode.

I kept the news to my family vague and unemotional: "Just wanted to drop you a quick note to let you know we're all OK," I wrote in an email. "There was an attack at a base in another province, but I know sometimes the news just says 'eastern Afghanistan' so I didn't want you to worry."

I remember the cloud of fear choking the FOB, slinking beneath the plates of my body armor. I know sadness swept over us too. The emotion most evident from my emails during that time, though, is anger. A Camp Chapman colleague wrote that he had been friends with some of those Killed in Action. My response should have been one of compassion. Public affairs training stressed condolence statements as a necessary, upfront element of any casualty communication. Even without that, compassion was my default setting. Like my mom, I moved through life sponging up everyone else's pain. In the wake of the Chapman attack, however, anger snuffed out everything else.

Instead of sympathizing with my colleague, I wrote: "You know, I'm starting to adopt the attitude that we've been risking our lives and spending our tax dollars to help these people for eight years, and all they do is whine and ask for more money and try to kill us . . . maybe it's time to leave."

* * *

Time passed. Anger wavered. Fear returned. The body armor requirement lasted three days. I avoided the gym much longer. Eventually we reestablished our routines, just a notch or two closer to paranoia. All visitors were now subject to gate searches. The FOB Gardez mall closed at sunset. The weekly traveling bazaar was canceled indefinitely.

Three times after the attack I encountered an unfamiliar Afghan man in the gym. He had a bushy rust-colored beard and wore a green camouflage Afghan National Army uniform. He always used the same machine, the elliptical closest to the door. For just five or ten minutes, the man's heavy breathing blended with mine. My heartbeat quickened, not from exertion. I thought about leaving, sprinting behind the man, out the door and to the relative safety of the qalat, while my abandoned treadmill continued its squeaky, lopsided loop. Always before I could decide what to do, the man left.

I realized later that that man marked a turning point. For the first seven months of my deployment a thought had been edging into my mind. The Camp Chapman attack took away my sense of control, my power to fight back. Now, moving forward, I could trust no one.

17

Collateral Damage

NOT LONG AFTER THE CHAPMAN ATTACK, I stared at my half-dressed reflection in the slab of my qalat room mirror. Olive green socks, tan uniform undershirt, red underwear (I had to squeeze in color some-where), hair still damp from the shower. The deployment had changed me. My feet flaked with ugly callouses. Both of my big toenails horseshoed into my toes, ingrown from nearly a year in combat boots. I'd all but given up shaving my legs. Under a layer of stubble they glared shockingly pale, several shades lighter than my arms and face, but they were carved with muscles that even swimming and marathon training had never revealed. The Body Armor Workout Plan seemed to counteract the Deployment Diet around my belly, too. Inside I felt soft, bloated from months of greasy, preservative-packed food. Yet I had to cinch my belt tight to keep my uni-form pants in place. My hair fell to my rib cage, the longest it had been since I was eight years old and grew it out for the first of two ill-advised perms. A salon-free year and day after day of tight hair buns gave me a new sort of frazzled perm, frayed at the ends and kinked at regular in-tervals where the rubber band scrunched. Once again I was thankful I'd brought makeup to Afghanistan. Without it my face looked weathered and splotchy. Dry patches along my cheeks and chin fed into a scaly rash that ran down my chest. The perpetual dark circles I'd been so self-conscious of as a teenager were angrier than I'd ever seen them. I'd long since sur-rendered my contacts, and the tint of my glasses cast my eyes in a sunken, purplish tinge.

Then there was the tattoo. Less than a year ago, skin raw with the new ink, I had held up my left arm to proudly show my Florida Bible study group. I told them I wanted the cross to be the first thing I saw when I got dressed every morning. I said I knew Afghanistan would be challenging, but I felt like I was supposed to be there to help the Afghan people and to be a beacon of light for the other soldiers. I actually said "beacon of light," and I meant it.

Now the tattoo stared back at me through the mirror. That's all it did. It didn't inspire comfort or centeredness. It certainly wasn't a beacon of light, and neither was I. If anything, the markings made me realize how silly I'd been. I was spliced again: joining Paintball Wimp Lauren and Combat Barbie Lauren now were Naïve Holier-Than-Thou Lauren and Lauren the Cynic.

I'd kept in haphazard touch with the Bible study group while in Afghanistan. I admitted in a mass email that the deployment was indeed challenging, but I didn't elaborate, with them or anyone else. Chris remained the outlet for my day-to-day emotions. Bits and pieces leaked into phone calls with family and emails to different friends. I sprinkled small truths around. No one knew the whole story. I was protecting everyone, I reasoned, the same way my parents had protected us kids when Mom deployed, keeping fear between the two of them.

In late January I emailed the good friend who'd introduced me to the Bible study. "I've seen some things that make me disgusted with Afghanistan, the military, and humanity in general!" I wrote. "Sometimes I feel myself turning into this bitter, cynical person I don't recognize. It's so hard to not get jaded. If I could ask a favor, could you pray for me and my buddies out here? We're all going through that to some extent. We're getting close to the end (about six weeks now!) but every day has its challenges, especially emotionally and spiritually."

That email was the most revealing I would get. Over the next six weeks, the quiet season would roar, and I would disclose nothing further. My shutdown would be complete.

The Camp Chapman attack was the first big domino to fall. Its aftershocks rumbled into the next month. On January 7, two nearby attacks once again escalated our alert status and confined us to body armor for twenty-four hours. A suicide bombing threat at FOB Gardez then put us on alert for forty-eight hours. Two weeks later, we received reports of possible suicide bombers attempting to access FOB Gardez—or potentially already on base. Alert procedures were beginning to feel unnervingly routine: Armor outside hardened structures, 100 percent ID checks, heart rate increase with approaching footfalls, body jolting at every sharp noise. This time all base units dispersed in teams, canvasing the FOB, searching every shadow for suspicious activity. Shining my flashlight into qalat alcoves, running the beam along cracks in the curdled wall, I was transported back to training in Indiana:

In Camp Atterbury's auditorium, I watched the Army trainers flip through PowerPoint slides about IED recognition. The Before photos showed potential hiding spots: a pile of trash, an animal carcass, a patch of shrubbery, a disturbance in a dirt road. The After photos x-ray visioned through the object: buried explosives, a hidden pressure plate, wires curled around branches.

My brain jumped to training on the IED Lane, scanning through Humvee windows for real-life versions of the images from the slides. *There's what looks like magnetic tape dangling between trees, better call it in . . . That could be wires protruding from that rock pile. Let's set a perimeter . . . What's that shiny thing there? Does that look weird to you? BOOM!* The instructor signaled an explosion. *Good thing this isn't real.*

Next, I saw myself bursting through a door in a plywood village. I lay sprawled on the gravel, covered in pink paint.

My brain leapt back to Afghanistan, to the shredded Humvee on display at Bagram, to emails with my parents. "I'm sad to report there was another suicide attack in Gardez this afternoon," I'd written recently. "This is really getting old." My mom emailed that in Saudi Arabia, "Even the scud attacks became part of everyday life because they didn't hit too close to home. I hope you have as benign a threat as we did and never have to use any of that training."

On my Gardez surveillance check I gripped my flashlight tight enough to etch its imprint on my palm and crept slowly outside the qalat. I breathed harder than my bulletproof vest wanted me to, spitting puffs of exhaled air into the beam. The sun was setting, night's suffocating blackness soon to follow. I surveyed the low wall of HESCO barriers and the few spindles of concertina wire that had never failed to inspire confidence—however mis-guided—but now wavered flimsy and inadequate in the shaking triangle of light.

War is full of irony. By early 2010 coalition forces' presence in Afghanistan was becoming increasingly controversial, both with the Afghan people and the international public, fueled by a string of high-profile incidents of mass civilian casualties. Mounting reports of green-on-blue insider attacks on coalition forces by Afghan forces left us feeling vulnerable to threats from our Afghan colleagues.[9] All the while, we were ever more encouraged to play nice. Efforts had begun for the Afghan government to reconcile with members of the Taliban and reintegrate them into civilian society. Presi-dent Karzai would formalize the initiative at the January 28 International Conference on Afghanistan in London, but the impact had preemptive-ly filtered down to Gardez. We no longer referred to the Taliban in radio broadcasts; we called the enemy "criminal insurgents." Instead of capacity building, the focus shifted to Combined Team Operations. Hierarchical re-lationships were to be replaced with partnerships. We would train, plan, and execute missions side-by-side with the Afghans with the goal of improving communications, transparency, trust, and ultimately effectiveness, on both sides.

Military personnel in the northern Paktia district of Dand Wa Patan practiced Combined Team Operations. U.S. soldiers there partnered di-rectly with a unit of Afghan Border Police charged with securing the nearby Pakistan border. When I hosted an embedded reporter in mid-January, he was eager to visit Dand Wa Patan to see Combined Team Operations in ac-tion and joined us for a government outreach mission there. Dand Wa Patan was the smallest district in Paktia and home to the smallest combat out-post. When our two helicopters plowed in for landing, they splattered dirt and gravel across the entirety of the small compound. Rotor wash pelted the shack that served as the outpost's kitchen, the plywood outhouses, the plywood barracks where soldiers slept like cattle and the adjacent Afghan barracks (sleep being the one activity the nations did separately), and the single two-room building where we would hold our *shura*.

When we landed, we were greeted by our local PRT civil affairs officer, a smattering of Army soldiers, and three stray dogs that had been adopted by the Army unit. Military regulations strictly forbade pets and mascots. Animals carried disease, and we were valuable government property. Sometimes, though, we couldn't help ourselves. My weakness was the black and white cat named Cheeto, and Garfield, a big orange tabby who liked to sleep on the sunbaked hoods of the Humvees outside the qalat. Before they were shot, I'd snuck the Gardez dogs scraps from the dining facility. Skittles the goat resided in the qalat courtyard for a month, eating the few plants that managed to poke through the course dirt and braying late into the night, annoying me but charming everyone else. Even Nick—tough, crude, grunt-to-the-core Nick—loved the little goat. Every time he passed the courtyard, Nick stopped to spend a few minutes with Skittles. He would scratch her chin and offer a bite of apple, cooing in a voice reserved for a different type of man. He always looked refreshed when he came back to the office, like he'd just had a good chat with an old friend. When Skittles ultimately served her purpose as a Ramadan ceremonial meal for our Afghan employees, Nick was crushed.

The Dand Wa Patan dogs, called Target, IED, and Rufus, were scruffy but deliriously happy creatures. They wove through my legs and whipped me with their tails and pranced their filthy paws across my uniform pants, and I couldn't help but laugh. I tossed each a few crumbles from a granola bar and giggled when their soft tongues lapped at my hands. The reporter laughed too and snapped photos as the dogs zipped between soldiers, jockeying for attention and treats.

The high from the animals carried me through a *shura* of stale promises and complaints and a meal of rice and sand and grisly meat that now always made me think of Skittles. After, as we waited for our helicopters, I climbed to the top of a corner guard tower. The view lacked the glory of the Gardez qalat tower. Mountains didn't pierce the skyline before bleeding into a valley. Sunlight didn't rupture behind the peaks. The stretch of Dand Wa Patan lay flat, bland, and brown. But there, a few hundred meters before me, was the invisible line of the Pakistan border. Seeing Pakistan felt like an accomplishment, somehow. I wanted to scratch my name into the wood of the tower railing: *Lauren was here.* Proof that I'd been somewhere significant. That's what I told myself when I returned to FOB Gardez, to hot meals, indoor plumbing, and my own bedroom, to at least some level of separation from the local nationals I'd come to resent or fear. I reminded myself of that feeling of significance when I boasted the mission's success to the embedded reporter and when I copied and pasted another overly optimistic storyboard, when we got the next threat increase a week later, and again in February after a suicide bomber dressed in an Afghan Border Police uniform snuck onto the Dand Wa Patan outpost and attempted to get inside the U.S. barracks. The insurgent didn't reach his target; he was attacked by three dogs, forcing him to detonate himself outside the structure, wounding five soldiers but killing none. Just one dead dog. Acceptable collateral damage.

Yes, I told myself, the military's work here is important, the mission is worth the cost, and my contribution matters.

18

The Fog of War

FEBRUARY 12, 2010. The day after the Dand Wa Patan suicide bombing.

I remember how the day started, with my new IO Army colleague Markus standing in front of the PRT office, jittery with news. And I remember how the day ended, with my other new colleague Alex, his hands shaking as he flipped through the photos of bullet-ridden corpses.

Between the beginning and the end—utter chaos.

At the beginning, Chris and I walked back from breakfast, stomachs heavy with scrambled eggs from a carton, soggy bacon, and crusty pancakes made soft with a drenching of chocolate syrup. I needed coffee to counteract the grease and the grogginess from another restless night. Even without body armor I felt weighed down. My boots scuffed along the ground as I walked, little cyclones of dust swirling around my legs. The promise of caffeine alone propelled me to my office. I could smell a chocolate-hazelnut brew as we approached.

On this morning, though, I didn't follow the smell inside. Markus, Jacob's replacement after his unit rotated out, stood by the door waiting for me. Markus had swagger and unfussy good looks, with black hair he greased into a rebellious spike. He reminded me of the cool guys back in college, the ones who seemed to exist in a parallel universe full of keg stands and casual sex and other hedonistic things that I was too scared to admit intrigued me. Loud, brash, and crude, Markus always teetered near the edge of inappropriate, and he was almost unnaturally happy. None of those traits bothered me; from my perspective, his worst feature was that he was a morning person. Whenever our paths crossed before my second cup of coffee, I had a strong urge to punch Markus in his grinning, babbling face.

Today I didn't have time for annoyance. As soon as he saw me Markus blurted, "Lauren, the Taliban fucked up! There was a shooting downtown." His wide eyes glinted with the kind of excitement that shouldn't be generated by death and destruction. "A couple civilians were killed. Some women. Alex is on his way out there to take pictures." He spat a wad of dip next to his boot. "Fucking bastards."

Rage flared in Markus's eyes too, a complicated mesh of emotions I was beginning to understand. War seeded rage at everything, everyone; sometimes justified, sometimes petty. I directed mine at Paktia's governor and President Karzai and his not-so-legitimate government, or President Bush, President Obama, and military leadership for trapping us in this black hole of a campaign. I raged at the bad guys—whoever they were today. At Afghan men. All of them, de facto bad guys for lack of a more defined target. I resented my shoddy internet connection and the stupid single qalat toilet. I hated the Tweedles and their tweedling, Markus's energy, and Chris's jealousy. I hated that I felt so weak and emotional. I despised the security threats and attacks, but also the moments between, the waiting, the blandness that makes up so much of war. Fingers that twitch from the absence of a rifle, that find their way to barbells and video game controllers and wrap themselves around cigarettes to steady the tremors. Minds that spin through the nothingness, lurching for the chance to translate training into action, distorting shadowed corners and sudden noises, molding suspicion from every conversation. And morphing death into excitement.

Markus was excited because here was a chance to *do something.* The insurgents had fucked up, and in their mistake they dropped a nugget of IO gold into our laps. I found myself smiling. I was excited too.

The need for coffee replaced by adrenaline, Chris and I followed Markus to the operations center, which was busier than I'd seen since Election Day. At the front of the room, the projection screens displayed a grainy image of a qalat in a Gardez neighborhood. I don't remember if we could see people. They must have been there, little ants marching around the screen. I know we couldn't see the bodies. I would remember the bodies.

From somewhere, maybe multiple places, we got an update: The night before, there had been a raid at a qalat in town to capture a man suspected of insurgent activity. As a Combined Team Operation, both U.S. and Afghan Special Forces were involved. The joint team had converged on the compound and conducted a "call out," hollering for the wanted man to come outside. Someone appeared with a weapon. Shots were fired. Inside the qalat, the team discovered five dead bodies. Or maybe six. Three were women. No one knew how long they had been dead. They had bullet wounds, there was blood, but their mouths and feet were bound for burial. Had they been dead before the raid?

The villagers blamed U.S. forces. The Special Forces team denied responsibility for the deaths.

This was not the clear-cut IO victory we expected.

In public affairs training we learned to gather all possible facts and send out an initial news release within sixty minutes of an incident, part of the overall sixty-minute battle drill following a SIGACT, a significant action. We were taught to "go ugly early"; if shit happens, broadcast details as soon as possible to prevent the perception that you're hiding anything and to minimize gossip. And if casualties are involved, always, *always,* include a condolence statement.

In Gardez, I couldn't draft a press release. Because of the national implications of civilian casualties, that responsibility went up the chain of command to people with stars on their shoulders. There would be no condolences, we were told; that was as good as admitting blame. "Facts" were a tricky notion in Afghanistan. Securing an area and preserving evidence weren't priorities for Afghan security personnel. By the time a FOB Gardez investigation team arrived, they were left scrambling to connect an ever-shifting set of dots. The story had changed multiple times—the number of casualties, their identities, speculation on the time and cause of death—with various, conflicting versions reported in local and international media. In Gardez, there would be no PA sixty-minute battle drill. Here, I was nothing but a conduit for rumors.

In the aftermath of the raid, the cultural advisors monitored local news coverage and took calls from media and community members. Markus got real-time updates from the operations center. The Tweedles called. The Tweedles emailed. Markus emailed from his desk in the operations center that he couldn't get anything done because the Tweedles kept calling and emailing.

Afghanistan's Pajhwok news agency reported: *Paktia's deputy chief of police said that U.S. Special Forces have killed the security officer of Zormat district along with four members of his family.*

Ariana TV reported: *Based on a statement from Paktia's governor's spokesman, an unknown gunman killed an Afghan National Police officer who was working in Zormat district, an employee of the attorney's office, and three women.*

From the PA Tweedle: "They're saying the chief of intelligence was at that house. Is that true?"

From Markus's leadership: "We're literally sitting in a meeting with the chief of intelligence right now. He's very much alive."

A representative for two local TV stations told Aamir that a district prosecutor, one Afghan National Police officer, and three women from the officer's family were killed. The reporter also claimed coalition forces took six individuals into custody.

A Paktia radio employee called Aamir and said his brother, a police officer, was detained during the operation.

A Pajwok News agency headline: "Foreign Forces killed National Directorate of Security Officer and his four family members."

Afghan Sharq TV reported: *Afghan officials say that American soldiers killed an officer of the National Intelligence Department of Afghanistan and four of his family members in Paktia Province.*

An email from me to Chris in the operations center: "Today sucks and I miss you and I'm hungry."

Rumors churned through the local news:

There was a party in the house where the operation was carried out.

The party was to celebrate the birth of a security official's infant child; the security official was among those killed.

One of the dead men worked for the police. The second man worked for the attorney general's office.

One of the women was pregnant.

Aamir called: "Media is asking about the reason the operation was carried out?"

Aamir emailed: "Media is asking too much about this incident."

Aamir again: "Do we have anything to tell media?"

My response: "If the media asks questions, please tell them that we do not know yet who was killed, but we will contact them as we get more information. Tell them that Afghan National Security Forces, the Afghan government, and the International Security Assistance Force are all working together to get the details of the incident."

I hated the way the words tasted coming out of my mouth, and how easily they came, even when I fought against them. I hated that there was nothing I could do but tap dance, stall, and repeat hollow command messages. I put my head on my desk. The cold wood felt soothing against my skin.

The previous day's attack on the Dand Wa Patan outpost still gathered media steam too:

The Taliban claimed responsibility for the suicide bombing.

Ariana TV reported that the five wounded U.S. soldiers were killed.

The next hour, Ariana TV reported that the five Dand Wa Patan soldiers were wounded, not killed; however, they also said that the Taliban claimed the death of up to twenty Afghan Border Patrol and coalition forces soldiers in the attack.

A little past one o'clock, several hours after we learned of the Gardez incident, with speculative accounts roiling through local and international news, the International Security Assistance Force public affairs office issued a press release:

KABUL, Afghanistan (February 12) – The Interior Ministry and the International Security Assistance Force (ISAF) are conducting a joint investigation in the incident in Paktia Province in the Gardez district near the village of Khatabeh today. A joint Afghan-international security force found the bound and gagged bodies of two women and dead bodies of two men in a compound during an operation last night.

"'ISAF continually works with our Afghan partners to fight criminals and terrorists who do not care about the life of civilians. The Interior Ministry of Afghanistan has sent a high ranking delegation today to jointly investigate this incident. We will cooperate fully in this joint investigation and provide any assistance the Interior Ministry requires," said Brig. Gen. Eric Tremblay, ISAF Spokesperson.

The joint force went to a compound, after intelligence confirmed militant activity. Several insurgents engaged the joint force in a fire fight and were killed. Subsequently, a large number of men, women, and children exited the compound. Eight men were detained for further questioning.

Afghan and international security forces work together to eliminate the insurgents and terrorist threats and to ensure the safety and well-being of the Afghan people.

I read the release, thinking it terse and cold. Later that day, Markus, Alex and I pestered the Tweedles: *Where are the condolences? Regardless of blame, where is any indication that we care that people have been killed in our area of responsibility?* The response came as a snide comment from the IO Tweedle: "Oh they're just Hazaras," a minority ethnic group. "No one cares about them."

Later still, amid claims of inaccuracies, the press release was removed from the ISAF website.

By five o'clock Afghan government and security officials arrived at the Gardez neighborhood qalat with an investigation team from Kabul. The FOB Gardez investigation team returned to base, including Alex, Nick's replacement, who had been photographing the scene for IO documentation. I don't remember Alex's arrival at our shared office. Maybe I wasn't there. He probably went to his b-hut first to unload his gear, then to the operations center to rally with Markus. In the IO office, they likely found me gaping at my computer screen, waiting for . . . something. Something concrete. Something un-morbid. Something giving me permission to do anything other than channel rumors and imagine years of relationship-building unraveling in a matter of chaotic hours. Maybe that's why I looked at the photos. I needed to *do something*.

Alex inserted the SD card into the laptop I kept as the FOB photo computer. His hands shook. That's what I noticed first. Other than his muscular arms, Alex bore little resemblance to my previous office mate. Alex had served two deployments in Iraq. He left the military after his second tour, earned an MBA, and landed a cushy job in a Manhattan high rise. Then, the Army plucked him out of his civilian career, long-term relationship, stable life, and recalled him for this deployment with the National Guard. Unlike Nick, Alex did not want to kill people. He didn't want to be here at all. He hated the Army. He hated Afghanistan. He marked his days with Xs on his calendar, long weightlifting sessions to "get something out of this hellhole," late-night phone calls to his girlfriend in New York, and apathy—except when he was rebelling. Alex talked back to the Tweedles in ways I wished I could. "What are they gonna do?" he joked, "Send me home? Kick me out?" At another Forward Operating Base before taking Nick's place in Gardez, Alex had leaked information to the press about a Pentagon contract with a public relations firm to profile reporters looking to embed in Afghanistan and direct them to favorable coverage. In the ensuing investigation, a team from *Stars & Stripes* newspaper won the George Polk Award for Military Reporting. The Pentagon canceled the contract. Alex had broken a cardinal military rule to serious consequences, and he was proud to boast about it.

I saw Alex as a kind of anti-hero, a fuck-the-system well-meaning vigilante. His audaciousness both frightened and impressed me. I admired him, but I knew I could never be like that. I was too strait-laced and non-confrontational, and far too loyal. Even when my emotions ran counter to the tasks of my job, duty always won out. Alex was as resolute in his bitterness as in his indifference. I'd never seen him waver. That's why I noticed his shaking hands. While he uploaded the photos to the laptop, I traced my vision from Alex's hands up his thick arms, across his dusty Army shirt, and to his face. His brow didn't hold its usual skeptical crease. His mouth didn't twitch with a sarcastic remark. His face wasn't his own; it was made of ashen clay, and his lips had been squished into an unnatural rigid line. Alex's eyes looked at the laptop but focused elsewhere, someplace deep and terrible. I couldn't stop watching him. I wanted to push the corners of his mouth upwards. I yearned for him to blink and sneer and say something off-color that told me everything was normal.

Instead, Alex started rambling. "It was crazy there . . . blood everywhere . . . fucking shit show . . . just a girl . . . tied up like that . . . it's barbaric . . . she was pregnant. Fucking pregnant . . ."

The pregnant woman flashed in a photo on the computer screen. I looked when I heard the mouse click. *A camera angle from the opposite side of the room. Concrete floor. A woven rug of yellow, green, and blue. Splotches of dark red that don't belong. Discarded shoes. A blood spatter on the wall behind a white-robed figure. CLICK. Zoomed in now. It's not a white robe but a sheet pulled taught around a woman's body. The lumps of her breasts. The swell of her pregnant belly. Flowers of dried blood. CLICK. A pretty face. She's my age, maybe younger. I've never seen skin that color, like a bruise when it's beginning to fade. That must be the color of death. CLICK. Death from the left. CLICK. Death from the right. CLICK. Death from above. CLICK. CLICK. CLICK.*

"Why am I looking at this?" Alex suddenly asked. He gave a nervous half-laugh, but his finger kept clicking. I'd been asking myself the same question. Markus hovered behind me, disturbingly quiet. *CLICK.* More figures, more angles. Finally, I ripped my vision away. On the office door, the Achmed skeleton decoration shot Valentine's hearts with his cupid bow and arrow. "I KILL YOU . . . with love." Everywhere I looked I could see the woman's sallow, waxy face. The blood. Alex's eyes and shaking hands.

A montage I want to forget, but in the end it's what I remember most.

Information emerged no clearer in the following days. CNN referenced an unnamed senior official saying the victims were shot "execution-style" in what appeared to be an Afghan honor killing.[11] In a *New York Times* article, the Paktia chief of police asserted that the women were "killed by Taliban militants." The same article quoted an Afghan military spokesperson saying that the men had been "killed by coalition forces after they opened fire on a joint patrol."[12]

Many headlines and comments were rabid.

The Revolutionary Association of the Women of Afghanistan reported: "Villagers accuse U.S. special forces for killing five civilians."[13]

Witnesses "told the Associated Press that the victims were executed after being ordered from the house, forced to kneel and had their hands tied."[14]

The AP interviewed a Paktia provincial council official, who said, "The Americans conducted an operation in a house and killed five innocent people, including three women. The people are so angry."[15]

Press TV reported: "Angry locals said the killings had been 'deliberate' and called for legal action against the perpetrators. At one point, they began throwing stones at a convoy of the U.S.-led troops."[16]

An Arab news website scoffed: "Let us launch an investigation which will invariably exonerate U.S. occupation forces."[17]

As the days passed, rumors swelled. No Afghans were involved, officials said; the government didn't know the raid was taking place. Others claimed that Americans requested air support and bombed the house, or that the shooting was an assassination.

Thousands of protestors gathered outside the governor's compound in Gardez, chanting anti-American slogans.

I watched the events unfold with horror, resigned to inaction. Anything left of my *Three Cups of Tea* fantasy faded with those protest chants. Whatever happened in that raid, Americans, myself included, clearly weren't the heroes of this story.

The Afghans demanded reparations, condolence payments for the grieving families. In the appeal I discovered a new kind of anger for the fact that Afghan women really were worth more dead than alive.

A new kind of fear stalked me too. Maybe I was not only not changing the world for the better; maybe I was actually making it worse. What if my IO messages, radio broadcasts, and media talking points—all promoting support for the war, the American military, and the Afghan government— what if those messages sent ripples. And what if, on either side, people got caught in those ripples. And what if people died. *My job isn't life or death*, I'd always told myself. But what if it was?

A few days later a PRT officer stood at the corner of the conference room, opposite where I sat. I don't remember his exact words, but I know the feeling they left me with: a vice clamp tightening against my chest, the air sucked out with a sharp exhale, wanting to flail and kick and yell but my body shackled to the chair.

In February's cruel trick, the days following the Gardez raid stretched like weeks. The PRT officer had spent the time partnered with ISAF agents to investigate the raid-gone-wrong and the five dead Afghans. Now he summed up the investigation results. His speech went something like this: "It looks like American forces might be responsible, but there's really no way to know for sure. The Afghan reaction has been very localized, and if we accept a level of responsibility the news will probably spread, and it will damage relations even further. So, we're not going to say anything. We'll make condolence payments, but we won't admit fault."

We're not going to say anything.

We're not going to say anything.

The words spun through my brain like the omitted line from the detainee's interview. *We're not going to say anything. We're not going to say anything. I don't know why I was taken. We're not going to say anything.*

My head screamed. My body wanted to scream. My hands clenched into fists, digging their nails into my palms. My teeth gritted together so I could feel my heartbeat behind my eyes. Then, when my stomach unwound itself enough to let in a gulp of air, I interrupted the meeting.

"Can we do that?"

I didn't scream into the room. In my memory my voice is shaky and tentative, almost like the words weren't coming from me at all but a stage-whisper from somewhere above the conference table. My protest was not one of strength. Astonishment may have come through. Perhaps resignation did too. Maybe I didn't even speak out loud; the echoes might just have been in my mind.

Ultimately, what I thought or said or didn't say was of little consequence to the U.S. military. I had no control over what happened—or didn't happen—next. Alex suggested we go to the press, like he had with the Pentagon PR contract. If coalition forces insisted on lying, he said, the public deserved the truth. Markus and I talked him down. I didn't agree with silence, but whistleblowing was the opposite extreme. We didn't know for sure U.S. forces were responsible, I reasoned. We had no evidence other than hearsay. Like the PRT investigating officer said, admitting fault could further stoke the flames. Despite my anger at inaction, I shrunk from the possibility of action. Selfishly, Markus and I had careers to preserve. Even if I left the military, a dishonorable discharge would be a big stain to wipe away. Whereas Alex didn't care about his reputation, I still did. And after everything, I still wanted to be a good officer.

19

The End

ON A COLD SUNDAY IN FEBRUARY, somewhere amid the Camp Chapman CIA attack, the Dand Wa Patan suicide bombing, and the Gardez raid, I lost my faith. My faith in God had been slipping away for a while, but sitting in the tiny white chapel, in the second seat from the aisle of the third hard wooden pew, singing the chorus of a worship song, I realized it was gone.

I know people who've been through terrible tragedies, much worse than corruption and lies or witnessing death secondhand. Some find faith in the aftermath; faith becomes their salvation, their something-to-hold-on-to. For those with a religious foundation, trials seem to beat against the walls of their faith, either strengthening or shattering it. I don't know why mine did the latter.

I do know, in the wake of the Gardez raid, I gave up on Truth. That which I was supposed to reveal in my PA campaigns and news releases. That which meant we were the good guys, or that such a thing as "good guys" even existed in war. Truth, I realized, was nothing but a storyboard, a pixelated photo where everyone stood a little taller, smiled a little wider. Truth was the tempered, warped reality viewed through the water of a swimming pool. My IO reports were pretty enough to obscure what lurked between the lines. We could track performance, but not effectiveness; dollars spent, but not effectively applied; buildings constructed, but not utilized. The sermon at the local mosque contained Truth, just like my talking points and radio messages, what I wrote in my election commentary, what we released as the final detainee interview, and what would be in the Gardez raid investigation report. Like the military, the government media, and religion itself—filtered, unchallenged, through an official mouthpiece—Truth was open to interpretation and easily perverted.

Nothing here was black and white. Sitting in church that February morning, what hit me was that faith—at least what I thought of as faith, a pure and sure and crystalline thing—couldn't exist in the gray area. So, for me, it ceased to exist.

Chris didn't accompany me to the chapel that day, so it might have been the Sunday after the Gardez raid, when he was called away, like the other PRT investigating officer, to look into the Dand Wa Patan suicide bombing. That would make sense. My emotions were peaked and my confidence in just about everything shaken. With Chris gone, I had no one to be strong for. A chaplain from the new Army unit stood up front, a small, boyish man who swayed when he sang. Around me, new arrivals sat in uniforms that still smelled of starch, their sharp camouflage exposing how dirty and sun-bleached my own had become. I glanced at the closed eyes and clasped hands and listened to the reverent, off-key voices of strangers. I didn't know anyone here. I didn't have the energy to try to know them in the month before I would never see them again. So, I let the gulping sob escape. I let tears tumble down my face. When others looked at me with concern, when the captain next to me put a comforting hand on my heaving shoulder, I wondered if they could tell that I no longer belonged.

Later that day at the lookout tower, I pushed through the creaky, rusted gate, steadying myself on the railing so as not to slip on the worn wood, and willed the FOB to fall away below me. A single story up, I could still hear the voices of my colleagues, the occasional scrape of the PRT office door, the rumble of vehicles over gravel. Yet I usually found tranquility in that small separation. Everything kept moving, but I, for a moment, could be still. Now, it felt the opposite. Beyond the tower, past the connexes and HESCO barriers and concertina wire, in the miles of emptiness that stretched through Gardez Valley and spilled into miles of mountains—*there* was stillness. I was turbulence and noise. Even the sun dipping behind the farthest ridge of mountains and splintering into wavering slivers of color and shadow, a sight that typically left me breathless, brought no repose. Beauty, peacefulness, harmony; these things could only be temporary. The sun would rise tomorrow over parched land and suffering. That was the truest truth I could find in Afghanistan.

Three punches in the gut, a fall from grace, and a round of leapfrog—that's how my deployment ended.

His recall orders complete, Alex left in late February with a "Fuck Afghanistan" and a promise to toast us with a tropical drink or several from the Bahamas, where he was headed with his girlfriend. PRT personnel filed out with departing helicopters. Just a small core, including Chris and me, would remain until the bitter end. I focused my energy on packing and shipping boxes home (actually to the PA office at Hurlburt Field, the only local address I had, though the office itself had relocated since I left), and on compiling continuity for my replacement. Always a perfectionist, I wanted to set up the incoming IO captain for success, though my definition of success no longer stretched anywhere close to world peace. I would give the captain candidness and accurate reporting. The sooner she learned the spectrum of suck in Gardez, the sooner she could embrace it, and the sooner I could leave Afghanistan behind. If I could anticipate my replacement's questions, I thought, if she knew where to find what she needed, if she could step seamlessly into the IO role, then I could leave and forget about everything. I could get on with my life.

Other FOB units, too, did the change of command dance. Most incoming teams, including the PRT, were larger, swollen with the troop surge. What scraps of privacy we'd once enjoyed disappeared with their arrival. The USO building where Chris and I watched movies was gutted for a barracks expansion. The old Olive Gardez became the new morale center, dense with sweat and spit bottles and men screaming at video games. Connexes zigzagged with new industrial tents where soldiers slept on cots. The qalat women's bathroom worked overtime to serve eighteen women. I moved into a four-bunk qalat room with Major London and the supply officer, the last from our PRT's cohort of women. Two days later, my replacement arrived.

The day floated by like a wonderful dream, the counterpart to the recurring nightmare that I woke up at training at Camp Atterbury and still had the entire deployment ahead of me. On the morning of March 2, 2010,

I found myself at the Helicopter Landing Zone, shielding my eyes from the dust and gravel kicked up by the landing helicopters. When they touched down, I watched a handful of soldiers stumble off and stagger, hunched over, past the reach of the rotor blades, and then straighten up and gape as they took in the first view of FOB Gardez: the brown mountains and swirling brown air, the brown shack of the Air Control Center and post office, the churning gravel, the HESCO barriers, the beaten-down exuberant remains of our team; this snow globe that would hold them—trapped, isolated, shaken—for the next nine months. As one of only a few women, my replacement was easy to spot.

"You must be Captain Douglass!" I squealed. After weeks of emailing, I felt like I knew the rosy-cheeked blonde in front of me. In fact, I thought I might love her. On their own accord, my arms reached out and hugged her. "Sorry," I said, stepping back hastily. "I'm just really happy you're here."

To my great relief, the captain laughed. "I completely understand," she said. "I'm sure I'll hug my replacement too."

"Here, let me take your bag," I said. "It takes a while to get used to the altitude!" I couldn't keep the exclamation points out of my voice. "And here's the qalat, isn't it cool!?" . . . "Your room is this way, not bad at all!"

I glided through the afternoon like I'd been drugged with a magical pill that left me googly-eyed and deliriously happy. Suddenly, I didn't care that I had to wait an hour and a half for the shower. I didn't mind walking in the cold to stand in line to sit squished against the dripping wall of the dining facility tent to eat rubbery chicken nuggets and freezer-burned lettuce. Chris rode the same high. We planned to watch a movie that evening, projected on the peeling wall of a dingy qalat meeting room, but instead we made out like teenagers. Before bed I emailed my parents: "Guess what? MY REPLACEMENT ARRIVED TODAY," followed by sixty-seven exclamation points.

A few days later, I called home one last time. It was Grandpa Johnson's eightieth birthday, and the family threw him a big party. With his cancer raging, they suspected this might be his last birthday. I didn't know what I was missing, just that I'd soon be reunited with the people on the other end of the line. Dad put me on speakerphone, and I spent most of the conversation in giggling confusion over who was yelling and whether they were yelling at me or at something burning on the stove or at one of the pets. Then Grandpa got on the line.

"Hi Grandpa," I said. "Happy birthday! I wish I could be there!"

"I wish you could too, sweetie. There's lots of good food."

"There always is!"

Then Grandpa's voice caught. "I'm so proud of you, Lauren. We all are." The rest came out in a sob. "We love you so much."

That's the only time I ever remember him crying.

My replacement's arrival and my phone call with Grandpa are my last vivid memories in Gardez. Captain Douglass proved willing and competent, which gave my brain clearance to start heading home. (She even dressed the Achmed skeleton in St. Patrick's Day attire; my work was officially complete.) I know on March 10 we held an IO Conference with the PRT, Army, and Agribusiness Development Team replacements, the PA mentoring team from FOB Lightning, the director of information and culture, a few local media representatives, the cultural advisors, and the Gardez DJs. The conference was one of my pet projects, a way of introducing everyone and getting all parties on the same page, as well as empowering the Afghans to expand their own communication efforts. The event is one of the few things I look back on with pride and think that maybe, just maybe, I *did* do some good after all. But I remember nothing of that day.

I vaguely recall taking pictures with Aamir and Rahim and the Gardez DJs in an Afghan dress—heavy velvety fabric, maroon with gold embellishments, a parting gift from the cultural advisors.

There's a PRT photo from March 11, the afternoon my team left Gardez. The final thirteen of us pose against a backdrop of HESCO barriers, flanking the sign at the entrance to the HLZ:

**WELCOME TO FORWARD OPERATING BASE
GARDEZ. WE'RE DEDICATED TO A BETTER
AND SAFER AFGHANISTAN**

The Air Force camouflage clashes slightly with the Army's. I and another rogue cold-blooded type wear green fleece jackets. Half the team is smiling, half giving tough guy grimaces, at least one wears an expression of why-the-fuck-are-we-taking-another-photo. Only Chris's head is visible poking over the top of the sign. I'm the solitary woman. Crouched in front, I'm gripping Annie like she belongs with me and grinning bigger than anyone.

A short helicopter flight later, we spent the night at the PRT compound in neighboring Paktika Province. I high-fived the newly arrived PRT IO rep there, none other than the young PA lieutenant from my office at Hurlburt who I'd welcomed to the Air Force eighteen months prior. "Good luck, dude," I told him. "It kinda sucks. But at least you have Pizza Hut." I didn't elaborate.

Then we were at Bagram, and I was handing over my weapons. The parting was not sorrowful. Only later would I balk at the phantom weight and miss the illusion of safety from the pressure against my thigh, the comfort of sameness in the solid, steadying grip.

Bagram's transient "tent city" where we had stayed on our first nights in Afghanistan nine months prior had grown into a thriving suburb of the main base with its own fast food kiosks. I gorged myself on Dairy Queen and Pizza Hut, not caring that my stomach responded with angry pitches. The tent city bunkers had also been completed. We tested them on our second night when the INCOMING sirens jolted us awake for a mortar attack. I knew the chances of a mortar landing within the Bagram perimeter were low, the odds of one hitting our exact location nearly impossible, but my body trembled, grating against everything in me that ached to be away from this place. The faces around me in the bunker stretched taught with fear. Some women I wouldn't know for more than tonight as we shared a tent full of bunkbeds and this bunker. Then there was Sergeant Rivera, who herded us inside with steadfast urgency, at once a soldier and a mother, her long hair loose and matted with sleep; and Major London, her expression both soft and firm, resolved to handle whatever came to pass with what had become her customary resilience and calm. These two women would always have a piece of me.

I remember holding my breath as the C-130 jerked up and away from Bagram, and, when the pilot announced, "We have left combat air space," releasing a slow *whooooooo* and watching my armor-clad chest deflate. Next to me, Chris's body relaxed. He squeezed my hand. I turned to him, and we exchanged Fertile Crescent-sized grins. That's how I'll remember him long after the deployment, after we fight other wars against distance and jealousy, expectations and logic. His bronze face glowing with sweat and childish delight. Green eyes crinkled beneath thick eyebrows. His smile curling into dimples.

We left by way of Manas, Kyrgyzstan, where we spent three days on standby and celebrated Saint Patrick's Day with mugs of Russian beer, two-drinks-per-person-per-day plenty to leave us dancing to a violin trio. We ate flavored popcorn by the bucket and watched movie marathons in a real theater with cushioned chairs that I appreciated so much I fell asleep during every showing.

At each stop, our team got smaller. We hopped from Manas to Turkey to Germany to England, and then finally to Baltimore-Washington International Airport, where we were herded through a small crowd of USO volunteers whose cheers and unfamiliar faces were as genuine as they were jarring, then through customs, then to separate terminals for separate flights back to wherever home might be; barely registering that after nearly a year of living, eating, working, and surviving together, those jet-lagged, bewildered minutes might be the last we ever shared. I sleepwalked through dinner with Chris on the Baltimore Harbor and a few hours in a hotel, my first proper bed since Christmas Eve. The next morning Chris left for a new posting in Texas, and I made the final leg of my journey alone.

I was the only military passenger on my flight. When the plane landed at the Tampa International Airport, no celebration waited for me. There were no screaming spectators or clicking flashbulbs, no important hands to shake. The air didn't fill with patriotic music or glitter blowing off home-made signs. I didn't need to elbow through throngs of camouflage to find who I was looking for.

I had been in transit for eight days, including nearly twenty-four hours of straight flight time. My internal clock remained stuck halfway around the world. My head groped through a thick fog to make sense of the sleek terminal and bright windows, the people in civilian clothes, the neon restaurant signs, the discordant symphony of music and newscasts and flight updates, the missing weight against my thigh where Janie should be holstered. I felt like I was on another planet.

Then I saw my family. It had been almost exactly eighteen years since our last deployment reunion. My six-foot-two brother was easy to spot at the end of the terminal ramp. Next to him his girlfriend held a small American flag, and my parents strained against the security rope. All my senses zeroed in on them. My mom yelled, "There she is! There's Lauren!" And I was seven years old and running into her arms.

Part Five

STRUGGLE *verb*

Definition: Common

1. Make forceful or violent efforts to get free of restraint or constriction.

2. Strive to achieve or attain something in the face of difficulty or resistance.

3. Have difficulty handling or coping with.

4. Engage in conflict.

5. Make one's way with difficulty.

Definition: in Military/War

1. An earned right, e.g., through combat.

2. A feeling to be pushed through or ignored, to "soldier on."

3. Conflict shifting from external (recognized/acceptable) to internal (less easily or readily recognized or accepted).

4. Inducing of guilt.

20

"Home"

I MUST HAVE BEEN AN AMUSING SIGHT, standing on the Florida sidewalk outside the Winn-Dixie grocery store, cursing and gesticulating at the Redbox movie rental machine in front of me.

"Rent! I said RENT!" I squealed, jamming my finger into the screen. The machine refused to respond. I had used Redbox once before, a year earlier when my parents were in Florida helping me pack my belongings pre-deployment. We'd passed up Blockbuster in favor of the new video vending machine, more for novelty than anything. "It's an interesting concept," my dad had mused. "I wonder if it will last."

Not only had Redbox lasted, it had multiplied. I'd noticed machines outside grocery stores all across the panhandle. They'd run Blockbuster out of town; this morning I'd driven to two of the old locations only to be greeted with shuttered doors and a sign: "This Blockbuster Video location is permanently closed. Thank you for your business." At one, the name had been partially scratched off the side of the building, like a ragged connex storefront at the FOB Gardez mall.

"I AM swiping up or down!" I growled. "I'm swiping up AND down! What more do you want?" I kicked the machine for good measure. The exertion made me cough. Though I'd swapped the altitude and dry air for sea level humidity more than a week ago, Afghanistan still clung to my lungs. "Stupid fucking thing," I sputtered. I couldn't recall if my dad had done anything special with his credit card when he'd completed last year's rental. A year felt like a lifetime. Blockbuster had gone extinct. At movie theaters, entertainment seemed no longer acceptable in two dimensions. My sister had twin girls. My grandfather had cancer. My old slider cell phone was declared obsolete (as were my MP3 player and my laptop). In Tampa, my brother showed off how he could wiggle his finger across the touchscreen of his new smartphone and make a coherent text message magically appear. He laughed when, eyes widening in amazement, I asked, "How does it know what you want to say?"

Upon deployment, I resigned myself to missing a year of life events, and I did: Shavonne's pregnancy and the birth of my nieces, the wedding of one of my oldest friends, Matt's twenty-first birthday, Thanksgiving, Christmas, and New Year's. I never thought to anticipate playing catch-up to a year of technological advancements as well.

Finally, the machine spit out my DVD, one of the *Twilight* movies. I expected it to be bad, but I didn't care. I just needed to not think for a couple hours. I climbed into my Toyota Corolla, with the "FREEDOM ISN'T FREE" bumper sticker that I'd plastered on the back windshield years ago, believing I understood the sentiment. The driver's seat felt foreign. Despite earning my Humvee driver's license at Camp Atterbury, I'd never operated a vehicle in Afghanistan. Chris had been my chauffeur during mid-tour leave, chugging our little rented Peugeot up and down the Alps while I read or slept. Matt borrowed my Corolla during my absence, and it was waiting for me when I arrived in Tampa. "I put all your radio presets back in," he said, handing me the keys.

In the pop culture realm, music left the most catching up to do. I'd had access to movies in Afghanistan—at least the grainy, bootlegged variety—but the top forty radio loop I'd deployed with had long since fallen off the charts. Half the artists were unfamiliar. Two in particular had stormed the music world in my absence. I encountered the woman who called herself Lady Gaga in the grocery checkout line, staring at me from a photo teaser on a magazine cover. She had bright yellow hair and wore what looked like cellophane wrapped in concertina wire. I gaped at the image until the cashier repeated my total for the third time. Then there was the teenage phenom. I heard his name before I heard his music. The first time a song of his played on my car radio, I assumed the singer was a woman. When the radio announcer named the artist, I exclaimed out loud, "*That's* Justin Bieber?!"

Pulling out of the Winn-Dixie parking lot, I merged haltingly onto the main highway. At least this stretch of road remained familiar. Farther east a new multi-million-dollar construction project had transformed the beachside strip into luxury condos and a boardwalk of restaurants and souvenir shops. I'd wandered through there a few days ago, stopping to read menus and run my hand over bright racks of sarongs, feeling not quite like a tourist. Heading west, though, the Gulf on my left, Hurlburt Field on my right, seemed almost like home. Almost. I'd been back to base briefly to sign paperwork and then promptly sign out for two weeks of "reconstitution time" in the local area. For the first time since arriving at Hurlburt in 2006, I needed a base map to find the public affairs office, which had relocated a few months after I deployed. Most faces there were new too.

Just past the base I turned down a cul-de-sac of cute two-story houses. The driveways were all empty, their owners still at work. Part of me felt eager to get back to work as well. My natural inclination pulled me to do what I'd always done and leap in headfirst, let the job consume me, give me direction and purpose. But I was also afraid. Not the excited fear of a new unknown, but fear of confirming what I thought I now understood: I wasn't changing the world. My job was both less clear-cut and packed with greater implications than I'd been able to fathom from my air-conditioned office on the Gulf Coast.

And yet, maybe that was just my deployment hangover talking. That was IO and that was Afghanistan. PA was a job I did well. I was comfortable at Hurlburt Field. The stakes were lower. I would be supported by a whole public affairs team. What I said, or didn't say, wouldn't have international implications. My job wouldn't be life or death. At the same time, I didn't want to return to work at all. "I wish they could continue to pay me to do nothing!" I joked. In truth, though, nothingness didn't suit me. As much as I feared what might be looming on base, this purgatory of waiting was worse.

I would reflect on those first two weeks back as a period of numbness. After a frenzied week-long tour of the Orlando theme parks with my family, I'd returned to the panhandle and spent the first couple days "reconstituting" by driving aimlessly around town and puttering aimlessly around the mall. I killed an afternoon in the cat adoption section at PetSmart. My cats remained in Seattle, and I might have brought home a second litter if I had an actual home, not just a borrowed room at a friend's house. I bought almost an entire new wardrobe. My storage unit contained two closets worth of clothes, and I had a full suitcase to tide me over until I could unpack. Clothes shopping just seemed easier, more fulfilling than other activities. Wearing anything besides boots and camouflage felt immensely satisfying. After a year as a soldier, clothes could re-brand me. In a cute sundress, I looked normal, even if I didn't feel that way. The town didn't quite fit me anymore, but a pair of designer jeans did. Ironically, as soon as I got "home," I put on the same Eeyore pajamas I'd worn in Afghanistan.

Home was my friend Alsbeth's guest bedroom. I would stay there until she left for a posting in Japan. A medical officer at Hurlburt, Alsbeth became one of my first friends in the area, and now she was one of the few who remained—at least for another month. Alsbeth and I had attended concerts together, taken road trips, run 5Ks, spent weekends partying until the sun came up and Mondays exchanging regretful texts from opposite sides of the base. We even deployed to Afghanistan at the same time. Before we reported to our separate versions of Army training, she'd joined me in the prophetic meeting where we were advised to "embrace the suck." We held a joint going away party at the local Irish pub. Once in country we emailed frequently between our Afghanistan FOBs, swapping news about the various layers of our realized suck, lessons learned, the food and people we missed, and the kind of so-stupid-it's-funny jokes that reach new levels of hilarity in a war zone.

Coming off a six-month deployment, Alsbeth had been home three months by the time I returned and had graciously offered her spare room while I figured out a more permanent living situation. I was of course grateful for the space, and I had looked forward to talking with Alsbeth, as old friends and as newly returned soldiers. I thought she might get some of the inside jokes and share some of the frustrations. Maybe I could talk to her normally, which I seemed to have lost the ability to do with others. As much as I wanted to rip it away, my brain lingered in Afghanistan. I had trouble following conversations on any other topic, yet when Afghanistan came up I could only babble erratically, my mouth and my head hopelessly stuck on different continents.

I'd first noticed the disconnect the day my flight arrived in Tampa. My parents, brother, and I went to dinner with Matt's girlfriend and her family. I was exhausted but eager to meet them. The young couple had been together nearly a year; this marked a critical step in catching up on Matt's life. I was excited to wear civilian clothes and go to an American restaurant with real silverware, even though I wouldn't need silverware to eat pizza. I was very excited for pizza.

I held up through the initial introductions, the awkward hugs and welcome-homes and thank-you-for-your-services, dazed but smiling until my cheeks hurt. At the restaurant I sank into the padded booth and savored each glorious bite of gooey mozzarella, spicy sausage, fresh peppers, and crispy crust. The meal seemed to languish in luxury. Programmed by the frenzy of the Gardez dining facility, I finished well before everyone else. Staring at my empty plate, it hit me: I had nowhere to go. No meeting to rush off to. No daily reports to file. No night-before mission intelligence brief. No weapon to clean and hope I wouldn't need to use. Elation swung quickly to anxiety. I had *nowhere to go*. My heart hammered. The air conditioning blasted but sweat bloomed on my forehead. I wrung my napkin beneath the table, wishing I had the grip of a rifle to steady my hands. What was wrong with me? I didn't want to be holding a weapon. I didn't want to be in Gardez. I wanted to be here. But I felt trapped. The others chatted and laughed around the table. Their presence and their voices surrounded me. They made eye contact, directed conversation at me, acknowledged my returned words and gestures, but I remained separate, as if I were a movie character inserted into a scene from a different movie where I didn't belong. This scene had played without me for a year. It would keep playing whether or not I was here.

The group circled plot points I couldn't track. They talked about an earthquake in Haiti, the dismal economy, the recent Winter Olympics, the movie *Avatar*. Then suddenly the scene zoomed in on me. "So, Lauren," Matt's girlfriend's mom said, "I'd love to hear about Afghanistan. You were working directly with the locals? That must have been very interesting."

"Um, yeah," I stammered over my thumping heart. "Interesting is a good word for it." I let out a forced little laugh. "Um . . . It was . . . long . . .? Not a vacation destination I'd recommend." I chuckled again. Heat crept into my cheeks. "We were there for the second presidential election, which was interesting." *Where did that come from?* I grasped for talking points.

My brain felt scrambled. "Yeah, so we were sort of working with the locals, in the sense that we were capacity-building. Not like hands-on building schools and stuff but more working with contractors so they can build the schools. Mentoring government officials. That sort of thing. Like, helping them help themselves." Then I added, mumbling into my plate, "Easier said than done."

"And you ran training programs," my mom prompted.

I jumped on her lead too eagerly. "Yeah! Well, not ran them, but we sponsored civics training programs so women could learn about their rights. You know, they have a constitution but eighty percent of the population is illiterate so they can't read about their rights, or even if they can read they might not have access to it, so they don't know that they *have* rights. Like, it's not OK to beat your wife . . ."

I kept rambling. My mind flipped through storyboards from civics training, carpentry and welding classes, a midwife graduation ceremony, splicing the sound bites together on the way to my mouth. Then I launched abruptly into politics and the troop level discrepancy between Iraq and Afghanistan and the extremists' perversion of Islam and the Christian interpreter named John who worshipped at the little white chapel. Then, just as quickly as I'd accelerated, I ran out of steam. "It's just a very complicated situation," I said.

In the ensuing silence, my dinner companions started at me wide-eyed.

"So," Matt's girlfriend's mom finally said. "Is it worth it? What do you think is the way forward from here?"

The words skipped right over my brain this time. "I think we need to cut our losses and get out." It was the first time I'd said anything like that out loud. The confession fell like an elephant on the dining table.

My face must have indicated I'd hit my limit. The girlfriend's mom nodded and said, "It sounds that way," and the conversation shifted elsewhere. A few minutes later I excused myself to go lie down in the car. I curled up in the back seat, feeling the weight of exhaustion and so many things I couldn't name, and I cried until I drifted into a brief sleep.

Despite my intentions, I didn't talk much with Alsbeth. It was easier to retreat to my borrowed room, to movies and seclusion. I'd planned my afternoon Redbox rental excursion so I'd get back to an empty house. I called Chris, as I did most evenings, though I didn't feel like chatting. He'd recently told me he wasn't a phone person. "Well, in a long-distance relationship that's kind of a critical element!" I'd snarled. "Can you at least try?" To his credit, he was trying. Now I was the one itching to hang up. Chris's voice invaded my solitude. Every petty little thing that had started to annoy me in Afghanistan amplified across the phone line. I bristled at his unusual vocal inflections, his bleating Popeye laugh. Instead of making me laugh, his cheesy jokes grated on my nerves. I snapped when he pried into who I was hanging out with, knowing he was imagining other men.

More than anything, I just wanted to be alone. In hindsight, I recognize my reclusiveness as an indicator of depression. At the time I reasoned that I hadn't had much privacy in the last year or much opportunity to relax. A lot of people came back from deployments and yearned to stay active because they missed the sense of purpose. I felt the opposite, like I'd filled my productivity quota for the next several months and needed to just *stop*. The problem was, of course, that my brain always kept moving.

21

Death

I WAS HOLED UP IN ALSBETH'S SPARE ROOM when, after nine months in Afghanistan and nearly one more back on American soil, the thing that had been chasing us, the thing we feared, arrived.

Death. It didn't' come from a war zone. It wasn't caused by insurgents. Death happened on vacation, on a country road outside Edinburgh, Scotland.

I had last seen Eli and his wife, Amanda, the fellow Air Force civil engineer, when our flight home stopped briefly in England, where they were stationed, before heading to the U.S. Chris and I hugged them goodbye and watched them walk, hand in hand, down the concourse. They both looked exhausted, but they grinned at each other, obviously relieved to be home, so obviously in love. I held their faces in my mind three weeks later as I read Eli's email.

"On our R&R trip to Scotland, Amanda and I were in a terrible car accident," he wrote. "She's in very bad condition and at this point needs a miracle. Please if you can find a spot in your prayers, please include Mandy."

I remembered the adoring glances Eli and Amanda had exchanged when our PRTs crossed paths at Camp Atterbury, the handholding under the table in the dining hall, an evening stroll when Chris and I intruded on a private moment and couldn't help but pause and admire their cuddled forms on the bleachers of the base baseball field. I thought of the way the stress and crankiness melted from Eli's face when he spoke of his wife, how his voice softened when he called her from the adjacent engineering office.

I hadn't talked to God since that February morning in the Gardez chapel, but I slid off the bed onto my knees and prayed with everything in me.

I asked my Bible study group to pray too. They assured me that God has a plan and does everything in perfect love.

A few days later, Eli emailed again: "Amanda's condition was very bad and in the end there was nothing that could be done. She left us on a sunny day."

I read the email three times. It didn't make any sense. How could God be with Eli and Amanda in Afghanistan, getting them through separate deployments, and bring them home together safely, only to desert them? I had Googled the details. On the road in Scotland, their car tire exploded. Amanda had survived an IED blast in Afghanistan only to die on vacation when her car tire fucking exploded.

I stumbled out of the room and down the stairs, blubbering with tears. Alsbeth looked up from the couch where she was watching TV with her boyfriend. "Oh my God, Lauren," she said. "Are you OK?"

"Amanda died," I sobbed. "She fucking died." Alsbeth hurried to my side, where I stood frozen on the bottom step. "The wife of one of my teammates from Afghanistan," I said. "She was deployed too. Then they went on vacation and their car tire fucking exploded and she died." I let out a wail. "Oh Eli! Poor Eli!"

"Oh Lauren, I'm so sorry," Alsbeth said. Her arms twitched for a hug. Her face contorted with concern. "That's terrible. Is there anything I can do?"

I looked at the door. "No, I just need to . . . I need to . . . go somewhere."

"OK, let me know if you need anything."

But I was already gone. I got into my car and turned onto the highway, driving too fast. The road bottlenecked with weekend beachgoers and spring breakers, gawking at the Gulf on one side and Hurlburt's runway on the other. I would go back to work for the first time Monday morning. I continued past the flight line, past the downtown strip of bars, past the tattoo parlor where I'd been branded a year earlier. I didn't know where I was headed until I pulled into a dead end behind an apartment complex where a friend used to live, where a wooden slat pathway led to a secluded stretch of beach. I staggered down the trail, collapsed into the soft sand, and cried.

By the time I returned to Alsbeth's house, she had left for the evening. I texted Chris, "OMG babe, Amanda died!" because I needed to tell someone who would understand, who knew Amanda in the brief but poignant way I did. He texted back: "I saw that. So awful. Poor Eli. I'm here if you want to talk." I didn't respond. I didn't call my parents. I said nothing more to Alsbeth. Maybe I felt I didn't deserve to hurt so deeply. After all, death hadn't come for my family. *I* wasn't the one who'd been betrayed by God. For whatever reason, I made an agreement with myself to grieve alone.

Monday morning, I reported to Hurlburt Field before sunrise for the PA office workout. At the back of the crowd, I moved trancelike through stretching and calisthenics. Then everyone took off for a run and I moped to the gym to ride the stationary bike and nurse my nagging knee pain. I wondered how the new airmen saw me. Perhaps they had heard stories about the jovial, pseudo-sadistic marathon-running/triathlon-competing workout leader lieutenant. The person they met now was haggard and gimpy.

Later, I organized my new desk, a spare workstation jammed into the conference room, a temporary arrangement since my future was uncertain. Approaching four years at Hurlburt, I was due for my next assignment—or I was done with the military. I was almost positive it was the latter, but I didn't tell anyone. Not yet. I wanted to hold off talking to people until I had to. I took my time setting up the desk space, avoiding interactions as much as possible. My computer account had been disabled in my long absence. My phone line wasn't yet hooked up. Through in-processing appointments, meetings, and introductions to new staff, I went through the motions.

Then on Friday, death came again.

Before Afghanistan, I'd gotten used to the uncanny way shit always happened at four thirty p.m. on a Friday. The routine became a caustic joke. As we packed our bags, shut down our computers, confirmed weekend plans, that's when the local military beat reporter called requesting an interview for a breaking news story (deadline five o'clock!), or when a hurricane started barreling straight for the panhandle, or an angry civilian called to complain that an aircraft was flying too low and disturbing her horses. This time the call came from the base commander's office as a cryptic message: something happened downrange, command meeting at 1700 hours.

My boss's face creased with the same preemptive fatigue I felt. Mine overlayed the bone-deep post-deployment exhaustion that I still hadn't managed to shake. My boss and I usually attended command meetings together, for company as much as business. When the pilots and logistics officers started discussing operational aircraft movements, frag breaks, and chalk loading times, she nudged me with her elbow and gave a look that asked, *What are they talking about?* and I shrugged in reply. I'd missed her companionship during Paktia's grueling election meetings. We had a practical reason for our tag-team as well. As the public affairs chief, my boss needed to be informed about any major incident involving base personnel or equipment, but her schedule hinged on two kids who needed to be picked up after school and ferried to a variety of activities. I, the next in command, had nothing but leftovers, a rom-com, and, previously, my cats.

Just before five o'clock, the two of us joined a procession of colonels and senior enlisted advisors entering the secure command center. We dropped our cell phones in a basket in the atrium and then continued into the windowless room. This marked the first time I'd been inside since returning from Afghanistan. The faces had changed, each replaced by a matching uniform with matching rank. Even the worry lines looked familiar. But I missed the friendly smiles of recognition, the hollers of "Hey, L-T, how's life in PA?"

No one smiled on Friday, April 9, 2010. There would be no playful ribbing from my boss. A slide projected at the front of the room settled the crowd into a morbid, all-business mode. The slide flashed two lines in bold print: A CV-22 crashed in Afghanistan. Two wounded. Two KIA.

I stared at the letters. KIA. Killed in Action. In Afghanistan, I'd seen the acronym in official paperwork, in newspaper clippings, in contingency planning documents, and far too often in my PRT email newsfeeds. Yet by some miracle of fate, death hadn't touched our team directly. Here at Hurlburt, I'd used "KIA" during base exercises, confirming fake information about fake casualties or a fake aircraft accident before passing the statistics along to a fake media representative on the other line. But there was no flashing red "Exercise Exercise Exercise" printed across the top of this slide.

Two KIA.

CV-22 crash.

My mind struggled to rearrange the letters into something that made sense. Something that didn't mean death. Something that didn't involve my friends.

It had been eighteen months, almost exactly, since I'd accompanied the unit that flew the CV-22 tilt-rotor aircraft, the 8th Special Operations Squadron, to the Republic of Mali. Eighteen months since I'd stuffed myself into the back of a C-130 cargo plane alongside the squadron members for the flight to Africa. En route, an aircraft needed repair, giving us a weeklong layover in a small Newfoundland village, where, by day, I hiked with my new friends to the top of an old lookout post, and, by night, I bought rounds of Irish car bombs for the Air Force-infested bar.

Once in Mali we'd huddled together in a makeshift operations center, swapping life stories while escaping the African heat. We'd gone running at sunset and collected gaggles of giggling local children scampering behind us. We'd meandered through the artisan bazaar and smoked hookah and danced salsa at a rooftop bar. I'd wheeled and pitched in the back of a CV-22, laughing when the gunner thrust his hands left, then right, to warn passengers of each sharp turn as we swept across the terrain; then they'd leveled out so I could scooch toward the open back door with my camera, the trail plane coming in so close I could see the pilot waving through my zoom lens. Eighteen months had passed since I'd led a *New York Times* investigative journalist around the steaming tarmac to talk to people I referred to as "some of the finest people I've ever met."

I wrote the series of articles that hung, pressed and framed, on the wall of the 8th SOS headquarters building. I attended the squadron Christmas party. I went for runs and out to dinner and got drunk with these men. One borrowed half my DVD collection before I deployed. Then I left. Then I got back. Then the call came at four thirty on a Friday.

At the front of the room, two men were talking. "Who was it?" one of them asked. I heard a name that sounded like "Germain," and I prayed I heard wrong. Then I cursed myself for praying for someone else's tragedy, for another broken family, another widowed wife.

We waited in tension until at five o'clock sharp the base commander confirmed: Major Benjamin Germain and Senior Master Sergeant Kevin Nguyen, KIA.

I didn't say anything out loud. The room fell into an eerie silence as death crept into our consciousness. This was different from the silence after the Camp Chapman CIA attack, not forged of anger or resignation, but a hollowness. The spaces between the letters: K. I. A. Nothing.

I couldn't hear what the commander said next because the silence was so loud.

Images reeled through my head: Jogging in Newfoundland, too early, the Irish car bomb revelry from the night before still heavy in my limbs. Ben Germain, another pilot, and I zigzagged up the side of a shallow mountain, steep enough to stress my spoiled sea level body. Near the top we entered a panorama of trees. I stumbled over loose gravel. Ben galloped easily ahead, impressively agile on much older legs, his tanned skin and salt-and-pepper hair jostling across my vision. At the top we enjoyed a dusting of snow and a view worth the climb. On the way down, we talked about running. Ben is a big runner. *Was* a big runner.

In the cockpit of a CV-22 with Ben flying. The dashboard held so many controls and levers, how could he keep them straight? A river snaked below around thatched-roof huts. I gawked and snapped photos, giddy at the tumbling views. Ben leveled out so I could maneuver back to the cargo bay. "Ready to switch career fields yet?" he asked with a smirk.

Going home, my first time on a massive C-5 cargo plane, sitting next to Ben. Someone baked cookies in the aircraft's oven, and everyone laughed when I exclaimed, "There's an oven here? No way!" We ate chocolate chip cookies and talked about music. Ben admitted to liking Katy Perry, blaming his teenage daughter. More laughing.

Silence.

In the Hurlburt Command Center, our collective mourning was brief. We all had jobs to do. My job would be different from exercises. Like the civilian casualties in Afghanistan, the press release would come from the International Security Assistance Force. There would still be phone calls and media queries to prepare for. Hurlburt Field was one of only two bases that flew CV-22s, so speculation would quickly lead to us. We wouldn't release names, not initially, just the line we practiced so often: "Names of those killed and injured are being withheld pending next of kin notification."

The base commander reminded us how important that notification would be. "We only get one chance to do this," he said. "We need to do it right."

Like "just in case" letters, my experience with next of kin notification was limited to movies. I had watched Colonel Hal Moore's wife in *We Were Soldiers* take it upon herself to carry the envelopes door to door, to witness heartbreak firsthand, over and over again. I knew the process happened outside Hollywood too. Heartbreak lurked behind each news article announcing a KIA, the Department of Defense casualty statistics that formed a sidebar to every discussion of war, the seventeen portraits on the FOB Gardez conference room wall, and the names etched into the memorial outside the Hurlburt Field chapel. Heartbreak sat in the front row of every memorial service I attended on base while I escorted news media who focused not so much on the tragedy, but on the heroism, selflessness, and sacrifice, the catchphrases of war.

I'd always known heartbreak existed, but I had the privilege of distance. I detached myself from the faces behind the statistics and the grief behind the names. I bought into the media catchphrases; the men and women had died honorably serving their country in a just and important war. Now, faces swam like holograms across my vision. Ben, Amanda, the seven CIA agents, the pregnant Afghan woman, the seventeen Fallen Comrades of Paktia Province.

My boss stood up beside me. "I guess we'd better get ready," she said. "It's gonna be a long night."

I volunteered to brief the casualty notification teams two hours later. I didn't want to sit in Alsbeth's spare room and think about all those faces. Long before seven o'clock, I arrived at the briefing room, a stack of freshly printed media information sheets in my hands. I wasn't the only early arrival. On the way in, I passed one of the few familiar officers left on base, the tall blonde chaplain with the southern accent who always smiled. He wasn't smiling now. We exchanged solemn greetings. I didn't ask, but he told me he had two dress uniforms. He kept one hanging in his office on base, just in case he needed to change quickly. In case he needed to stand on someone's porch to shatter a family's life. He looked down at his jacket when he spoke, as if resenting the uniform for what it meant.

Inside the room wasn't quiet, like I'd expected. Some men sat in pockets of silence with their heads down, lost in memories, in grief, in what to say when the door opened, in knowing there was nothing they could say. Yet I found clusters of something else too, something that almost felt like happiness. In one of these clusters, I saw Major Theo Ridley. He looked up when I approached.

"Hi, sir," I said. "I'm so sorry about Ben."

"Hi, Lauren!" He greeted me with a surprised smile and then pursed his lips and nodded. "Thank you."

Major Ridley, another pilot from the 8th SOS, would serve as the family friend on the four-man casualty notification team for Ben's wife and three children. His was the comforting face they would find above the sea of crisp blue uniforms. He would be the one they would hug, look to for confirmation, run to, scream at, the one whose uniform would be stained with tears.

I joined the group as someone recounted a story about Ben that made everyone laugh. More stories followed. I told them about eating cookies on a C-5 and extolling Katy Perry. "I was like, 'You're not supposed to like Katy Perry, you're *old!*'" I said. The others laughed.

"Yeah, that's the influence of a teenage daughter," Major Ridley said. His face fell at the final word. A daughter. A *fatherless* daughter.

At seven o'clock, the base commander addressed the room. He had known both Ben and Kevin. He understood, on a personal level, the weight of what was about to happen.

A third notification team was there to stand on the porch of the family of one of the two injured airmen, a young man who the commander assured us was stable. The team for the second injured airman would come from elsewhere and knock on a door without a family friend to notify out-of-town parents that their son might lose a leg, or he might not survive. I wondered if tragedy or limbo would be harder.

When my turn came to brief, the handouts shook in my hands. "I'm Lieutenant Johnson from public affairs." I caught Major Ridley's eye and steadied my voice. "I just want to let you know that we are here to support the squadron and the families in whatever way we can. The families will probably be contacted by the media when the names are released, and because they're civilians they're not restricted in talking to the media, and we encourage them to talk if they want to. Some people find it helpful to talk and pay tribute to their loved ones. But if they don't want to talk or if they want someone to speak for them or to help them handle the attention, public affairs can be their liaison. So, I have some information sheets you can give them to read through, with our contact information."

The words sounded shallow. I'd met Sergeant Nguyen in Mali, I considered Ben a friend, but that was nothing compared to the connection the men around me shared. I passed out the flyers. Black and white printing contrasted sharply with the blaze of emotions on each face. The teams filed out, twelve fluttering pieces of white paper. Three cars to three porches. Three doors to three families who didn't know they were waiting for their lives to change.

The base was quiet the following morning, a Saturday. Streetlights flashed in their weekend mode. I eased my car through the empty roads. Parking lots, usually a chaotic scene breeding fender benders and road rage, lay vacant. Except at the 8th SOS. I pulled my Corolla into the first free spot and walked through the double doors into corridors I knew well. Immediately, I found friends. We hadn't seen each other since before I deployed. We hugged. Someone said, "This is not how I wanted to see you again."

Major Ridley appeared, this time in his green flight suit. He shook my hand. "How are you, sir?" I asked, realizing immediately it was a ridiculous question.

"Hanging in there," he said. "Last night was rough."

Slowly—shaking hands, exchanging hugs, issuing condolences—I made my way to the auditorium, where the spouses of the deployed squadron members waited. I studied their faces as I shuffled down the aisle. They were frightened, expectant. They must have assumed that I, a person in uniform, knew why they were here. Did they have any idea? In the wake of last night's squadron recall and shutdown of deployed communications, had the rumor mill churned? Did they take stock, notice the absence of Mrs. Germain and Mrs. Nguyen?

I looked away and chose a seat in the far corner. I picked at my fingernails, traced patterned figures on my camouflaged pants. I took a drink from my water bottle to gulp down the pounding of my heart. My heart thumped in my throat and in my head; it burned behind my cheeks and eyes. Whispers fluttered across the aisle. I could feel the expectant stares.

The whispers stopped when the base commander entered. He walked more slowly than usual. At the front of the auditorium, he addressed the crowd. "Thank you all for being here," he said. "I know you're anxious for news, so I won't delay. There was a CV-22 crash in Afghanistan."

Gasps.

"Two airmen from this squadron were injured and two were killed."

Horrible, choking gasps. Hands to mouths, to each other's arms.

I closed my eyes. I saw Ben's face.

A desperate scream cut across the room. "Who?"

"The two killed were Major Benjamin Germain and Senior Master Sgt. Kevin Nguyen."

Sobbing. Cries of "Oh, my God!"

I blinked back tears. I couldn't bear to look at the audience, so I focused on the commander with his practiced poise. He listed the injured: one stable, one still critical.

"This is going to be a tough time for the families, and for all of you," he said. "And I will be here, and the base will be here to support you with whatever you need. Unfortunately, this is something we have a lot of practice with."

Other speakers followed. The squadron's director of operations announced that the deployed unit was standing down for twenty-four hours to honor the dead. Then they would resume flying, continue the mission, do their jobs. That's what Ben and Kevin would want, he said. *Is it?* I thought. *Or is that what you would want them to want?*

A representative from the Airman and Family Readiness Center gave a phone number people could call if they needed to talk. Social workers and chaplains would be standing by.

Then it was my turn. I stood on shaky legs. The retractable seat swung upward with a dramatic *thwamp*. The sound startled me, and I froze momentarily before walking, turning, and looking, finally, at the crowd. A hurricane had swept across the first three rows of the auditorium. The spouses looked different from how I'd found Major Ridley the night before and from what I'd seen around the command center when we first heard the news, different from what I'd felt dart across my own face. This was raw and unfiltered. Here, they had no pretense of stoic professionalism. They didn't need to put grief aside while they did their jobs. They could let it overwhelm them. Reflected, their grief overwhelmed me.

"I'm Lieutenant Lauren Johnson from public affairs," I began, hating the tremor in my voice. No one looked at me with expectation anymore. I had nothing to offer them now. "I had the pleasure of working with both Ben and Kevin," I said. "They were great men, and this is a great squadron, and I know they'll take good care of everyone. Um . . ." I took a ragged breath. "I just want to let you know that public affairs is here to support you in any way we can . . ."

My voice trickled off. Welling tears contorted the auditorium into quivering lines. I fought back the moisture and told the hazy faces that my office could assist them with media interaction. I passed out flyers and then sat down quickly, batting away a tear had leaked onto my cheek, the only one I would let myself cry for Ben until several years later.

I don't know how long I sat in the auditorium after the commander left. I didn't want to stay in the place where thirty hearts had broken in unison, where they were still breaking across the aisle. I didn't want to hear the sobbing or the breathless exclamations.

"I can't believe it!"

"My God, the poor kids!"

I didn't want to stay, but I felt rooted to my chair. I didn't trust my legs to hold my weight or my eyes to avoid the anguished faces. Mom and her "just in case" letters pulsed at the back of my mind, my own fortune of averted heartbreak in the crapshoot of war. I scribbled in my notebook to look busy, to look competent, to focus on something. I wrote notes to myself on what to do differently next time, what to say and how to hold it together when I came back in two hours to brief another group of spouses, whoever couldn't make this morning's meeting. My handwriting slanted drunkenly across the page. I closed my notebook, capped my pen, then took a deep breath and lunged out of my chair. At the back of the room, a young sergeant stopped me. I recognized her as one of the briefers, the representative from casualty affairs. She offered me a tissue.

"You OK, ma'am?" the sergeant asked. "You seemed pretty shaken up there. Is this your first time briefing for something like this?"

I sighed into the tissue. "Yeah, and I knew one of the guys killed."

"Oh, I'm so sorry. That must be tough."

"Thank you." I crumpled the tissue and shoved it and my hands into my pockets. Suddenly I was freezing. "How about you? Have you done this before?"

She nodded. "Unfortunately, I do this all the time."

22

Crossroads

THREE WEEKS AFTER BEN'S DEATH, I flew to Seattle. The promise of the trip had been my lifeline. My first month back from Afghanistan hit me like an AED on a heart still beating, a quick succession of jolts to an already quaking life: Amanda, Ben, news of Grandpa's cancer, wavering in nomadic limbo. Alsbeth would leave imminently for Japan. I'd found a condo to housesit for a deployed friend, but not for another month, so I leased a furnished short-term apartment, all sterile white walls and beige furniture and the lingering scent of Pine-Sol. The apartment was off the same road as my former rental house. I kept unconsciously driving past my new address, my body drawing itself toward memories of a more stable past. Once, I got all the way to the old house before a red pickup truck and neatly trimmed hedges reminded me that this was no longer my place.

As expected, I'd received orders for my next assignment. If I stayed in the military, I would report to a small base in South Korea in eighty-seven days. After months of waffling, the orders pushed me to decisiveness. I had to commit to another year in a remote corner of the world or the end of my military career. I declined the orders. I would be a civilian by Christmas.

The evening I turned in my military separation paperwork I got an email from my IO colleague Alex. "We were right all along," he wrote. "Now I kind of wish we had fed something to the press." I clicked on the link from the *New York Times*, "U.S. Admits Role in February Killing of Afghan Women"[18]:

> KABUL, Afghanistan—After initially denying involvement
> or any cover-up in the deaths of three Afghan women during
> a badly bungled American Special Operations assault in Feb-

ruary, the American-led military command in Kabul admitted late on Sunday that its forces had, in fact, killed the women during the nighttime raid.

The admission immediately raised questions about what really happened during the February 12 operation—and what falsehoods followed—including a new report that Special Operations forces dug bullets out of the bodies of the women to hide the true nature of their deaths . . .

I felt the same hot swell wash over me as I had the day of the Gardez raid investigation briefing. "NATO officials have also rejected the allegations that the killings were covered up," the article said. I scoffed into my laptop screen. Near the bottom of the story, the condolence statement we'd lobbied for, two months late: "'We deeply regret the outcome of this operation, accept responsibility for our actions that night, and know that this loss will be felt forever by the families,' said Brig. Gen. Eric Tremblay, a spokesman for the NATO command in Kabul."

"Wow. Just . . . wow," I wrote back to Alex. "Well, I officially put in for separation from the Air Force today by declining my next assignment (Korea in July). This bullshit reaffirms that I made the right choice. I'm tired of playing the game."

I proceeded to get drunk, not for the first time since getting back but for the first time with purpose. Early the next morning I stumbled out of bed, a hangover coiling around my head and stomach, to find I'd redecorated. Beer bottles scattered like grim, flowerless vases. Candy wrappers crunched under my feet. DVD cases tiled the floor. The bulging duffel bag I'd unloaded from my storage unit vomited clothing into a colorful cotton heap. I stumbled to the bathroom to do some vomiting of my own, thankful to be living alone again, to not have witnesses.

On the other side of the country, my childhood bedroom looked just as I'd left it: autographed boy band posters on the wall, swimming medals and plaques lining the shelves, frilly rainbow curtains. My cats were as I'd left them, only fatter. The air hung thick with familiarity. On this brief trip the slice of consistency rejuvenated me. Down a cul-de-sac outside Seattle, home was still home—just the assurance I needed. In time I would detect the undercurrent of foreignness, a gap of *close but not quite* just large enough to tip me off balance. It would take longer still to reconcile that feeling, to find comfort again, but in a new way. The house was the same. It was me who had changed.

My family gathered at the same restaurant where we'd met almost a year earlier on my four days leave between Indiana and Afghanistan, minus a pregnant Shavonne and her husband. In a few days I would meet my nieces, the babbling six-month-olds proving the best distraction yet, all chubby cheeks and gummy grins. This time we were joined at the restaurant by Matt, who had flown up from college in Tampa, plus the undeniable aura of war.

If my war had come slowly, creeping in over collective years, Grandpa's was shock and awe. He'd been diagnosed with lymphoma just after Christmas.

We didn't want to worry you," my mom said when my parents broke the news a few weeks earlier. "Grandpa asked us not to tell you until you got back. You were dealing with so much." Dad nodded solemnly from across the restaurant table. I stared at the menu. The loopy cursive of "Sonny's Real Pit Bar-be-que," the latest stop on my eat-my-way-through-the-Panhandle welcome home tour, shifted in and out of focus. I said I understood. I asked all the appropriate questions. Internally I wracked my brain, trying to read between the lines of our deployed communication: The postcards from the Oregon coast in Grandpa's scratchy handwriting. The boxes of trail mix and Riesen chocolates. Grandpa's tears when I called during his eightieth birthday party. The joint signature at the bottom or each email, always "Grandpa Norm & Grandma Dot," an inseparable entity after fifty-eight years. How many times had I neglected to respond?

By May Grandpa had won several battles: with chemotherapy, radiation, tumor removal, low sodium, and hospital Jell-O. He'd reached a break in the fighting, for now. Mom and Dad said he looked healthier than he had in months. Still, the man entering the Seattle restaurant was not the grandpa I knew. He plodded slow and hunched. He'd lost much of the paunch around his midsection, and his cloths fit baggy on his shrunken frame. Under his trademark flat cap his face hung pale and gaunt. The corners of his mouth drooped in an uncharacteristic frown.

I felt moisture at the back of my eyes, but it didn't materialize into tears. Crying would be appropriate here. Since that single tear in the 8ᵗʰ SOS auditorium, though, my emotions had turned inside out. I cried at silly things, sometimes for no reason at all. I cried over misplacing my keys, running out of cereal, a flash of jealousy in Chris's voice on the phone, Disney movies (any movies, really), inexplicably craving Little Caesar's Pizza and pulling into the parking lot to find it closed. A friend posted a video compilation of military homecomings on Facebook, and before the first soldier's arms wrapped around his loved ones, I was weeping. I watched the video over and over, crumbling into fits of deep, guttural sobs that left my stomach aching. My body recognized what my brain didn't, that I needed to grieve for Ben, for Amanda, for the parts of me I'd left in Gardez.

When Grandpa saw me his mouth stretched upward, and I recognized my grandpa in his smile. "Welcome home, kiddo!" he said, surprising me with the force of his hug. "We sure missed you."

I could feel the sharp bones of his shoulders. He smelled of something medicinal. I spoke around a fist in my throat. "I missed everyone so much." I pulled out a chair at the head of the table, and Grandpa sunk down with a sigh. "How are you feeling?" I asked.

He shrugged. "Oh, you know, pretty tired."

I nodded, as if I understood.

"I'm chugging along," he said. "But how about you? You getting settled back in?"

"More or less," I said. "I'm a bit of a nomad at the moment. I'm really glad to be here. This still feels like home."

"Well, we're sure glad to have you here," Grandpa said. A twinkle flashed in his tired eyes. "When do we get to meet this gentleman of yours?"

"He'll be here with me in August for a friend's wedding."

"Oh good," Grandpa said. "We owe him thanks for looking after you over there."

"Definitely," I said. "I don't know how I would have done it without him. He's my favorite Afghanistan souvenir." Grandpa chuckled at what had become my tagline for Chris (to which he always responded, "Yeah, me and respiratory problems!"). In truth, redeployment had warped our relationship. Distance magnified our differences. We subsisted on phone conversations, and more and more the conversations were stilted. I'd kept Chris as my main emotional outlet, but our interactions had dwindled so steeply that I could no longer mitigate the flow. What had in Afghanistan been a steady drip with just the occasional spurt now shot through the phone lines once a night in a torrent. I needed to vent my insecurities, and Chris needed reassurance to quell his. He demanded the sound of my voice, instant replies to text messages. He feared I was ignoring him, I was gossiping about him, I was leaning on anyone but him.

We made plans to see each other every month: in Florida and Texas, a Caribbean cruise, the Army Birthday Ball, the New York City Veterans' Day Parade. Like milestones in Afghanistan, these visits gave me means to track the time. Each provided an occasion to look forward to—and also a source of mounting dread. Pitiful as it was, I'd established a routine in Florida: Get up, go to work, try not to think about Afghanistan. After work I got takeout, too tired to cook and too anti-social to spend more time in a crowded restaurant than it took to pay for my barbecue pork combo plate, and then I went home, watched movies, tried not to think about Afghanistan, went to bed, and tried to sleep with my brain whirring through Afghanistan. My existence was insular. Chris's presence demanded more exertion than I had to give.

"Are we going to make it?" he'd asked one evening during our last visit. We were in a cab, between a New Orleans music festival and our hotel. In a few blocks, a passing accusation about me flirting with someone else had exploded into a shouting match about trust and jealousy. I'd hung out a few times with a former boyfriend and wouldn't agree to not see him again. Chris wanted me to go to grad school in New York so he could see me when he visited his family. I told him I wasn't ready to plan my life around him. Outside drunken people stumbled laughing down the sidewalk. I wanted desperately to be like them, uncomplicated and free.

I turned to Chris, the anger on his face replaced with concern. I loved him, yet I was beginning to question the nature of my feelings. Was this love of marriage and kids, like he'd caught me off guard by mentioning? Or was my feeling more like gratitude? Chris had gotten me through the deployment; for that I would always be grateful. But did I still need him?

Was I being selfish for holding on thinking I might? Or was I afraid to let go because so many other things were already slipping through my fingers? Did I *want* us to make it?

The cab stopped in front of our hotel. "I don't know," I said. I got out and slammed the door, hoping Chris wouldn't follow me inside.

In the Seattle restaurant, Grandpa said, "We're all very thankful he was there for you." The twinkle flashed in his eyes again. "But don't expect us to go easy on him."

I smiled. "I'll make sure he's prepared."

Grandpa shifted in his chair and discomfort rippled across his face. He quickly steeled himself. "And what's this I hear about orders for Korea?"

"They wanted me there in July," I said. "I told them no thanks!"

My grandmother chimed in: "I would have told them 'Up yours!'" I laughed as the soft-spoken, mild-mannered, polite-to-a-tee woman plopped down in the chair next to Grandpa's. She slid her hand across the table and into his.

Grandpa let out a feeble, airy chuckle. "You made the right choice," he said. "The Air Force isn't what it used to be."

I nodded, as if I understood.

"So, I'll be done in December!" I said. "I'm looking at grad schools for journalism or creative writing. Who knows? It's nice to have options!" I'd latched onto that line like a PA talking point for whenever someone asked about my future. Options *were* exciting, but also terrifying. For the first time in my adult life, my future lay in front of me completely unplanned.

"You've always been such a good writer," Grandpa said. "We enjoyed your Afghanistan blog. We shared it with the folks at the RAO." My grandparents volunteered once a week at the McChord Air Force Base Retired Activities Office.

"That's very sweet of you," I said. "I didn't do a very good job updating it."

"Well, we all knew how busy you were," Grandpa said. He nodded, as if he really did understand.

23

War & Peace of Mind

A SHORT WEEK LATER, THE COMFORT OF SEATTLE LEFT almost the instant I stepped out of the airport, back into the thick Florida air. I quickly fell back into my old routine, by day staring at my office computer and hoping my phone didn't ring, in the evening ordering takeout and watching movies until I fell into a fitful sleep.

I couldn't stop myself from researching Afghanistan. Even if I didn't actively seek out news from the region, headlines found me anyway. My IO replacement, Captain Douglass, emailed twice to say her PRT had been attacked. The first attack came at a school site, flying bullets and rockets with kids all around. The insurgents hid in a mosque. Then an attack hit FOB Gardez itself, leaving two Afghan security guards dead.

In June, three months after my return, General Stanley McChrystal was removed from his position as International Security Assistance Force Commander after making controversial comments about the Afghanistan war in a *Rolling Stone* interview. Shortly thereafter, Defense Secretary Robert Gates published a memo tightening the reins on military/media interactions—like the Tweedle's media crackdown, but on a national scale.

July brought the WikiLeaks release of the Afghan War Logs, which revealed colorful details about Paktia's governor and the corruption scheme that wound through the province and much of the country. Leaked cables accused the governor of "arresting contractors at job sites and holding them until they pay bribes," "funneling money from bribes and drug and jewel smuggling operations to an insurgent network," and "corruption involving U.S. funds and actively undermining the Afghan government's counterinsurgency policy." Some of the cables referred to my PRT teammates by name.

Especially at night, in the chasm between distraction and sleep, I couldn't look away from the train wreck of Afghanistan. I'd been on the train. Maybe I'd even steered it. I'd at least been complacent in its steering. I was invested and I was culpable for whatever the train crashed into. I learned to fall asleep in front of the TV. Otherwise, I lay on the plush white bed of my short-term apartment staring at the stark white ceiling in the glow of the streetlight. In the eerie quiet, I thought about the ripples I sent in my IO job, imagining them joining with other ripples sent by other naïve soldiers and aid workers, feeding a tsunami that swept across the country, swallowing people like Ben and the seven CIA agents and the pregnant Afghan woman. I couldn't close my eyes without seeing their faces, or conjuring other nameless faces yet to be swept away.

One night in July, I hit rock bottom. For me, rock bottom wasn't a crazy bender that sent my life flashing before my eyes. My rock bottom was the apartment's living room floor. I wore my Eeyore pajamas. The end credits of a movie scrolled over dramatic music on the TV. The beige carpet scratched against my cheek, wet from a stream of tears. The tears had stopped, for now. I scanned the floor-level horizon: soggy tissues, candy wrappers, beer bottles, mounds of dirty clothes. Another pathetic night in a string of pathetic weeks. "What the fuck is wrong with me?" I whispered to the carpet.

Then louder: "What the fuck is wrong with me? What. The fuck. Is wrong with me?"

Then nearly yelling: "WHAT THE FUCK IS WRONG WITH ME?"

Yelling felt good. I rolled over onto my back and stared at the blank white ceiling. Chris's voice jumped into my head, from last month's visit to Texas. In his living room, the scene began, like many others, with my tears.

"Why are you crying?" Chris huffed.

"I don't know!" I said.

"This is getting a little ridiculous."

"I know!" I sobbed. "I don't want to be like this! I don't know what's wrong with me. I feel like shit. I'm just all . . . BLAH!" I wailed into my hands. "And I'm so—I'm so tired. But I can't sleep. I keep thinking about deployment stuff."

Chris's voice softened. He put his arm around me, and I leaned into his solid chest. "I do that sometimes too," he said.

"Really?"

"Yeah," he said. "I don't think I'm quite back to normal. I've been thinking about talking to someone. A chaplain or something. Maybe you should too?"

Gazing up now at my apartment ceiling, I responded: "Maybe I should."

The waiting room was meant to be comfortable. Yet walking through the door of the Hurlburt Field Mental Health Clinic a few days later, I felt anything but.

Base leadership had debated changing the center's name because of the belief that people with "mental health issues" shouldn't be on the front lines. A quick glance around confirmed the stigma. Five other airmen waited, all with downcast eyes. I'd never felt so exposed while wearing camouflage. In any waiting room in any clinic anywhere else I would have been anonymous, just another stressed out twenty-something. But you can't be anonymous with a nametag, or officer's rank. The silver first lieutenant bars on my collar were supposed to declare me self-sufficient, competent, composed; walking through that door seemed as good as admitting I wasn't.

I trudged with my head down to the welcome desk, a Plexiglas-enclosed counter between two closed doors. The young airman receptionist checked me in for my appointment, typing at a computer in a way that sounded anxious, like he feared I'd leap up on the counter and smash my fist through the Plexiglas. He rolled up a stack of paperwork to fit it through a hole in the window. I unfurled an eight-page Intake Questionnaire designed, "to help your provider obtain a comprehensive picture of you in an effort to develop a treatment plan that will best suit your needs."

"Thanks," I muttered and turned to the selection of chairs. They were upholstered in pale pink fabric, the same shade as the waiting room at my childhood dentist's office, a soothing veneer to induce calmness in a place known for discomfort and pain. I took a seat and began with Question One.

Briefly describe the primary problem/concern that brought you here today.

I hesitated, trying to find a brief way to summarize the last year of my life. No tidy PA sound bites would suffice. I wrote "Depression, anxiety" and moved to Question Two.

What led to your decision to seek help at this time?

Other than crying on the floor and screaming at my ceiling? I wrote, "Seeking advice/guidance for dealing with stress and overcoming anxiety."

The form then asked me to use a scale to mark how upsetting this concern was. On the right end of the scale, I checked "Very Severe." The mark looked melodramatic.

Approximately when did your problem begin?

The easy answer would be January 2009, when that overzealous, idealistic version of myself volunteered to deploy. Wasn't that when my life began to shift?

Or was it Afghanistan itself, June 2009? Sure, my deployment had its challenges. But I hadn't been in combat. I hadn't seen anyone injured or killed, except in Alex's photos. I hadn't been sexually assaulted. My pen hovered over the page. *I shouldn't be here.* I thought. *I don't deserve to be here. Fuck. Just write something.*

I scrawled "March/April" on the form. My problem began when I got home and everything was supposed to get better.

The next section asked me to rate different problems in terms of their seriousness.

-Have you experienced loss of interest in pleasurable activities?

I marked "Extreme problem." Again, it looked melodramatic.

-Sleeping difficulty?

Another "Extreme problem."

-Occupational problems?

Just a "Moderate problem" to break the redundancy.

-Feeling sad or depressed? Temper outbursts? Irritability?

Severe, Moderate, Moderate.

Then the form listed a series of questions I recognized to be a screening for Post-Traumatic Stress Disorder. By 2010, the military and the world were acquainted with the poster boys of PTSD, those so tormented by their time in combat that they couldn't function back in "normal life." Loud noises like fireworks triggered flashbacks. They couldn't sit by windows or with their back to a crowd. They woke up screaming at night. The media latched onto the extreme cases, the ones who snapped and beat their spouses or went on a homicidal rampage.

I was not like those people. I had only been on the fringes of violence, only seen death secondhand. My concerns were trivial. *I shouldn't be here. I don't deserve to be here.*

–What solutions have you tried that have been most helpful?

I stopped writing in Afghanistan.

With my knee pain, I couldn't run anymore.

I couldn't bring myself to talk to family or friends. I'd gotten used to keeping everything inside. I didn't want to worry anyone. Mostly, I felt weak and inadequate.

I wrote, "Nothing."

Barely reading them, I checked "No" by all the questions about alcohol use. The last thing I needed was a referral to another agency.

–Do you belong to any groups or organizations that are supportive and helpful to you?

"I used to go to church." I looked down at my left forearm, where the cross tattoo hid under my sleeve. I could barely remember the girl with the faith so strong that she branded herself before she deployed.

The final question on the form:

–How do you think we can help you with your current problem?

Make this war end? Make the suffering stop? Make me not care so much?
I wrote, "Help me learn effective coping mechanisms."

I signed the form, walked back to the nervous airman receptionist, and slid my paperwork through the hole in the window next to a sign that read, "We value your privacy, please let us know if there's anything you would like to discuss in private."

Back in my chair, I picked at my fingernails. Camouflaged figures moved through my periphery. Consumed by self-pity, I thought about all the ways I must be different from those around me. Surely, they'd experienced things more horrible than I had. I was lesser. Deficient. The mathematics of my history confirmed it: Frequent, drawn-out illness. The extra-long swimming tapers and the time cuts I still couldn't make. The weight of body armor converging on my knee. The dust and altitude and that still clung to my respiratory system. Crying when Mom deployed. Crying over the failed media training. Crying at the restaurant in Germany. Always fucking crying. And when I should have spoken up, my silence. The addition was simple: I was unfit for the military and certainly unfit for war.

I didn't make eye contact with the other patients, but I imagined each of them looking at me, scrutinizing my rank and nametag.

Then, "Lieutenant Johnson?"

I looked up from my frayed cuticle to find a dark-haired middle-aged woman propping the door open with her sandal.

I hadn't expected a civilian. I hadn't known what to expect, really, but definitely thought I would be seeing someone in uniform. The woman had a genuine smile, not the dip-stained snarl of the drill sergeant I'd conjured in my mind. Forcing my cheek muscles upward, I crossed the waiting room and held out my hand.

"Hi," she said, "I'm Phyllis."

Her handshake was firm and reassuring, her eye contact unwavering. I felt vulnerable, naked without body armor, without the filter of a camera or a press release or an intake questionnaire. I sensed the gaze of my fellow patients following me through the door. Phyllis led me down a sterile hallway, the clip-clop of her shoes keeping time with my elevated heart rate. She stepped through a doorway on the left and beckoned me to follow. Inside, she pulled a high-backed leather chair out from her desk, smiled, and motioned to an armchair by the door, identical to the seats in the waiting room. "Have a seat, Lieutenant Johnson."

The office differed little from my old PA office, or any other office on base. A computer and military ID card reader sat on top of the desk. White walls held posters of nature scenes. Florescent lighting reflected off Phyllis's glasses, and air conditioning tickled the hairs at the back of my neck. The room's familiarity steadied my shaking legs; I'd half expected to recline on a Freudian couch. I sat in the armchair. Phyllis closed the door behind me and turned on a white noise machine.

"So," she said, wheeling her chair closer to mine and peering over her glasses. "I understand you're feeling a little out of sorts." The glasses magnified her eyes. They were kind eyes, but I imagined them boring into me, dissecting all the ragged pieces of my character.

"Yeah . . ." I spoke in a way that implied more, but I didn't continue. I crossed my arms over my chest. I felt hot and cold at the same time, like the clammy jitters I used to get before a big swimming race.

"And you recently got back from a deployment to Afghanistan?" Phyllis flipped over the top sheet of my Intake Questionnaire. "About four months ago?"

"Yeah," I said, "In March."

"It's very common to need an adjustment period after a deployment," she said. "You've been in a very stressful environment for a long time. The things you describe here"—she motioned to the form—"difficulty concentrating, trouble sleeping, work feeling trivial. Those are all normal reactions coming after a not normal situation."

I nodded, though nothing about me felt normal. I didn't feel like myself, and I didn't feel like anyone else around me on this special operations base full of badasses. As we talked, that word kept coming up. My childhood was *normal*, I insisted, meaning happy, stable, without abuse. Never mind the blip. Phyllis agreed that my reactions to Mom's deployment were *normal*. Shavonne hadn't been so overtly upset, but everyone demonstrates emotions in different ways. Being different was *normal*. Phyllis's assertion that it was *normal* to struggle with adjustment after deployment, though; that leap was too big for me to take. I'd never seen Mom struggle, and she had a family to take care of. In the Saudi Arabia hospital, they witnessed death and injuries every day. They faced nightly scud missile attacks. Mom thought her deployment was a suicide mission. No one at Hurlburt Field seemed to struggle, and many had deployed multiple times in much more intense capacity than PRT IO. I justified Chris's confessed struggles with the recent death of an uncle, me heaping my burdens on top of his own. Plus, I dwelled on what he'd said later in our conversation about talking to someone: "I'll probably find a place off base. I don't want to take up the time and resources from someone who needs it more."

"You've also had a big disruption to your local support network," Phyllis was saying. "We need to help you start feeling less isolated." She scanned her notes. "You mentioned a boyfriend?"

"Yeah," I said. "He was deployed with me. He lives in Texas now."

"Did you confide in him while you were deployed together?"

I nodded. "Pretty much only him."

"And do you still confide in him?"

"I think so?" I didn't mean to add the question mark, but it hinted at a deeper truth. In Afghanistan I'd warned Chris that someday he would get sick of my emotional baggage. I feared that was happening now. I couldn't decide, though, if a part of me hoped it was. Part of me was getting worn out of him, too. "It's hard doing the long-distance thing after being together all day every day for a year," I said. "He's not really a phone person. And after I get back from work, I don't really feel like talking either. He's the one who encouraged me to make an appointment here, though."

"That's good," Phyllis said. "He obviously cares about you and has an understanding of what you need."

"I think so."

"I would also encourage you to talk to your parents." I could tell by Phyllis's body language that she thought this point was important. She looked at me more intensely than she had the entire appointment. If she'd been writing notes on the blackboard, this would be in all caps and under-lined. "Your family has always been close," she said. "That's always been an important line of communication for you. They've always supported you. That won't stop now. And," she added, emphasizing with a head nod and a raise of her eyebrows, "you might find your mom understands more than you can imagine."

I didn't take Phyllis's advice right away. That night I argued with Chris on the phone and fell asleep in a tipsy heap on the couch. A few days later, bolstered by a feel-good movie and two beers, I called my parents. With the first ring, though, all the stomach-twisting, throat clamping, voice-in-my-head screaming barreled back. I hadn't necessarily called with the intent of opening up, but with each ring I became more certain that I would blurt everything out whether I wanted to or not. Talking to Phyllis unlocked the door. Talking to Chris in the following days cracked it open. The phone was still ringing, and I sucked back tears.

"Don't pick up," I whispered. "Don't pick up. Please don't pick up."

No one was home. I cried myself to sleep.

The next night I called again. This time, my parents answered. I didn't tell them everything. I didn't tell them nothing. Little confessions burst out between sobs.

Afghanistan was really hard. Really complicated. So much harder than I expected . . .

There were things I didn't agree with. But I did them anyway . . .

I can't stop thinking about it. About everyone still over there. About the Afghans. About what I could have done differently . . .

Then everything that's happened since I got back . . . It's all just too much.

I've been struggling for a while . . . went to the clinic last week.

I just feel so helpless.

My mom was crying too. My dad's voice brimmed with emotion. "Oh, Lauren," they kept saying.

We went on like that for quite some time, until I heaved a sigh and said, "I'm sorry I didn't tell you sooner. I didn't want to worry you."

"Oh, Lauren," my mom said again. "It's our job to worry!"

"We can worry a lot less now that you're back home," my dad said. "Yes!"

"I can't wait to be back home for real," I said. "In Seattle. Just six more months."

"Yes!" Mom said again.

Then I started laughing. It was the kind of laugh that only comes when you're all emptied out inside, bubbling up from the pit of your stomach and surging through your chest. I laughed until my abs hurt. "I'm really glad I'm not in Korea," I finally said.

My parents laughed too.

When the laughter stopped, my mom said, "I remember feeling a lot of those same things when I got back from my deployment."

"Really?"

"Oh yeah," she said. "It was not an easy transition. I'd only had to take care of myself, and then suddenly I was back to being a wife and mom. They wanted me back working in your classrooms right away. Dad, bless his heart, had been a single parent for four months and wanted me back doing everything I'd done before. I just wanted to hole up and cry."

"I don't remember you crying at all," I said.

Dad chimed in: "She cried all the time!"

"I still do!" my mom said, and we laughed again.

That phone call wasn't a magical healing moment. Our conversation settled like hydrogen peroxide in a wound, stinging and foaming and disinfecting, making way for proper healing to occur. My parents were the ones most deeply entrenched in the blockade I'd built around my emotions. After them, everyone else was easier—still not easy, but easier. I talked to Chris with less suppression. We still fought frequently, would continue to do so, but the flare-ups were more subdued. My emotions themselves would start leveling out too.

The phone call also served another purpose. Talking to my parents was a catalyst for a conversation that would go on for years to come: an open discussion with my mom and often my dad, sometimes my siblings and grandparents, about our wars: how they'd affected us, all the ways they were different, and all the surprising ways they were the same.

24

One Step at a Time

I CANCELED MY SECOND MENTAL HEALTH APPOINTMENT and took emergency leave to fly back to Seattle. Less than three months after my visit in May, following an all-too-brief reprieve in Grandpa's war, I sat on the edge of a hospital bed in his living room. The bed didn't belong between the floral print couches where the Christmas tree always stood. White sheets looked too stark atop the plush brown carpet, next to the heavy furniture and dark wood trim around the bay window.

In an optical illusion, nearly all the people from the photos that lined the bookshelves along the back wall had materialized around the hospital bed. Grandma, Grandpa's sisters, who flew in from California, Grandma and Grandpa Home, Dad and his brother, my mom and aunt, the five grand-kids, and Shavonne's husband. At the center, Grandpa grinned around an oxygen tube and bounced the great-granddaughters, now nine months old, on his frail lap. The crowd left barely enough space for my dad to maneuver the camera. Never had a Christmas Eve or Thanksgiving gathering packed so many people into that room.

A year had passed since the family had come together in such an un-planned collective frenzy, for brunch during my unexpected four days of post-Indiana training leave. Before that you had to go back almost twenty years, to a snowy Christmas in 1990.

The next night I slept on the couch beside Grandpa's hospital bed, snapping awake when the springs creaked or he moaned in his sleep. Earli-er, before I tucked him in and nested into the cushions, I turned on my voice recorder and asked him questions I'd been meaning to ask for a long time. The lamplight basked Grandpa in a deceptive glow, softening wrinkles and diffusing the blue veins that now spread with such prominence across his bald head. His skin looked almost transparent. Medical equipment dripped and buzzed in the background. The grandfather clock reminded us, in fifteen-minute increments, that our time was limited. Grandpa's voice came out weak, but clear. His mind took leaps I couldn't follow, but I let it empty itself into my recorder.

He talked about his childhood and how as the oldest he worked to shelter his sisters from their father's violent alcoholism. When he joined the Air Force, Grandpa sent half his paycheck to his family every month. He told me how he met my grandmother during his first period of military leave. At a feisty eighteen, she hooked him after just one date. His wistful smile affirmed that fifty-eight years later he was still hooked.

Grandpa talked about being stationed in Italy and Germany and Greenland, how the lure of travel had launched a career in the Air Force. I thought of the collectible plates that lined the walls of the downstairs basement. I remembered sitting in the orange polyester chair and marveling at all the places my grandparents had traveled, deciding that someday I would go to those places too. I smiled when I realized, at twenty-six, how many I'd already seen.

At the end of his career, Grandpa told me, he had been nominated to represent the entire Air Force enlisted service as chief master sergeant of the Air Force. We reminisced about winning the "best dressed family" award at my Air Force commissioning ceremony—Grandpa, the chief; my mom, the Army lieutenant colonel; Grandpa Home, the Navy commander; and me, the beaming new lieutenant. Grandpa's throat rattled when he laughed. He told me how proud he had been of me four years ago at that ceremony when he rendered my first military salute. He told me how proud he was of me now. He mentioned the Korea orders and mumbled, again, that the Air Force wasn't what it used to be.

"I guess a lot changes in thirty years," he chuckled.

"A lot changes in four years," I said.

A lot changes in twenty-four hours. That was Grandpa's last lucid night.

I left a few days later. The next month I would return for his memorial service.

Before the memorial I sat down, and, for the first time since stopping my blog in Afghanistan, I wrote. The result was a poem about my memories of Grandpa. The poem was cheesy and sentimental and silly and rhyming, but the words came from a place I'd closed off. Grandpa, who had always been so supportive of my writing, wouldn't be there to see me into grad school. He wouldn't follow along with the new blog I would start there or read my first published creative piece, which, incidentally, would center on him. But I credit him with the nudge over that hurdle to start writing again. I like to think that was Grandpa's last gift to me.

I saw Phyllis a few more times at Hurlburt, each session unfurling a little more. Between moving into my friend's condo and unpacking my storage unit, grad school research, memorizing GRE vocabulary words, visits with Chris, plus mounting job obligations, the pace picked up so much that I simply didn't have time to constantly dwell on Afghanistan. Invasive thoughts hit me in sharp pangs when something triggered a memory, and sometimes for no reason at all. Tears remained constantly poised at the corners of my eyes. For the most part, though, what had previously been a screaming pain receded into a dull ache. The black cloud still lurked around me, but it was losing force.

In September, Afghanistan held their parliamentary elections, and Hollywood came to Hurlburt to film a few scenes for the new *Transformers* movie.

A few weeks later, the Miami HEAT NBA team hosted their annual training camp at Hurlburt Field, and national media camped out to get their first glimpses of the new power threesome Lebron James, Dwayne Wade, and Chris Bosch, including eight-times-a-day live broadcasts with ESPN. I described "Hell Week" to my IO buddies Alex and Markus in an email as "almost feeling like I was back in Afghanistan with the hours we were working . . . except I got to choose my oddly timed meals off a menu and sleep in a comfy bed at night, and I didn't feel suicidal and/or homicidal at any point."

While I scheduled final medical exams and filled out reams of military separation paperwork, Afghanistan released the Parliamentary election results to claims of corruption and fraud. I channeled my anger into packing, preparing my belongings once more to be shipped to my parents' house in Seattle.

For one of my last PA journalism assignments at Hurlburt, I interviewed the sergeant who had been critically injured in the April 8 CV-22 crash that killed Ben and Sergeant Nguyen. I volunteered to write the article because I felt connected to the story. Selfishly, I was also chasing some sort of closure, a fragment of a happy ending. The sergeant had made a remarkable recovery. I knew the facts, that the crash left him with, as I wrote in the article, "significant blood loss and multiple fractures to his back, face, both legs, left arm, and pelvis." He'd been airlifted out of Afghanistan and hooked up to a ventilator at Walter Reed Army Medical Center. From there, he endured fourteen surgeries, skin grafts, pins and plates, hours and days and months of excruciating physical therapy.

Sitting beside the sergeant in his wheelchair at the 8th SOS building where I'd witnessed heartbreak six months earlier, I studied the dark purple scars crisscrossing his left arm. I traced the shrunken, misshapen muscles and the patchwork of mismatched skin. The sergeant shifted in the chair, scrunching his brow and clenching his jaw, obviously in constant pain. I surged with anger on his behalf. The military nearly destroyed this man. They killed Ben and Kevin, shattered two families, and left the sergeant in a broken shell of a body. And for what?

Yet, the sergeant smiled when he spoke. He said things like, "I count little victories every day. Whether it's just getting up. The other day it was opening a door, doing not one but two laps on the track. It doesn't have to be something amazing." He could have been bullshitting me, putting on a strong public face. But I knew in my gut that wasn't the case. Bullshitters don't go from near dead and maybe never walking again to walking six months later. The sergeant said the goal that had been driving him was not just to walk, but to walk back through the doors of his old squadron. The 8th SOS had been the backdrop to unfathomable pain and hardship, but those weren't the lessons he took away. His lessons were comradery, duty, resilience, and pride. This wasn't the place that had broken him but one that had given him the strength to heal.

"It's amazing what the human body can take and how it can come back together," he told me.

Later, as I watched the sergeant lift himself from his wheelchair outside the open squadron doors, squinting against the sun and the pain; as he paused, hunched over, to steady himself and then looked up with a grimace of pure, intense focus; as he hobbled forward, leading his right side with a lean of his shoulder and then dragging his left foot forward to meet it, his left arm cocked stiffly at the elbow; as the hallway erupted in clapping and cheers and "Welcome Homes" and the sergeant's lips parted and widened into a grin; as he continued to hobble—*lurch, drag, rest*—down the length of the tile hallway, extending his good arm for an occasional careful hug until he passed through the interior doorway and under the squadron logo "With the Guts to Try," I knew the sergeant's words to be undeniably true.

25

Welcome to
the Real World

MY MILITARY CAREER ENDED AS IT BEGAN, with a drive across the country with my mom. This time, we made the trip in reverse and at a frantic pace to arrive in Seattle before Christmas. Unlike our last road trip, we did no sightseeing. We listened to audio books and took shifts behind the wheel and napping in the passenger seat. I watched the land whip by my window, 2,200 miles of the same, flat plains along I-10, and then 1,000 more miles north through Los Angeles traffic, northern California rain, and snow in the Oregon passes, a familiar leg we'd traveled on family trips to Disneyland, and one I'd taken so many times back and forth to college. Now the drive felt different, final, but also uncertain. I felt like I was going home, for real, for good. At the same time, I knew something new lay ahead. I just didn't know what, or where, or when.

Grad school application deadlines awaited me in Seattle. I thought of them vaguely as the plains and cities and mountains trickled by. I thought of the impending holidays and warmed at the promise of spending Christmas at home with my family—everyone except Grandpa Johnson. His absence grew as we moved up the west coast. Growing too, was an anxiety that bubbled beneath the excitement of returning home. I was eager to make up for lost time with family and friends, to get to know my nieces, to belatedly celebrate birthdays, Matt's twenty-first, and Brittany's wedding. Yet I worried at the gap between us, one that had nothing to do with geography. We'd all aged since I'd been gone. But we had grown up separately. What if we no longer recognized each other?

I regarded my mom beside me in the car, a profile I knew so well: so much of myself in the light eyes and fine, stick-straight hair we'd both long ago given up perming; the long slender nose and freckle-smattered complexion my sister shared. As always, Mom radiated easy humor and comfortable silence, all overlaid with her usual compassion. *Was the temperature OK? Did I want to pick the next audio book? When did I need a bathroom break?* She was the same mom who had carted me to swim meets and five a.m. workouts, back and forth to Los Angeles, and nine states in ten days four years earlier.

Now, though, I was starting to glimpse new layers to my mom. That initial phone call confession had peeled the curtain back for both of us. Neither felt ready yet to yank it open. On the drive we talked only briefly about post-deployment and post-military life, deterred by the confines of the car, the long days of the long trip, the exhaustion building in our minds, and the winter storm biting at our heels. I thought of the last of my school Veterans' Day assemblies where Mom spoke, my senior year, 2001, in front of my entire high school. The wounds from 9/11 gaped raw. The room swelled with patriotism, perhaps the first time since 1991—and the last time—I felt my classmates and I existed on the same patriotic plane. For once in her decade of assembly speeches, I had the privilege of introducing U.S. Army Lt. Col. Deborah Johnson. I don't remember what I said, only that I beamed with pride. I hugged her when she approached the podium and then took my seat and beamed some more.

In her speech Mom told some of her standard stories. She shared an anecdote of her favorite Iraqi patient who had lost a leg and had his other leg and both arms broken. She talked about living as a woman in a segregated society, carrying her gas mask everywhere, and practicing inserting IVs with gloves like oven mitts. In a tone to match the new era—and with more foresight than she could fathom—Mom talked about the people who went to war. Eighty percent of our military strength comes from the reserves, she said, from moms and dads and aunts and uncles and brothers and sisters who are not expecting to go to war. "Try to imagine suddenly having a family member or a friend whisked away into a combat zone," she said. "And think about what you can do to help support your friends who find themselves in that frightening situation."

After nearly a decade, I was beginning to recognize that the snippets my mom shared at assemblies were her talking points, selected and crafted for specific audiences. She chose the stories purposefully. She didn't want to reveal too much. She wanted to keep her emotions in check. Even so, she'd choked up behind the podium in 2001. From the audience, I, too, struggled not to cry. For sponges like us emotions never flow far from the surface, and they carry more force when they've been repressed.

As The Beatles thrummed through the car speakers, my mind drifted to other music and my drive home from school on September 11, 2001. I recalled the signs of "God Bless America!" and "United We Stand" and honking and pumping my fist, then bursting into tears when Lee Greenwood's "God Bless the U.S.A." came on the radio. In all the years of Veterans' Day assemblies and class discussions and military reunions, I'd never seen Mom listen to that song and not cry. Until the afternoon of September 11, I didn't realize it had that effect on me too.

Two months later I'd stood behind the podium at the front of the high school gymnasium for the Veterans' Day assembly, hugging my mom, my hero. I had completed my ROTC scholarship application just to see what happened, to keep options open, without any inkling that those options might include "Deployment" and "Afghanistan."

In December 2010 the scenery shifted outside the car, and I watched the tectonic plates of my own history shift, and shift again. I got Mom's hair and eyes, her spongy emotions, her swimming talent, her tittering giggle. War, I was starting to understand, was part of my inheritance too.

Mom and I arrived home five days before Christmas. I let myself be swept up by the spirit of the holidays, compounded by delirium and joy and twenty-four months without a proper Christmas, and then caught up in the fervor of a four-generation celebration. For a few blissfully busy days, everything was done as "we." Then began the long process of rediscovering "me."

Like Mom's blip, what I remember of those few months in Seattle comes in snapshots. My brain still reeled from the nine-month whirlwind at Hurlburt and the nine months prior in Afghanistan. Now I spun, ever more gracefully, into another vortex. The winds blew softer this time, around the stabilizing mass of home.

In my childhood bedroom, I spent days hunched over my laptop on the old heavy oak desk. The document on my screen transported me to Afghanistan. I'd finished my graduate school writing portfolio, but the stories kept coming. Through my laptop I teleported to training in Indiana, bursting through the booby-trapped door. Then I was staring out a grimy MRAP window as brown fields, brown qalats, brown mountains jostled past. I felt a lurch of fear, a shot of anxiety. A gust of wind swept past my bedroom window, and an instant later the chimes trilled on the back deck. A cat adjusted against my feet. The low hum of the TV downstairs prompted my parents' synchronized laughter, and the piney warmth of the wood stove seeped through the floor vent.

Between writing, I sat next to Mom at the kitchen table, or on the family room couch, or on the floor of Dad's office, a photo album splayed between us. I passed Mom a tissue, and she dabbed at her eyes. "Goodness," she said. "I've never told anyone that before."

She told me this: *The first night U.S. planes dropped bombs we sat in the hospital hallway in our chemical gear. Everyone expected retaliation, chemical warheads or scuds. I just sat there in my gas mask waiting. That's all we could do. Just wait. For the world to end.*

And also this: *I was so happy to be going home, but we were like, wait a minute, we're not finished here! It was like we were leaving the job half done.*

And this: *I cried so much when I got home. Putting my uniform on and going on a drill weekend felt like saying goodbye to my kids again. I felt so guilty for missing four months of your lives.*

This too: *I still think about them sometimes, my Iraqi patients. I wonder if they're still alive. I wonder what more I could have done.*

I cried too. I said things too. We revealed fragments of ourselves, plucking them out by handfuls or one at a time. We arranged them on the table or the couch or the floor and found that, across decades and countries and wars, they fit together, like jagged puzzle pieces.

By August, I had unpacked my belongings from Florida, their contents priced and bartered for at an epic garage sale. Some items had been repacked into the seven suitcases Mom and Dad would drag with me to Boston, where I would soon begin a graduate school program in creative writing. An entire suitcase full of purses and shoes made Dad roll his eyes. "Non-combat footwear diversification!" I proclaimed. He grunted and heaved the bag into the back of the SUV, but he was smiling.

Other items got shoved into the storage room, adding to the growing time capsule of our lives. They would live next to shoe boxes of old photos, piles of homemade holiday decorations, bins of old schoolwork, award certifications, and newspaper clippings. Between the three kids, we'd collected enough sports trophies to open a scrap metal factory. The twins would soon wear the Easter dresses sewn by Grandma Johnson and play with the stuffed animals clawing against plastic bags. Buried somewhere among the treasure were cards and letters from Mom's deployment. Now, I added my own.

The storage spilled into the adjacent room, Shavonne's old bedroom. That's where I put my footlocker, next to the bookshelf and behind the foosball table. Inside I'd folded two sets of camouflage uniforms, a pair of boots rigid with dust, my Gore-Tex rain jacket, a handful of Air Force gym clothes, my Air Force dress uniform jacket and slacks, a stack of ribbons, and the set of silver first lieutenant bars Mom handed down for my first promotion. I had to keep the uniforms for three more years until completing my inactive reserve obligation, just in case, like Alex's deployment recall, the Air Force needed me back. But I wasn't ready to give them up yet anyway, these tangible reminders of places I'd been and things I'd done that now seemed alternatively all-consuming and surreal.

I opened the box one last time and traced my finger across the stitching on my camouflaged blouse. Double captain bars. "U.S. Air Force." "Johnson." Then I shut the lid, snapped the latches closed, and shoved the box snug beside the bookshelf. Industrial olive drab clashed against the pale pink of Shavonne's walls, next to stacks of *Babysitter's Club* and the *Chronicles of Narnia*.

Over time, the footlocker will be absorbed into the room, pillows and blankets tossed on top, plus the inevitable coating of cat hair. As years pass, the box will be pushed farther back to make space for pack-and-plays and the twins' toys, the new lives that have spawned in and out of this home; obscured, but never completely covered, a part of the room, but not commanding it.

One of my cats followed me into the room. I picked him up and he squeaked a protest before nuzzling into my neck. Then I turned, switched off the light, and closed the door.

Epilogue
(AUGUST 2021)

I JOLT AWAKE, THINKING OF BABIES. With two-month-old twin daughters, my life is a constant cycle of feeding, diaper changing, soothing, swaddling, washing bottles and breast pump parts, snatching at fragments of sleep. A baby hovers over me now, in my husband Ryan's arms.

"What time is it?" I mumble.

"Early."

"OK. Give me a minute to get set up."

On the living room couch I nest into my oversized twin nursing pillow. A minute later Ryan appears with baby number one. He passes her gently to me and I cozy her against one side while he retreats to the nursery to fetch her sister. We've finessed this sleep-walk routine by now.

"There you go, sweet pea," I coax, as baby number two settles in for her meal.

Ryan collapses onto the couch beside me. "Let me know if you need me," he says, closing his eyes. Almost instantly he starts snoring.

Exhausted as I am, I keep my eyes open. I study my daughters' tiny faces: the whisps of thickening hair, the flutter of long eyelashes, the perfect pink lips. I stroke a thumb across each forehead. "My baby girls," I whisper. "I'm sorry this world is so messed up."

My daughters were born into a global pandemic, political strife, a racial reckoning, rising gun violence, a climate crisis; here in the Pacific Northwest with wildfires raging, the world is literally on fire. And now Afghanistan reels violently amid the withdrawal of U.S. troops. That's what makes my mind jump to other babies, halfway around the world.

In many ways, my brain has spent the eleven years since my deployment withdrawing from Afghanistan. The summer after leaving the military I moved to Boston for graduate school, the progressive downtown liberal arts campus about as opposite from small southern military town as one could get. I crammed a whole accelerated life into Boston, flailing and lurching, anxious to both reinvent myself and make up for lost time. I relived the late-night barhopping of my early twenties, despite the protests of my late-twenties body. Uniform-free, I filled my closet with dresses and blazers and chunky jewelry. I learned how to accessorize and how to use a flatiron to tame my stubborn hair. Then in a spur of post-military rebellion, I chopped my hair into an asymmetrical bob.

Boston brought a master's degree and a close-knit circle of non-military friends. I simultaneously diversified my resume and tried to figure out what to do as a civilian grownup: an internship in book publicity, a stint as a personal assistant, a gig at a neighborhood toy store, a corporate office job with an insurance company. I bought a home and stayed put for nearly eight years, my longest stretch anywhere since childhood, and put down something resembling roots.

Still, the military always bubbled under the surface. My graduate school application essays on Afghanistan became my thesis, which became a book manuscript as I teased out more details, more nuances, more attempts at understanding. I found a passion for public speaking and sharing my military experiences. The more veterans I met, the more I recognized, as I had with my mom, the similarities running through all our war stories. I latched onto that connection so strongly that I let it sweep me into a dysfunctional relationship with an Afghanistan Army veteran, which evolved into a dysfunctional marriage.

It took five more years, one divorce, two job changes, and another cross-country move to get my bearings, to feel like I was finally moving forward in the right way. In early 2020, I bought a house outside Seattle with Ryan, my Massachusetts native, very non-military, soon-to-be second husband. After much wheel-spinning for both of us, we looked forward to carrying the momentum of our West Coast relocation into a new chapter of our lives. A month later, the world went on lockdown for COVID-19.

"I'm sorry this world is so messed up," I whisper to my nursing daughters. Their bodies huddle soft and warm against my ribcage. Gentle grunts find harmony with Ryan's snores. It's still a marvel to me to be here, the keeper of two tiny lives. I'm only beginning to appreciate the weight that carries.

"Someday," I say, "I'll tell you about this crazy year you were born."

Ryan and I didn't plan on having a COVID baby, let alone two of them. Six months into the pandemic, we made a deliberate decision not to put our lives on hold any longer, but we never expected to remain confined to our bubble a year later, with two infants and a new deadly COVID variant—and so much other turmoil—sweeping the globe.

Of the compounding series of events marking the year I became a mother, the Afghanistan withdrawal was one of the more predictable. The end has been a long time coming. Like so many things about American intervention in Afghanistan, the withdrawal was imbued with good intentions. And like so many things, it has not gone as planned. After two decades it took only nine days for Afghanistan to fall to the Taliban. Hundreds of thousands of men, women, and children have fled their homes. They've scaled walls and stormed the tarmac at the Kabul airport, a mini war zone with people literally dying to escape. They've clung frantically to the wings of departing aircraft.

There's a viral photo of a U.S. Marine at the airport, a hulk of a man, smiling under ballistic sunglasses and a Magnum P.I. mustache as he cradles an Afghan infant separated from family in the chaos. In a video taken outside the airport, a baby passes across a sea of extended arms and up over the airport wall. A Marine pushes aside a spiral of barbed wire to grab the child, and the crowd cheers. I try to wrap my head around the kind of desperation that would lead a parent to surrender a baby.

I picture myself there on the tarmac, in uniform; an alternative fate had I played my hand differently. I'm now older than my mom was when she deployed. When I passed that milestone on my thirty-fifth birthday, I told Mom, "I can't imagine going now. I don't know how you did it." With a bad knee and a quirky back, my body is no longer equipped for a war zone. But what about my soul? If I'd stayed in the military, I could be coordinating interviews with U.S. troops facilitating the evacuations and with Afghan refugees lucky enough to get a seat. Perhaps I'd write a press release like the one with the photo of the Magnum P.I. Marine. I would choose what stories to tell, and what to leave unspoken.

I hug my daughters closer. Every fiber of my being yearns to protect them. More and more, though, I'm wondering what it means to protect a child. The world is full of harsh realities to which no parent wishes to expose their children, but I know silence is not an option.

I've spent a decade reflecting on my military service, and on my mom's service before me. The soul-searching conversations with Mom continue to this day. We both hope our family military business ends with me. And yet, I must wrestle with the same uncomfortable questions she faced. Could I ultimately turn my daughters away from a choice I made myself? In my desire to protect, might I also be shielding them from knowledge or responsibility? On the other end of the spectrum, would I sully their idealism, their belief in *Three Cups of Tea*-type pursuits of noble and important efforts like "helping people" or "changing the world"?

I think of the little girl I met in the humble Paktia village eleven years ago during the PRT's nutritional supplement launch, the girl with the smudge of flour on her nose. She must be a young woman now, likely with children of her own. I hope she experienced a glimpse of the brighter future we promised. I worry she is among those seeking refuge, and that she may not find it.

One of my daughters lets out a squawk, her face scrunching in frustration. A moment later her efforts result in a diaper-filling rumble. I wriggle my hand out from under the baby and fumble on the couch for Ryan's leg. "Ryan, we've got poop."

He snaps to attention, arms outstretched. "Mmmkay, I got it. Give me the pooper."

As he shuffles down the hall with one baby, I snuggle the other against my chest. I lean down and kiss her fleshy cheek, breathe in her sweet powdery, milky scent.

"Someday I'll tell you everything." I whisper. "I promise I will."

Notes

[1] All common definitions come from the *Oxford English Dictionary*.

[2] Desert Shield/Desert Storm Employment or Reserve Component: Extracts of Lessons Learned, The United States Naval War College Operations Department. Retrieved from https://www.globalsecurity.org/military/library/report/1995/p162.pdf.

[3] Military personnel numbers from the 1970s vary, and numbers fluctuated drastically following the end of the draft and an increase in recruitment of female servicemembers, but estimates for 1972-1973 put female active duty strength around 45,000-55,000 (Department of Defense 2007 Demographics Report).

[4] Shah, Amir and Robert H. Reid, "Taliban kill 6 in attacks in two cities," Associated Press, July 22, 2009.

[5] Surveys conducted by the PEW Research Center suggest that roughly half of military veterans have a parent who has served, and veteran parents are more than twice as likely to have children join the military. http://www.pewsocialtrends.org/2011/11/23/the-military-civilian-gap-fewer-family-connections/.

[6] According to the office of the Special Inspector General for Afghanistan Reconstruction: https://www.sigar.mil/pdf/alerts/2010-09-09audit-10-16.pdf.

[7] The UN reported 169 polling sites opened on Election Day, though reports differ. For security reasons, 36 other planned sites were not used.

[8] Hoh, Matthew, letter to Ambassador Nancy J. Powell, September 10, 2009. TS.

[9] Prior to 2009, green-on-blue attacks were rare, only averaging one or two per year. 2009 and 2010 each saw five insider attacks which killed 12 and 16 coalition personnel (11 and 1 wounded), respectively. The number jumped to 16 attacks in 2011 (35 killed, 34 wounded) and a shocking 44 (61 killed, 81 wounded) in 2012. Green-on-blue attacks accounted for 15% of coalition deaths in 2012. (http://www.longwarjournal.org/archives/2012/08/green-on-blue_attack.php)

[10] Joint Publication 3-61, Public Affairs, 17 November 2015 Incorporating Change 1, 19 August 2016.

[11] "Bodies found gagged, bound after Afghan 'honor killing," CNN.com, February 12, 2010

[12] Nordland, Rod, "5 U.S. Soldiers Injured in Afghan Suicide Attack," *New York Times*, February 12, 2010.

[13] "Villagers accuse U.S. special forces for killing five civilians," *Morning Star*, February 13, 2010.

[14] Behind the Headlines with Bunn Nagara, " The more things change . . ." The Star Online, February 14, 2010.

[15] Shah, Amir, "NATO says insurgents killed; family says civilians," Associated Press, February 12, 2010.

[16] "Afghan protesters condemn US-led civilian killings," Press TV, February 12, 2010.

[17] "Innocent civilians? No way," The Angry Arab News Service, February 13, 2010.

[18] Oppel Jr, Richard A, "U.S. Admits Role in February Killing of Afghan Women," *New York Times*, April 4, 2010.

Seven-year-old Lauren (bottom left), her sister, and brother welcome Major Deborah Johnson home from her deployment at McChord Air Force Base on March 15, 1991.

"Best Dressed Family" at Lauren's Air Force commissioning ceremony, June 2006: Retired Air Force Chief Master Sgt. Norman Johnson, Retired Army Lt. Col. Deborah Johnson, Air Force 2nd Lt. Lauren Johnson, Retired Navy Cmdr Jerry Home.

Lauren poses with local children outside a school in Gardez, Afghanistan, 2009.

Lauren takes photos during a groundbreaking ceremony for a construction project sponsored by Provincial Reconstruction Team Paktia in Gardez, Afghanistan, 2009.

Lauren, her pistol, Janie, and her rifle, Annie, during a mission in Paktia Province, Afghanistan, 2009.

Photo by Alice Malia Photography

Lauren and her husband, Ryan, with their newborn twins in July 2021.

Acknowledgments

I've recently learned that it does, indeed, take a village to raise a child. So, too, does it take a village to write a book. This book would not exist without the love and support of many people over many years.

I've always liked to write, but two English teachers at Meadowdale High School helped me discover the power of words: Ms. Sparks and Brother Reitan, look what you inspired!

When I arrived at Emerson College to begin my MFA, I had a lot of anxiety and a vague idea for a book-like thing. I left with the framework of an actual book and the confidence to complete it. I'm grateful for my amazing nonfiction classmates, particularly Emily Avery-Miller, Jennifer Crystal, Shannon DeScioli, John Fantin, Martin Hansen, Catie Joy, Caitlin McGill, Paige Towers, Elliot Tetreault, Krysta Voskowsky, and Ashley Wells; and professors Jabari Asim, Richard Hoffman, Jerald Walker, Doug Whynott, and Joan Wickersham for challenging me to dig into the hard places and always encouraging me to Just. Keep. Writing.

From the Emerson community came the Rest Haven Writers, a writing group and so much more. Thank you for helping clean up the slop of many drafts, and frequently, too, the slop of life.

Andria Williams and Brian Castner generously read early versions of this manuscript. Without their insight this would be a much clumsier book.

Before there was a book, Matt Mabe, Molly Birnbaum, Dario DiBattista, Colin Halloran, and Olivia Kate Cerrone were champions of my work and supported some of my first writing and speaking endeavors.

Thank you to The Bread Loaf Writers' Conference, Virginia Center for Creative Arts, Wellspring House, and the Squaw Valley Community of Writers for providing the space to write, reflect, and commune, and GrubStreet and the *Wrath-Bearing Tree* for keeping literature ever-present when life pulls me in different directions.

I stand on the shoulders of many who have written beautifully and insightfully about contemporary Afghanistan, warfare, or military culture—including, but certainly not limited to, David Abrams, Elliot Ackerman, MC Armstrong, Kim Barker, Jerri Bell, Anuradha Bhagwati, Adrian

Bonenberger, Randy Brown, Benjamin Busch, Ron Capps, Brian Castner, CJ Chivers, Dario DiBattista, Ryan Leigh Doste, Teresa Fazio, Matt Gallagher, Jesse Goolsby, Anand Gopal, Colin D. Halloran, Brooke King, Phil Klay, Matthew Komatsu, Jay Moad, Peter Molin, Qais Akbar Omar, Jennifer Percy, Shannon Huffman Polson, Joydeep Roy-Bhattacharya, Katey Schultz, Brian Turner, Amy Waldman, and Kayla Williams. In an industry that can be competitive and challenging to navigate, I'm grateful for the war writing community for providing such a welcoming, nonjudgmental space and supporting every kind of war story. (Looking forward to the next AWP reunion!)

I'm thankful for my agent, Janet Silver, who believed in this book—and me—from the very beginning, and for Tracy Crow and the MilSpeak team for seeing value in my story and ushering it into the world as the best possible version of itself, with the brilliant design of Michelle Bradford Art (how gorgeous is that cover?!).

I will always be grateful to "Chris" for getting me through Afghanistan. To you and the rest of PRT Paktia 9-10 and my Army colleagues: This book cannot do you justice. These pages are not enough to render each of you in your full wonderful, colorful, quirky glory. Whatever our differences, I appreciate each of you for your role in this pivotal time in my life.

Shout outs to my fat tabby cat Milo, my number-one writing buddy; to the Brookline Village Starbucks baristas for keeping me caffeinated throughout the writing process; and to Twizzlers and Ben & Jerry's for the creative fuel.

Finally, to my family, my lifeblood: a book's worth of words cannot express how much you mean to me. Thank you for supporting me through my many journeys, including those portrayed in this book, and, of course, the long journey of writing about them. Mom, you're still my hero. Thank you to Ryan, my partner, for all the journeys to come. And to my girls, Freya and Aurora: I can regret nothing that led to you.

Photo by Becky Fuller Photo

Lauren Kay Johnson's essays, fiction, and poetry have appeared in the *Washington Post*, the *Atlantic, Glamour, Yale Medicine Magazine, CONSEQUENCE* magazine, *Drunken Boat, Pleiades*, and several anthologies. Her writing and interviews have been used in the creation of dance and theater productions, and she has lectured at schools, conferences, and veteran centers across the country, including the Association of Writers and Writing Programs national conference, the Boston Book Festival, and the University of Iowa. She is a writing consultant with GrubStreet, an editor at the *Wrath-Bearing Tree*, and a former editor-in-chief of *Redivider*.

Lauren lives with her family in Seattle. By day, she works for IGNITE Worldwide, a non-profit that aims to combat the gender imbalance in STEM fields. By night, she writes (with the help of her fat tabby cat) and eats copious amounts of ice cream.

Thank you for supporting the creative works of veterans and military family members by purchasing this book. If you enjoyed your reading experience, we're certain you'll enjoy these other great reads.

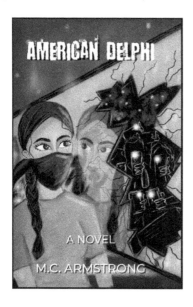

American Delphi

by M.C. ARMSTRONG

During America's summer of plague and protest, fifteen-year-old Zora Box worries her pesky younger brother is a psychopath for sneaking out at night to hang with their suspicious new neighbor, Buck London, who's old enough to be their father. Their father, a combat veteran, is dead—suicide. Or so everyone thinks, until Buck sets Zora and her brother Zach straight, revealing their father as the genius inventor of a truth-telling, future-altering device called American Delphi.

Salmon in the Seine

by NORRIS COMER

One moment 18-year-old Norris Comer is throwing his high school graduation cap in the air and setting off for Alaska to earn money, and the next he's comforting a wounded commercial fisherman who's desperate for the mercy of a rescue helicopter. From landlubber to deckhand, Comer's harrowing adventures at sea and during a solo search in the Denali backcountry for wolves provide a transformative bridge from adolescence to adulthood.

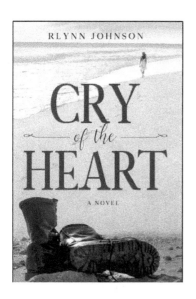

Cry of the Heart

by RLYNN JOHNSON

After law school, a group of women calling themselves the Alphas embark on diverse legal careers—Pauline joins the Army as a Judge Advocate. For twenty years, the Alphas gather for annual weekend retreats where the shenanigans and truth-telling will test and transform the bonds of sisterhood.

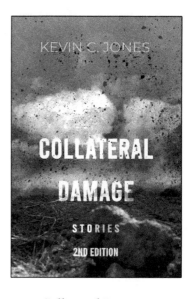

Collateral Damage
2nd edition

by KEVIN C. JONES

These stories live in the real-world psychedelics of warfare, poverty, love, hate, and just trying to get by. Jones's evocative language, the high stakes, and heartfelt characters create worlds of wonder and grace. The explosions, real and psychological, have a burning effect on the reader. Nothing here is easy, but so much is gained.

—ANTHONY SWOFFORD, author of *Jarhead: A Marine's Chronicle of the Gulf War and Other Battles*

Sub Wife

by SAMANTHA OTTO BROWN

A Navy wife's account of life within the super-secret sector of the submarine community, and of the support among spouses who often wait and worry through long stretches of silence from loved ones who are deeply submerged.

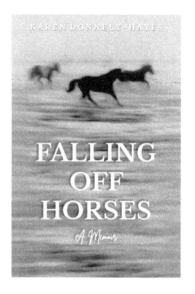

Falling Off Horses

by KAREN DONNELY-HAYES

A mutual love for horses unites two young women as teenagers who forge an undying friendship that will steady them after countless falls from horses, a roller coaster of love losses and triumphs, the emotional pitfalls of equestrian breeding and competing—and finally, through the heartbreaking diagnosis of a fatal illness.

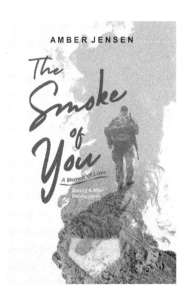

The Smoke of You

by AMBER JENSEN

A young couple's love and marriage are tested during and after a military deployment with the National Guard to Iraq that results in a battle with chronic pain and the slow-burning challenges of married life. A story of selfless love and self-discovery, of hardship and hope, *The Smoke of You* will resonate with anyone who has ever suffered, and still bravely loved.

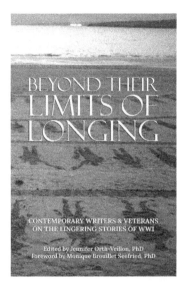

Beyond Their Limits of Longing

Edited by JENNIFER ORTH-VEILLON, PhD

In America, WWI became overshadowed by WWII and Vietnam, further diluting the voices of poets, novelists, essayists, and scholars who unknowingly set a precedent for the sixty-two successive, and notable, war writers who appear in this collection to explore the complexity both of war's physical and mental horrors and of its historical significance in today's world in crises.